Microsoft® Project 200[ ] For Dummies®

Cheat Sheet

1. **Determine the project's scope.** What are you going to do? What's the product?

2. **Identify stakeholders.** Who has a vested interest in the project, either in work to perform or in project outcomes? Plan how you'll report to them.

3. **Determine standards.** What constitutes quality for your project? Is there universal agreement about this?

4. **List constraints.** What unavoidable limitations exist in regard to time and the availability of resources?

5. **Assess your muscle.** How much support do you have for this project? Are there built-in organizational problems? Is so, what will you do about them?

6. **Face risks.** How will you develop the necessary contingencies?

7. **Set goals.** Set achievable goals consistent with the project's scope.

8. **Create categories or phases.** What are the groups of functions (called summary tasks)?

9. **Break down the project into tasks.** Identify the individual planned activities of the project.

10. **Define task durations.** Set a realistic length of time for each task.

11. **Set milestones.** Determine key points throughout the project that represent significant stages of completion.

12. **Identify resources.** Assign individuals or groups to perform the tasks.

13. **Determine the critical path.** What must be accomplished and in what order to keep the project on schedule?

14. **Refine your project plan.** Double-check each of these steps to ensure that they're consistent with the project's scope and goals.

15. **Enter data into Microsoft Project.**

16. **Take a very long break.** You can use this step as a recurring task throughout your project.

Six Ways to Correct Overallocated Resources

- **Set overtime rates.** In a resource view, choose Project⇨Resource Information.

- **Change the work calendar.** Choose Tools⇨Change Working Time. Highlight days on the calendar and then choose Nonworking time or Working time. If you want to change the working time for a specific reason, select the resource in the For List. Change the calendar as you want and click OK when you're finished.

- **Get assistance.** Click the Resource Assignment button on the standard toolbar. Either assign an additional existing resource or add a new one.

- **Relieve some of the duty.** Highlight a task and press Delete.

- **Extend a deadline.** Select a task's duration in the Gantt Chart Duration column. Up and down arrows appear. By clicking the up arrow, units of time increase in minutes, hours, days, and weeks. To change from one unit to another, such as from minutes to hours, type the number of units and then type **m**, **h**, **d**, or **w**.

- **Take your project home and work evenings and weekends.** Nah!

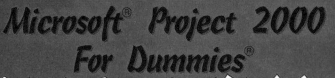

BESTSELLING BOOK SERIES

Microsoft® Project 2000 For Dummies®

Cheat Sheet

Where'd You Say That Was?

Here are some helpful hints for your hunt.

How Do I . . .	Answer
Know whether a project file is a template?	Its extension is .MPT.
Identify a workspace file?	Its extension is .MPW.
Temporarily hide a project?	Place it under your desk or make it the inactive window by choosing Window⇨Hide.
Make a consolidated project?	Choose Window⇨New Window. Hold down CRTL, click the projects you want to consolidate, and then click OK.
Create an outline?	Select the tasks and click the Indent button. The preceding task becomes a summary task.
Make a split view?	Choose Window⇨Split.
Change a form in split view?	Highlight the lower pane, choose View⇨More Views, and select a form.
Make a highlighted filter instead of an isolated filter?	Holding down the Shift key, choose Project⇨Filtered For, and then choose a filter.
Change the timescale on the Gantt chart?	Double-click the date area. Choose major and minor scales.
Change the font style of items in the Gantt chart?	Choose Format⇨Text Styles. Select the Item to Change, and have at it.
Draw on the Gantt chart?	Use washable crayons on the monitor or choose Insert⇨Drawing to display a floating drawing toolbar. (The crayons work better.)
Put a movie in the Gantt chart?	Choose Insert⇨Object. From the list box, select Media Player. Open an AVI or an MOV file. A movie object appears on the screen. Double-click it to run the movie. Get out the popcorn.
Find project statistics?	Choose Project⇨Project Information⇨Statistics.
Update tasks as completed to the present date?	Highlight the tasks, and then choose Tools⇨Tracking⇨Update Tasks. In the Update Tasks dialog box, type **100** in the % Complete box.

Creating a Schedule

1. Enter the project tasks by typing in the Task Name column.

2. Enter task durations (m — minutes, h — hours, d — days, w — weeks, 0 — milestones).

3. Link tasks by selecting them and then clicking the Link button on the standard toolbar.

4. Change predecessors and successors using the Task form in split view (Window⇨Split).

5. Add resources using the Task form.

6. If necessary, change constraints using the Task Details form (View⇨More Views⇨Task Details Form).

7. Set the baseline by choosing Tools⇨Tracking⇨Save Baseline.

IDG BOOKS WORLDWIDE

For Dummies®: Bestselling Book Series for Beginners

TM

BESTSELLING BOOK SERIES

References for the Rest of Us!®

Are you intimidated and confused by computers? Do you find that traditional manuals are overloaded with technical details you'll never use? Do your friends and family always call you to fix simple problems on their PCs? Then the ...*For Dummies*® computer book series from IDG Books Worldwide is for you.

...*For Dummies* books are written for those frustrated computer users who know they aren't really dumb but find that PC hardware, software, and indeed the unique vocabulary of computing make them feel helpless. ...*For Dummies* books use a lighthearted approach, a down-to-earth style, and even cartoons and humorous icons to dispel computer novices' fears and build their confidence. Lighthearted but not lightweight, these books are a perfect survival guide for anyone forced to use a computer.

Already, millions of satisfied readers agree. They have made ...*For Dummies* books the #1 introductory level computer book series and have written asking for more. So, if you're looking for the most fun and easy way to learn about computers, look to ...*For Dummies* books to give you a helping hand.

Microsoft® Project 2000 FOR DUMMIES®

by Martin Doucette

IDG Books Worldwide, Inc.
An International Data Group Company

Foster City, CA ◆ Chicago, IL ◆ Indianapolis, IN ◆ New York, NY

Microsoft® Project 2000 For Dummies®

Published by
IDG Books Worldwide, Inc.
An International Data Group Company
919 E. Hillsdale Blvd.
Suite 400
Foster City, CA 94404
www.idgbooks.com (IDG Books Worldwide Web site)
www.dummies.com (Dummies Press Web site)

Library of Congress Catalog Card No.: 99-66331

ISBN: 0-7645-0517-3

Printed in the United States of America

10 9 8 7 6 5 4 3

1O/RV/QW/QQ/IN

Distributed in the United States by IDG Books Worldwide, Inc.

Distributed by CDG Books Canada Inc. for Canada; by Transworld Publishers Limited in the United Kingdom; by IDG Norge Books for Norway; by IDG Sweden Books for Sweden; by IDG Books Australia Publishing Corporation Pty. Ltd. for Australia and New Zealand; by TransQuest Publishers Pte Ltd. for Singapore, Malaysia, Thailand, Indonesia, and Hong Kong; by Gotop Information Inc. for Taiwan; by ICG Muse, Inc. for Japan; by Intersoft for South Africa; by Eyrolles for France; by International Thomson Publishing for Germany, Austria and Switzerland; by Distribuidora Cuspide for Argentina; by LR International for Brazil; by Galileo Libros for Chile; by Ediciones ZETA S.C.R. Ltda. for Peru; by WS Computer Publishing Corporation, Inc., for the Philippines; by Contemporanea de Ediciones for Venezuela; by Express Computer Distributors for the Caribbean and West Indies; by Micronesia Media Distributor, Inc. for Micronesia; by Chips Computadoras S.A. de C.V. for Mexico; by Editorial Norma de Panama S.A. for Panama; by American Bookshops for Finland.

For general information on IDG Books Worldwide's books in the U.S., please call our Consumer Customer Service department at 800-762-2974. For reseller information, including discounts and premium sales, please call our Reseller Customer Service department at 800-434-3422.

For information on where to purchase IDG Books Worldwide's books outside the U.S., please contact our International Sales department at 317-596-5530 or fax 317-572-4002.

For consumer information on foreign language translations, please contact our Customer Service department at 1-800-434-3422, fax 317-572-4002, or e-mail rights@idgbooks.com.

For information on licensing foreign or domestic rights, please phone +1-650-653-7098.

For sales inquiries and special prices for bulk quantities, please contact our Order Services department at 800-434-3422 or write to the address above.

For information on using IDG Books Worldwide's books in the classroom or for ordering examination copies, please contact our Educational Sales department at 800-434-2086 or fax 317-572-4005.

For press review copies, author interviews, or other publicity information, please contact our Public Relations department at 650-653-7000 or fax 650-653-7500.

For authorization to photocopy items for corporate, personal, or educational use, please contact Copyright Clearance Center, 222 Rosewood Drive, Danvers, MA 01923, or fax 978-750-4470.

 is a registered trademark under exclusive license to IDG Books Worldwide, Inc. from International Data Group, Inc.

About the Author

Marty Doucette is an author, a technical writer, an educational program developer, a video producer, and a multimedia author. He was introduced to project management in 1991 while producing a series of teleconferences with the Public Broadcasting Service. Marty resides in Indianapolis with his beautiful wife Lorita and their four children, Nicole, Ariel, Lindsay, and Eve.

ABOUT IDG BOOKS WORLDWIDE

Welcome to the world of IDG Books Worldwide.

IDG Books Worldwide, Inc., is a subsidiary of International Data Group, the world's largest publisher of computer-related information and the leading global provider of information services on information technology. IDG was founded more than 30 years ago by Patrick J. McGovern and now employs more than 9,000 people worldwide. IDG publishes more than 290 computer publications in over 75 countries. More than 90 million people read one or more IDG publications each month.

Launched in 1990, IDG Books Worldwide is today the #1 publisher of best-selling computer books in the United States. We are proud to have received eight awards from the Computer Press Association in recognition of editorial excellence and three from Computer Currents' First Annual Readers' Choice Awards. Our best-selling ...For Dummies® series has more than 50 million copies in print with translations in 31 languages. IDG Books Worldwide, through a joint venture with IDG's Hi-Tech Beijing, became the first U.S. publisher to publish a computer book in the People's Republic of China. In record time, IDG Books Worldwide has become the first choice for millions of readers around the world who want to learn how to better manage their businesses.

Our mission is simple: Every one of our books is designed to bring extra value and skill-building instructions to the reader. Our books are written by experts who understand and care about our readers. The knowledge base of our editorial staff comes from years of experience in publishing, education, and journalism — experience we use to produce books to carry us into the new millennium. In short, we care about books, so we attract the best people. We devote special attention to details such as audience, interior design, use of icons, and illustrations. And because we use an efficient process of authoring, editing, and desktop publishing our books electronically, we can spend more time ensuring superior content and less time on the technicalities of making books.

You can count on our commitment to deliver high-quality books at competitive prices on topics you want to read about. At IDG Books Worldwide, we continue in the IDG tradition of delivering quality for more than 30 years. You'll find no better book on a subject than one from IDG Books Worldwide.

John Kilcullen
Chairman and CEO
IDG Books Worldwide, Inc.

Eighth Annual
Computer Press
Awards ≥1992

Ninth Annual
Computer Press
Awards ≥1993

Tenth Annual
Computer Press
Awards ≥1994

Eleventh Annual
Computer Press
Awards ≥1995

IDG is the world's leading IT media, research and exposition company. Founded in 1964, IDG had 1997 revenues of $2.05 billion and has more than 9,000 employees worldwide. IDG offers the widest range of media options that reach IT buyers in 75 countries representing 95% of worldwide IT spending. IDG's diverse product and services portfolio spans six key areas including print publishing, online publishing, expositions and conferences, market research, education and training, and global marketing services. More than 90 million people read one or more of IDG's 290 magazines and newspapers, including IDG's leading global brands — Computerworld, PC World, Network World, Macworld and the Channel World family of publications. IDG Books Worldwide is one of the fastest-growing computer book publishers in the world, with more than 700 titles in 36 languages. The "...For Dummies®" series alone has more than 50 million copies in print. IDG offers online users the largest network of technology-specific Web sites around the world through IDG.net (http://www.idg.net), which comprises more than 225 targeted Web sites in 55 countries worldwide. International Data Corporation (IDC) is the world's largest provider of information technology data, analysis and consulting, with research centers in over 41 countries and more than 400 research analysts worldwide. IDG World Expo is a leading producer of more than 168 globally branded conferences and expositions in 35 countries including E3 (Electronic Entertainment Expo), Macworld Expo, ComNet, Windows World Expo, ICE (Internet Commerce Expo), Agenda, DEMO, and Spotlight. IDG's training subsidiary, ExecuTrain, is the world's largest computer training company, with more than 230 locations worldwide and 785 training courses. IDG Marketing Services helps industry-leading IT companies build international brand recognition by developing global integrated marketing programs via IDG's print, online and exposition products worldwide. Further information about the company can be found at www.idg.com. 1/26/00

Dedication

To Nicole, Mike and Kathy, John and Teresa, Bob and Debbie, and Rich and Edy. *I will leave as a remnant in your midst, a people humble and lowly, who shall take refuge in my name.*

Author's Acknowledgments

Although this book has a single author, many people have put long hours into its creation. This is an acknowledgement of just a few of them. First, Kyle Looper, my project editor, thank you for caring so much about quality and value. And Christine Berman, thanks for your determination that the reader will actually understand what I'm attempting to convey. Laura Moss, thank you for your enormous and kind patience while I finished another book. And thank you Scott Linn of NX Communications (slinn@nxco.com) for your technical consulting on Microsoft Project Central and for solving a bunch of networking problems.

Publisher's Acknowledgments

We're proud of this book; please register your comments through our IDG Books Worldwide Online Registration Form located at http://my2cents.dummies.com.

Some of the people who helped bring this book to market include the following:

Acquisitions, Editorial, and Media Development

Senior Project Editor: Kyle Looper

Acquisitions Editor: Laura Moss

Copy Editors: Christine Berman, Beth Parlon

Technical Editor: Dennis Cohen

Media Development Editor: Marita Ellixson

Associate Media Development Editor: Megan Decraene

Associate Permissions Editor: Carmen Krikorian

Media Development Assistant: Eddie Kominowski

Editorial Manager: Leah Cameron

Media Development Manager: Heather Heath Dismore

Production

Project Coordinator: E. Shawn Aylsworth

Layout and Graphics: Amy Adrian, Barry Offringa, Tracy K. Oliver, Jill Piscitelli, Brent Savage, Brian Torwelle, Dan Whetstine

Proofreaders: Laura Albert, Beth Baugh, Corey Bowen, Vickie Broyles, John Greenough, Marianne Santy, Susan Sims

Indexer: Mary Mortensen

Special Help Amanda Foxworth

General and Administrative

IDG Books Worldwide, Inc.: John Kilcullen, CEO

IDG Books Technology Publishing Group: Richard Swadley, Senior Vice President and Publisher; Walter R. Bruce III, Vice President and Publisher; Joseph Wikert, Vice President and Publisher; Mary Bednarek, Vice President and Director, Product Development; Andy Cummings, Publishing Director, General User Group; Mary C. Corder, Editorial Director; Barry Pruett, Publishing Director

IDG Books Consumer Publishing Group: Roland Elgey, Senior Vice President and Publisher; Kathleen A. Welton, Vice President and Publisher; Kevin Thornton, Acquisitions Manager; Kristin A. Cocks, Editorial Director

IDG Books Internet Publishing Group: Brenda McLaughlin, Senior Vice President and Publisher; Sofia Marchant, Online Marketing Manager

IDG Books Production for Branded Press: Debbie Stailey, Director of Production; Cindy L. Phipps, Manager of Project Coordination, Production Proofreading, and Indexing; Tony Augsburger, Manager of Prepress, Reprints, and Systems; Laura Carpenter, Production Control Manager; Shelley Lea, Supervisor of Graphics and Design; Debbie J. Gates, Production Systems Specialist; Robert Springer, Supervisor of Proofreading; Trudy Coler, Page Layout Manager; Troy Barnes, Page Layout Supervisor, Kathie Schutte, Senior Page Layout Supervisor; Michael Sullivan, Production Supervisor

Packaging and Book Design: Patty Page, Manager, Promotions Marketing

◆

The publisher would like to give special thanks to Patrick J. McGovern, without whom this book would not have been possible.

◆

Contents at a Glance

Table of Contents

Introduction

· ·

*H*ere's a scary picture. At this very moment, thousands of people are busily managing projects without knowing anything about the professional discipline of project management. This is a humongous crisis, folks! Well, actually, you know it isn't a crisis at all. You've been doing it for years.

You've probably performed a layperson's version of project management many times and muddled along just fine. You organized the plan, created a schedule, made assignments, and mothered the project to completion, sometimes even on time and under budget.

So why put yourself through all the trouble of figuring out a project management software program? Even more basic, why find out about project management? The answer is self-evident. Because you've managed projects before, you know there has to be a better way. You're ready to discover what all this project management hoopla is about, and you'd like to use Microsoft Project to do the job. You've just made two good management decisions.

Confidentially Speaking

Deep down, you're probably wondering whether this is going to hurt. Between you and me, finding out about Microsoft Project is straightforward and kind of fun. You don't have to know anything special about computers or project management to begin. As you'll see in the upcoming chapters, a simple wisdom is evident throughout the software program. You're going to look very good throwing all those Gantt charts and reports around at the office. And what's really neat is that you can let people assume that it took grueling labor and a steel will to figure out the program. It's our secret.

Using This Book

As this book's title so subtly implies, the following chapters show you how to use Microsoft Project. But what the title doesn't say is that this book also gives you a basic explanation of project management. Two for the price of one. You are some manager!

You'll enjoy the logical sequence of this book's chapters if you want to read it from soup to nuts. But you can also use this book strictly as a reference tool. If you're like many managers, you don't have the time for a full-course meal. You're lucky to get fast-food carryout: Smorgasbord to your heart's content.

As you read this book, you may notice that whenever I specifically tell you to choose a command, certain letters are underlined. You can use these underlined letters, known as *hot keys,* instead of clicking with a mouse. If you press Alt and then press the underlined keys, you quickly activate the command.

About the CD-ROM

In the book, I assume that you have Microsoft Project 2000 and that you can use it as you read the chapters. The book is written in a way that lets you master your project management skills by practice. I've also provided a CD-ROM with a number of project files so that you can read the material and practice. (I tell you exactly when you can use the files from the CD-ROM.) At any time, you can use information in your own project instead of practicing with the sample files.

See Appendix C for instructions about using the sample project files and for information about other valuable tools and information you'll find on the CD-ROM.

How This Book Is Organized

This book has seven parts. Each part is a logical grouping of chapters, with each chapter focusing on a major point about project management or Microsoft Project. The chapters are kept as brief as possible without sacrificing important details.

In each chapter, individual sections describe a specific function. Navigating the chapters' headings, you can easily find an explanation or specific information you need.

Part I: Starting a Project

The beginning is often the right place for most of us to start. And that's what you do in this part — you start by making a very simple project. Immediately, you find out two important facts. First, Microsoft Project 2000 is easy and fun to use. Second, the best way to use Microsoft Project is know a little bit about the discipline of project management.

Quite frankly, there's nothing embarrassing about asking a question like "What's a project?" Most people may be surprised by the answer. In this part, you check out your knowledge of project planning, you find out about the three basic ingredients of project management, and you see how Microsoft Project works to provide you with information.

Part II: Building a Project

Part I shows you what you need to know to begin a project. Part II shows you how to enter the information into Microsoft Project. In this part, you create tasks and set their duration. You customize the work calendar or make multiple work calendars for different groups. You create a schedule of events and define the relationships of the tasks in the schedule. You create deadlines and determine where you can permit slack. You identify who's going to do what for how much and when. Your project manager muscles start to show a little tone. You're ready to strut around in Microsoft Project.

Part III: Analyzing a Project

The place where your work starts to pay dividends is the use of project views. How much work is assigned to each resource? Which tasks are critical? How can you find a specific piece or group of information and exclude unrelated information? In Part III, you become familiar with the multitude of ways that Microsoft Project can organize and calculate your information. Searching and sorting information is surprisingly simple after you get the hang of it, and it's where you start realizing how smart you're getting to be with this project management stuff.

Part IV: Refining a Project

After you enter the project information and find out how to view tables, charts, and forms, you're ready to trim the fat and build up areas of weakness. Is anything overbudgeted? How can costs be reduced? Is the schedule tight? Are resources being used in the best manner? In Part IV, you get to tweak and poke and test and mold till you're satisfied that you have a project that's ready to fly.

Part V: Tracking and Reporting a Project

When the project is off the ground, you keep it on course with Microsoft Project's tracking tools. Compare the actual course of events against the original plan. Update the project with up-to-the-moment status reports. Analyze variances in cost or work or time. Create interim plans. Customize your work environment to better suit your style and needs.

Ready to flaunt your expertise a little? Microsoft Project provides all kinds of nifty ways to communicate project status. In this part, you print views and reports. You find out how to isolate specific resource information. You turn your information into graphs and charts. And you say it all in different kinds of reports. What's more, if you don't like the options available to you, you can customize your presentation. You're wearing your project manager status well — it looks good on you.

Part VI: The Part of Tens

Part VI takes you to the toolshed and out on the highways and byways. You find out about the many Microsoft Project toolbars and you discover various services for your continuing growth as a project manager. If you're interested, this could even be a new career path.

Part VII: Appendixes

The final part includes a glossary and provides some basics about using data from other applications in Microsoft Project. I also show you how to load the sample project files from the *Microsoft Project 2000 For Dummies* CD-ROM.

Icons Used in This Book

This icon points out a feature that's new to the Y2K version of Microsoft Project.

This icon signals something technically wild and wonderful (if you're into technospeak). It may be interesting and useful to you, but it's not essential to doing business in Microsoft Project.

Here's a friendly little shortcut on your road to project management success. This icon usually tells you a way to do your work more easily or more quickly.

This icon tells you that the information is worth committing to one of your memory banks. Otherwise, if you don't recall it, you'll have egg on your face and on the keyboard. Don't worry, the book doesn't have many of these icons.

In some parts of Microsoft Project, a keystroke or a mouse click can take you to a point of no return. This icon warns you when you're approaching one of those places.

Once in awhile, you'll see this icon. I included some sample files and some great resources on the CD-ROM to help you be a little less busy and a lot more organized in your project management.

Where to Go from Here

Project managers are decision makers. Here's your first one in this book. You can begin with Chapter 1 or Chapter 2. Or you can smorgasbord. In any case, have fun.

Part I
Starting a Project

The 5th Wave   By Rich Tennant

"IT'S NOT THAT IT DOESN'T WORK AS A COMPUTER,
IT JUST WORKS BETTER AS A PAPERWEIGHT."

In this part . . .

Two questions are usually floating in people's minds when they begin using a project management software program. Is the program too complicated to learn? And is project management too tough to do? The answer to both questions is no. But don't believe me, find out for yourself.

Part I begins by taking you right into Microsoft Project 2000. Within moments, you're building your first project. And you're finding that either this program is simple to use or you're awfully bright. I'd put my money on both.

Part I also shows you the kinds of information you should know to use Microsoft Project 2000 successfully. First, you need to have a workable plan. Simple, you say. Well, maybe so. But then again, maybe not. You need a project plan that can face reality eyeball to eyeball. You need contingencies for the unforeseen. You need to assess the strength of the support you have for carrying out this project to completion. Okay, I'll lighten up. The point is, using Chapter 2 to define your project's scope and clarify your goals may be worth your while.

Chapter 1

Getting Started with Microsoft Project 2000

In This Chapter

▶ Starting up your program

▶ Getting used to the view

▶ Finding your way around Microsoft Project

▶ Creating your own simple project

▶ Saving a project and shutting down

I'm guessing that you didn't purchase Microsoft Project 2000 for its entertainment value. And I bet you didn't buy this book because you thought it would make a nice alternative to a fiction novel on the best-seller list. Rather, you're probably getting into this computer-aided project management stuff because you *don't* have time to waste and you hope this book will help you hit the ground running. Congratulations! You've already made two very astute project management decisions.

Microsoft Project is a powerful planning, analysis, management, and reporting tool that gives you and your project team the ability to see the broad scope of your project and its details simultaneously. The program is so encompassing that it even helps you identify risks and solve problems before they occur. Empty, boring days may even be an occasional possibility.

However, because Microsoft Project is so incredibly muscular, getting started can be a bit intimidating. But project managers don't let silly little things like software programs kick sand in their faces. Don't be intimidated! In this chapter, I show you how to start the program, get acquainted with it, create a simple project, save your project, and shut down. After you know Microsoft Project's basic steps, you can jump head first into creating your own project.

Starting Microsoft Project

Some people buy a new car and then read the owner's manual before even touching the keys. And then there's the other 95 percent of humanity who can't wait to *drive the car* and put off reading the instructions until later. Based on those odds, you probably don't want to read a lot of stuff about Microsoft Project, you just want to get going. Well, buckle your seat belt because it's time to take off.

After you buy the Microsoft Project software, you have to install it on your computer. To install, simply put the CD into your CD-ROM drive and follow the instructions on-screen.

To start Microsoft Project 2000, simply choose Start⇨Programs⇨Microsoft Project. When you open the program for the first time, a Welcome screen offers you the option of watching a preview or following a tutorial (although the tutorial may leave you feeling a bit numb). Here are your choices on the Welcome screen, as shown in Figure 1-1:

- ✔ **What's New:** A series of short descriptions of the major differences between Microsoft Project 98 and Microsoft Project 2000.

- ✔ **Quick Preview:** A short description of Project's features for building, managing, and reporting on the status of a project. If you know the basics of project management, this selection has some helpful information.

- ✔ **Tutorial:** A brief step-by-step guide for planning, tracking, and communicating results of a project. The tutorial won't teach you how to use Microsoft Project 2000, but it contains some useful pointers about the relationship of Project to project management.

- ✔ **Project Map:** A logical layout of the phases of a project plan. Project Map describes common project management activities throughout the life of a project.

After you see all you care to see of the Welcome window, you can temporarily banish it by clicking the X in the upper-right corner of the window. Or, if you'd like to hide the Welcome window but keep it available, click the minimize button in the upper-right corner as shown in the margin.

To keep the Welcome window from automatically appearing the next time you open Project, click the Display Help at Startup check box to deselect it. Now you see Microsoft Project waiting patiently to serve your project-management needs, as shown in Figure 1-2.

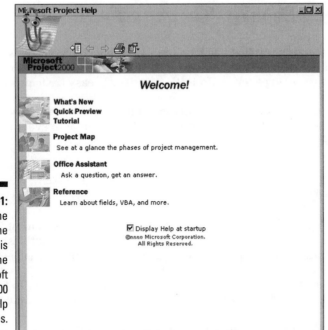

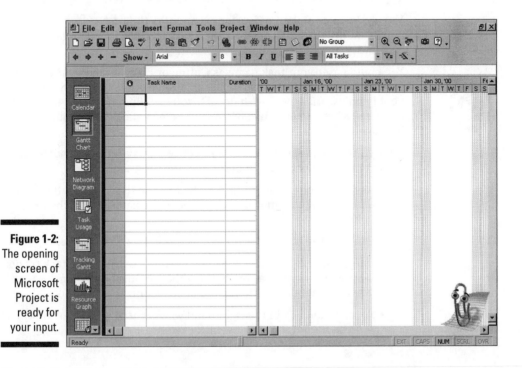

Figure 1-2:
The opening
screen of
Microsoft
Project is
ready for
your input.

Creating a (Very) Simple Project

Although Microsoft Project has more project management answers than any number of questions you may throw at it, you're probably better off getting started by practicing a few of Project's surprisingly easy basic procedures.

Granted, this project barely gets Microsoft Project's motor running above idle, but the steps in this simple project are fundamental to every project you create and manage.

Entering tasks

You begin a project by defining tasks. A *task* is a step that you must finish to complete a project. A good way for you to understand the relationship between a task and a project is to compare it to the chores you need to do to clean your home. The project is cleaning. But cleaning is actually a number of distinct chores — dusting, sweeping, vacuuming, and mopping. To tell Microsoft Project what tasks make up your project, follow these steps:

1. **Click the first white space in the Task Name column.**

2. **Type a short description of the task and press Enter.**

   You could enter **Make Coffee**, for example, as the first step among many important projects. (At least, for me, making coffee is an important first task in any project starting before 10 a.m.!)

   You could enter your task name as **Coffee** or even **Make decaffeinated coffee**. Microsoft Project works just as easily with tasks of any length (but I don't work as well with decaf). You may find, however, that short task names are easier to use when your screen starts filling with information.

   After you enter a task, Microsoft Project gets busy right away doing its project management stuff. In particular, the program

   • Assigns a sequence number to the task, so that the first time you enter a task, the number 1 appears on the same row in the first column.

   • Displays the task description in the task box on that line.

   • Dares you to guess how long you need to complete the task by displaying a prompt that reads 1 day? in the Duration column. (I tell you more about duration in the next section.)

   • Posts a blue box in the right-hand window that's a sort of graphical representation of your new task (Figure 1-3).

3. **Repeat Steps 1 and 2 until you've entered all the tasks in your project.**

   Each time you enter a new task, Project assigns it the next number in sequence and puts another little box in the right-hand window. You don't need to do anything to tell Project when you're done entering tasks.

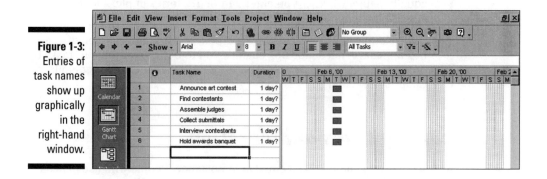

Figure 1-3:
Entries of task names show up graphically in the right-hand window.

Setting task duration

Estimating the time it takes to complete a task *(task duration)* is part of your job as a project manager. By default, Microsoft Project measures task duration as one day, but you can set it to minutes, hours, days, weeks, or months. Microsoft Project places a question mark next to the default duration until you either commit to a one-day duration or change the setting.

To enter an expected duration of a task, follow these steps:

1. **Click the duration box to activate it.**

2. **Type a duration and press Enter.**

   Project recognizes m to mean minutes, h to mean hours, d to mean days, w to mean weeks, and mo to mean months.

Figure 1-4 shows the process of entering duration values to your tasks.

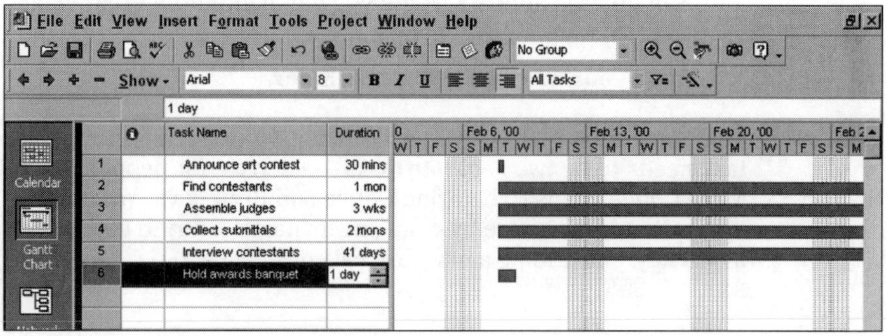

Figure 1-4:
Duration units can range from minutes to months.

Here are some important things to remember about duration:

- ✔ You can assign duration to any task, at any time, in any order. You're the driver.

- ✔ Don't be concerned about how you enter duration. Microsoft Project is equally happy whether you enter **24h** or **1d,** for example, and it doesn't gripe if you enter **36d** or **50,400m.**

- ✔ If you double-click the Task Duration box, the Task Information dialog box appears. This dialog box enables you to better control your tasks by providing you a number of fine-tuning details. I cover the task details in Chapters 3, 4, and 5.

Editing tasks and duration

A pencil has two ends — each equal in importance. People who use pencils need to be able to change their minds and erase things. The same is true of project planners who use project planning software programs. Project planners change their minds a lot. Fortunately, implementing a change is easy with Microsoft Project. Inserting and moving tasks and changing task duration is a breeze.

Forgot something! (Inserting tasks in the middle of a list)

Microsoft Project enables you to insert a task anywhere you want in the task column. Big deal, you say. Well, actually this is a big deal. Seldom will you correctly anticipate all the tasks that will need to be performed to create a project. More commonly, you'll make a task list, study it, and realize you've overlooked some steps. Remember that you can insert a new task by clicking the place where you want existing tasks to drop down. To insert a task, follow these steps:

1. **Click an existing task name.**

2. **Press the Insert key on your keyboard.**

   You can also choose Insert⇨New Task.

   A blank task appears where you highlighted the existing task and pushes the other tasks down beneath it.

3. **Type your new task and press Enter.**

Inserting is also a way to break a task into pieces. Suppose you decide that a task needs to be two separate tasks — such as, for people with grinders, Make Coffee needs to be Grind Coffee and Brew Java. You can edit an existing task called Make coffee by changing its name to Grind coffee, pressing the Insert key, and adding a new task called Brew java.

Moving tasks

Moving a task at the early stages of your project planning is simple. Later in a project, as you see in Chapter 4, moving a task can get sticky. This is because early in your project planning, you probably haven't associated (*linked*) tasks to each other. Moving tasks is no big deal. Later in a project, when you have linked tasks to one another, you create a relationship between them that doesn't easily permit moving tasks without first unlinking them.

Moving unlinked tasks is a snap. You just have to know one simple little trick — where to place your cursor for dragging. Follow these steps to move a task:

1. **Click the number of a task.**

   Microsoft Project highlights the entire task row.

2. **Drag the cursor up or down to the place you'd like to move the task.**

   As you drag the cursor, a gray sideways T, indicates where you're moving the task, as shown in Figure 1-5.

3. **Release the cursor.**

   The task is now renumbered and residing in its new location.

Place where task will be moved

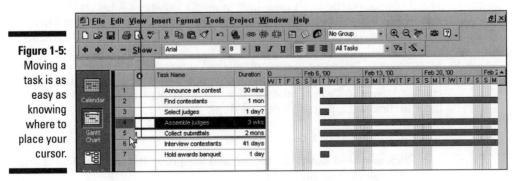

Figure 1-5:
Moving a
task is as
easy as
knowing
where to
place your
cursor.

If you enter sequential tasks and then discover that you need to add something else between them, insert the new task. Microsoft Project won't get upset (see Figure 1-5).

Editing duration

Changing the duration of a task is simple and painless in the early stages of building your project. You simply click on the task duration that you want to change and type a new number and time unit. To change a task's duration, perform the following steps:

1. **Highlight a task duration by clicking it.**

2. **Type a new duration.**

   If you prefer, you can click one of the spinner buttons next to duration to add or subtract time. Just be aware, that the spinner button won't change your selection of minutes, hours, days, weeks, or months. For example, if your minutes exceed 59, you might consider changing your designation from minutes to hours.

   Microsoft Project changes both the duration in the duration box and on the graphical chart (called a Gantt chart) to the right.

3. **To exit the task duration, press Enter or click anywhere on the screen.**

Linking tasks together

Two of the most important decisions you need to make as a project manager are the order of your tasks and the dependency those tasks have on other tasks. For example, Task 2 depends on Task 1 to finish before Task 2 can start. This dependency is called a *task relationship*. Fortunately, Microsoft Project likes ordering tasks and pondering relationships. In Project, linking is the way you create the order and the relationship among tasks in your project.

Each of the task's durations appear graphically in the Gantt chart to the right. The timescale on the chart measures in weeks and days. A task with a duration of less than one day appears as having a bar filling only a portion of a day. Other tasks are longer and have bars extending from here to Timbuktu.

Most projects' tasks can't be accomplished simultaneously. More often than not, a project requires one task to be completed before the next one can be started. Microsoft Project provides a very simple way to order tasks sequentially. To link tasks, just follow these steps:

1. **Click in the Task 1 box.**

2. **Click and hold down the mouse and then drag it downward until you have selected all the tasks.**

3. **Release the mouse.**

   All the tasks are highlighted on-screen.

4. **Click the Link Tasks button.**

   The tasks link together on the chart (see Figure 1-6).

In Project, the default task relationship is called *finish-to-start* because you have to finish one task before you start the next one. Microsoft Project offers you three other task relationships — finish-to-finish, start-to-start, and start-to-finish. Chapter 4 explains relationships in more detail.

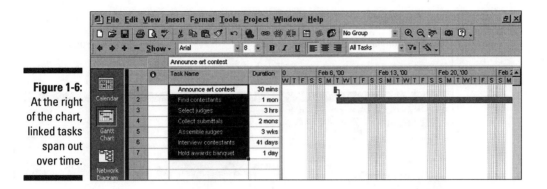

Figure 1-6:
At the right
of the chart,
linked tasks
span out
over time.

Nice, you say. But where did all the tasks go? They were here a moment ago, but seem to have taken off east at breakneck speed. Actually, everything's just fine. When you linked the tasks, they expanded over time. The Gantt chart doesn't show all the time covered by the linked tasks. Nothing to worry about. Microsoft Project enables you to see your work in its entirety. You simply need to know some facts about getting around in the Project interface.

Getting Comfortable with the Microsoft Project Interface

Microsoft Project is like a telescope, microscope, and radar, all rolled into one and all attentive to your project. Microsoft Project is ready at any moment to provide you with numerous perspectives and insights about your project. Figuring out how to access and use Microsoft Project's capabilities is the trick. You need to familiarize yourself with the program's *views*.

What's this weird interface? The Gantt Chart view

Projects are all about time management. You need to know when particular tasks begin, when they should end, and when your overall project needs to be completed. How can you find out when tasks occur after they're linked together? Microsoft Project's default view splits the screen between a task sheet where you enter your tasks, duration, and other information, and a *Gantt chart* that enables you to see the project graphically (as shown in Figure 1-7).

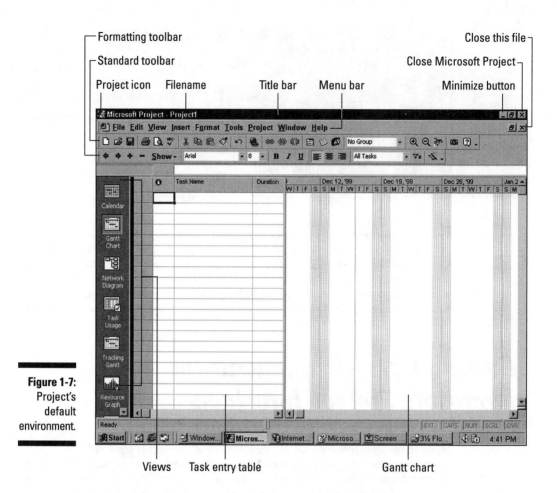

Figure 1-7:
Project's
default
environment.

The following list describes some of the important elements in the Project
environment:

✔ **Title bar:** The title bar reassures you that you're using Microsoft Project
(like, duh) and shows you the name of the current document. Until you
save the file with a better name, the filename shows up as `Projectx`.
The *x* represents a number that increases as you create new projects
(Project1, Project2, and so on).

✔ **Menu bar:** Chances are good that you're familiar with the *menu bar* even
if you couldn't care less what it's called. Clicking one of the words in the
menu bar (such as File, Edit, View, and so on) reveals a menu of options
from which you can choose. If an option is unavailable at any given time,
it appears grayed out. If an option is followed by an ellipsis, clicking it
brings up a dialog box into which you can enter information and make
additional choices.

When you open a menu, you'll probably see a few of the menu choices plus a double arrow. Click the double arrow and the menu expands to show all the choices available. Every time that you select something from a menu, it moves up in the list. So don't be surprised to see items move around on these lists, but if this irritates you, you can choose Tools➪Customize➪Toolbars, click the Options tab, and deselect the check box that reads Menus show recently used commands first. Your menus return to pre-2000 style.

✔ **Toolbars:** Microsoft Project displays two toolbars by default. The *Standard toolbar* contains most of the buttons necessary for performing basic functions in Microsoft Project such as starting a new file, opening an existing file, saving your work, printing, linking and unlinking tasks, and assigning resources. I discuss the Standard toolbar in more detail in the following section. The *Formatting toolbar* contains a mixture of buttons common to other Microsoft Office programs and buttons unique to Microsoft Project, such as the Gantt Chart Wizard button. I discuss the Formatting toolbar a bit later.

You can display additional toolbars by choosing View➪Toolbars and then selecting the toolbar of your choice. Chapter 21 is devoted entirely to toolbars.

✔ **Entry bar:** The long empty box beneath the formatting toolbar is the *entry* bar. The entry bar is an editing tool for writing or editing the contents of project tables and sheets, such as tasks in the Task Name column. You can use the entry bar to write or modify task names.

The Standard toolbar

The following buttons on the Standard toolbar are common to most Microsoft Office applications. Table 1-1 lists these common buttons.

Table 1-1		Common Buttons on the Standard Toolbar
Button	**Name**	**What It Does**
	New	Opens a new project window
	Open	Opens the default or current folder
	Save	Saves the active project
	Print	Prints a copy of the active project with current print settings
	Print Preview	Shows how the printed document will look

(continued)

Table 1-1 *(continued)*

Button	Name	What It Does
	Spelling	Provides a spell check of your active project
	Cut	Cuts a selection from Project and stores it in the clipboard
	Copy	Copies a selection to the clipboard
	Paste	Pastes from the Clipboard, replacing the selection
	Format Painter	Copies and applies text format
	Undo/Redo	Undoes or redoes the last command (unlike Word, Excel, and PowerPoint, which have separate Undo and Redo buttons)
	Microsoft Project Help	Opens Microsoft Project Help topics

Table 1-2 tells you about the buttons on the Standard toolbar that are unique to Microsoft Project.

Table 1-2   Buttons Unique to Project on the Standard Toolbar

Button	Name	What It Does
	Insert Hyperlink	Opens the Edit Hyperlink dialog box for selecting a hyperlink to associate with a task
	Link Tasks	Links selected tasks with a default finish to start relationship
	Unlink Tasks	Breaks the link between the selected tasks
	Split Task	Enables you to create a nonactive period within a task
	Task Information	Clicking this button is the same as double-clicking a task to open the Task Information dialog box

Button	Name	What It Does
	Task Notes	Opens the Task Information dialog box in the Notes tab
	Assign Resources	Opens the Assign Resources dialog box
	Zoom In	Zooms the Gantt chart to a shorter period of time on the timescale
	Zoom Out	Zooms the Gantt chart to a longer period of time on the timescale
	Go To Selected Task	Causes the Gantt chart to jump to a selected task
	Copy Picture	Opens the Copy Picture dialog box allowing you to take a snapshot of the portions or all of the Gantt Chart view

If you click a toolbar button to perform a basic operation, you don't have a choice of settings. For example, if you click the Print button, your computer automatically prints using default options or the latest options you set. You can't modify the print properties. On the other hand, choosing File⇨Print enables you to choose the print properties for the document.

Buttons, buttons everywhere

Microsoft Project has a bunch of buttons that provide great shortcuts to performing project management functions. Knowing and remembering these buttons is the trick.

Even if you use Microsoft Project daily, you may find it hard to remember what each button does. Not a problem! You can find out what buttons are and what they do easily by using two online Help features in Microsoft Project — the Tool Tips and What's This.

Tool Tips is simple but immensely helpful. Place your mouse over one of the toolbar buttons (but don't click). Almost instantly, a descriptive phrase or word appears.

If the tip doesn't appear, the Tool Tips feature is probably turned off. You can turn it on by choosing View⇨Toolbars⇨Customize. Click the Show Screen Tips on Toolbars check box in the Options tab. Select one of the Menu animations, such as Unfold. After you finish, click Close.

If you want information about the function of a specific button, choose Help⇨What's This? and then click the button you want to know about. A nutshell description of the button's purpose appears.

The Formatting toolbar

The *Formatting toolbar* is the fourth horizontal bar. The formatting toolbar is a mixture of buttons common to other Microsoft Office programs and buttons unique to Microsoft Project. Some of the more interesting ones are included in Table 1-3.

Table 1-3	Interesting Buttons on the Formatting Toolbar	
Button	*Name*	*What It Does*
✚	Show Subtasks	Causes Microsoft Project to display all subtasks of tasks
▬	Hide Subtasks	Causes Microsoft Project to hide all subtasks of tasks
Show ▾	Show	Opens a drop-down list to enable you to select the level of subtasks you would like to display
▽=	AutoFilter	Turns on a filter function for each column in a task or resource sheet
⟍ ▾	Gantt Chart Wizard	Opens a wizard for formatting Gantt bar charts

Megahelp for Many Needs

Help comes in many ways and in varying amounts in Microsoft Project. That's good, because the program is so powerful and the features are so expansive, you could spend half your time just trying to remember what a particular button does or what a particular view presents.

One of the great things about new Microsoft Office products is the large selection of Help options. By selecting the Help menu, you can get suggestions from a variety of Microsoft Office Assistant Help procedures.

Choose Help⇨Microsoft Project Help or press F1 to launch the Microsoft Office Assistant. The Office Assistant offers you a variety of humorous, animated forms, such as the default Clippit. Clippit and the gallery of other animations serve no real function other than to provide an always-available help function. The Office Assistant is an interactive guide that helps you find answers to questions right where you are on the interface or within a procedure. Personally, this little procedure drives me crazy. A bunch of people must like this feature, because Microsoft continues to expand the role of the Office Assistant.

Choose Help⇨Contents and Index to see the standard linear approach to finding information or solutions to your questions. The Help program leads you to a three-tabbed, old-fashioned hierarchy of contents, indexes, and search functionality. Aaah. This is more like it.

Choose Help⇨Getting Started to access some tutorials that lead you through the basics of the program and some basics of project management.

Saving Your Work and Shutting Down

Saving a project file and exiting Microsoft Project is basically the same process as in any other Microsoft Office program. The only curveball you'll encounter is a Planning Wizard that asks if you want to save the project file with or without a baseline. A baseline is a snapshot of a project file that you use for comparison later on when the project has actually begun. Typically, you would select the Save Without a Baseline option until you're finished adding all the ingredients to your project plan. To save and shut down, follow these steps:

1. **Select File⇨Exit.**

   The Office Assistant asks if you want to save your project.

2. **Click Yes.**

   The Save As dialog box appears.

3. **Select a folder where you'd like to save your file.**

   If you want, create a new folder for your project files, such as "Project files." Pretty clever, huh?

4. **Name your file and click the Save button.**

   A Planning Wizard appears, asking you if you want to save your project with or without a baseline. (I explain baselines in detail in Chapter 17.) For now, click Save your file without a baseline. You can now exit Microsoft Project.

Chapter 2

Gathering Your Project Information

● ●

In This Chapter

▶ Finding out what makes a project a project

▶ Identifying your goal

▶ Drawing up the phases of your project

▶ Breaking down phases into tasks

▶ Putting together your information

● ●

*M*icrosoft Project has a voracious appetite: It gladly consumes just about any information you want to give it. One of your most important jobs as project manager is to feed the program the proper data. The information you program into Microsoft Project can be basic or complicated depending on how much work you want the software to do.

If you want to use Microsoft Project for conducting a neighborhood yard sale, your data can be limited and simple. If you need Microsoft Project to organize and manage an expedition to find the Sasquatch in the outer regions of Borneo, you may need to input all kinds of important information. Properly directed, Microsoft Project can handle the complexities of even the largest quest. This chapter helps you assemble and organize the information you need for a project — big or small.

What's a Project?

A *project* is a series of actions initiated to create a unique product or service. This may seem a little highfalutin, but it makes sense (as I show you in this chapter). Project management is what you and your team members do as you apply your knowledge and experience to meet your project objectives.

More important than defining the terms project and project manager is defining your own project. What information do you need to collect to assemble your project plan? How do you begin? What do you need to know and control to ensure success? This chapter helps you through these and other tough questions.

You can read the suggestions in this chapter and at the same time begin work on your project. Do this by using either Microsoft Word or WordPerfect to open `Defining.doc` or `Defining.wpd`, respectively, in the forms folder of the *Microsoft Project 2000 For Dummies* CD-ROM. The Defining form (see Figure 2-1) is written to complement the sections of this chapter. You may find it helpful to complete the Defining form and print it as a reference tool for upcoming tasks. You may want to print additional copies of the form for your team members.

First of all, projects aren't things you tackle at your workplace every day. You can generally break down your work into the following categories:

✔ **Operations:** Operations comprise work you perform routinely.

✔ **Projects:** Projects have specific goals apart from normal functions.

Defining The Project		
Category	Question	Your Answer
Temporary	What marks your project's beginning?	
	What is the project beginning date?	
	What will be the determining factor to mark your project's end?	
	When (what date) does your project need to be completed by?	
	When (what date) does your responsibility as project manager begin?	
	What will be the determining factor to mark the end of your project managing responsibility?	
	How many people will you temporarily need for your project team?	
	Who are the project team members that you can name at this time?	

Figure 2-1: The Defining form and other forms on the CD-ROM can help you begin the pick-and-shovel work for your project.

For example, when I sit at my computer to work, I usually do these things:

- ✔ Write letters
- ✔ Send invoices
- ✔ Answer the phone

Those are normal operations. Today is different. I'm sitting at the same computer, doing what appears to be the same things, but I'm performing a project. I'm writing a book.

For work to be considered a project, it must have these elements — it follows a *temporary* timetable; it has its own *unique* factors; it *progresses;* and it ends with a *product* or service.

Limiting your project's timeframe

By definition, your project is temporary. It has a beginning and an end, and usually, as the project manager, you have to see the project all the way (or significantly) through its lifetime.

To ensure that your project finishes successfully, you have to take responsibility for keeping the project on schedule and allocating the resources necessary to finish the project.

This book, for example, had a definite beginning with the submittal of the proposal to the publisher. This book project ends (for me) when it's approved in its final version for publication by or before the deadline. A project is temporary in that it usually involves a project team that exists for the sole purpose of the project.

So why is it important for you to consider the temporary nature of your project? There are lots of reasons. For example, temporary projects mess up people's "normal" days. If someone has been assigned to help you with your project, you may have a major conflict if the person isn't able to genuinely make room in her schedule for the out-of-the-ordinary demands you'll be making on her time or if she is powerless in staving off other assignments from low-flying work delegators.

Other examples of potential problems stemming from the temporary nature of a project can be as mundane as permitted access to copy machines or an assignment of petty cash.

You have to be able to distinguish what temporary changes are occurring in your workday and in your work environment and you need to be able to verbalize these changes to anyone impacted by the circumstances.

Microsoft Project helps you handle the gargantuan task of managing a project when you program it with the following types of information:

- ✔ Your project's start date and/or particular events that mark the project's beginning

- ✔ Your project's ending date and the criteria that determine its completion

- ✔ The circumstances under which you start and conclude your duties as the project manager

- ✔ The resources you need for your project, including people and technology and team members who can help you complete your project successfully

Considering the uniqueness of your project

Your project has unique factors. Every product that's the outcome of a project differs in some way from other products or services. If you're managing a project, you're developing something that didn't exist before. It doesn't matter whether the project involves engineering a Mars landing, planning a party, or researching a new species of garbanzo bean. If it's a project, it's unique.

Dummies Press publishes oodles of useful and fascinating books. But the *Microsoft Project 2000 For Dummies* project has its own focus, deadlines, project team, marketing strategies, and so on. This book is unique.

Considering the uniqueness of your project is important because in pondering its uniqueness, you're less likely to make assumptions about your project before you start it. If you allow yourself to be lulled into thinking that you've done projects before, you risk missing the differences between your project and others.

You need to give a lot of consideration to identifying and fully understanding what's unique about your project. The uniqueness of a project is its lifeblood. Here are some things to consider when you put your project under a microscope:

- ✔ What's unique about your project?

- ✔ Have other projects produced similar goals?

- ✔ In what ways were other projects similar to yours? How were they different?

- ✔ In what ways have past projects succeeded or failed?

Following your project's progression

A project involves placing separate but related events on a timeline for completion with the goal of creating a product or service. A project is created in that something comes into existence.

Most projects go through several phases on their way to becoming a product or service. People who are involved in the project during its phases have a stake in the project's outcome. As a project manager, you need to keep those people (stakeholders) apprised of the project's status as it follows the timeline. Communication about your project's status throughout its phases is critical and often difficult. Microsoft Project is a powerful tool for collecting and organizing information from the people responsible for project tasks. And, using Microsoft Project, you can help stakeholders understand the technical concepts involved in each phase.

Crafting Your Goal Statement

A *goal* is something you identify to measure the progress and success of your project. Your project is successful if it advances along the timeline and culminates in fulfillment of your goals. Consider these three things when formulating your goal:

- ✔ **Is your project's goal clear?** Fuzzy goals are of little value. A good goal statement is specific and measurable. For example, the goal "I will lose 23 pounds of unwanted fat within 3 months" is specific and measurable. In contrast, "I will lose weight" is fuzzy.

- ✔ **Is the goal attainable?** A good goal statement gives your project the best chance for success. Admirable goals are not necessarily attainable ones. Can your project realistically and definitely achieve what it's being created to perform? If you have taken care to design your goal statement for reasonable achievement, you're most likely to exceed your project goal.

- ✔ **Does the goal need a reality check?** In order for a goal statement to be a good one, it has to be written to work within the environment where the project is to be created. Maybe your goal statement is specific and measurable and maybe it's attainable, but can it happen at the time you want to do it? For example, maybe your project goal doesn't fit the reality of vacation schedules of your team members.

Thinking About Phases

A project *phase* is a group of tasks that represents a project within a project. A phase usually results in the completion of a step or an intermediate goal within a project. In Microsoft Project, a summary task and its subtasks make up a phase.

Understanding the advantages of phases

Small projects with few tasks don't need phases. Projects with any degree of complexity or with more than a few tasks tend to have phases. The reason for this is logical. Usually, work within projects is performed in clusters. Phases are made up of tasks that need to be performed in order for the phase to be complete. For example, your project may be to move from your old location into a new one. That project may include phases such as:

- ✔ Provide temporary customer support
- ✔ Move furniture
- ✔ Advertise move

The above phases are unrelated, but each phase is necessary to complete the project. The phases have tasks. For instance, the temporary customer support phase might have tasks such as:

- ✔ Rent computers
- ✔ Set up temporary office
- ✔ Transfer phones

The following list describes some characteristics of phases:

- ✔ **Phases proceed in cycles.** A phase begins, is carried out, and ends in another phase's beginning.

- ✔ **Phases produce an intermediate product or service.** The project management term for an intermediate product is a *deliverable*. An example of a deliverable is an architect's blueprints. The blueprints are the intermediate product created during the design stage in order for the project to move on to the construction phase.

- ✔ **Phases have an end-review process.** A phase needs to be judged as having met its objectives in order to make the next phase possible.

Most projects have five to seven phases, but some have a lot more. Simple projects usually have at least three phases, as follows:

- ✔ **Project planning phase**
- ✔ **Project execution phase**
- ✔ **Project closure phase**

Upon review of all contracts and other administrative considerations, the bills are paid, the project team is disbanded, and the maintenance of the product is turned over to ongoing operations for the product's life. Although the product lives on, the project has ended. (In Chapter 3, you see how Microsoft Project uses phases to create task groupings.) Figure 2-2 shows how a series of phases ends with a successful project.

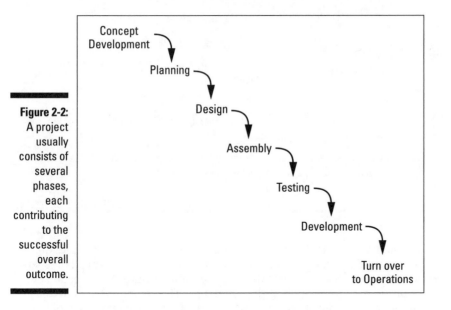

Figure 2-2:
A project usually consists of several phases, each contributing to the successful overall outcome.

Identifying project phases

Breaking down your project into phases is a good way to see its details. To reach completion, the phases of your project use resources, reach milestones, and pass along deliverables to the next phase.

In a way, phases define their own existence. Certain tasks belong together to create a deliverable. If you're building a house, the wallboard installers won't show up before the walls are framed (hopefully). The wallboard installers are part of the phase that happens after the house is framed.

The many hats of a project manager

If you are a project manager, you wear a lot of hats. Fortunately, Microsoft Project is a great valet and will help ensure you don't don the wrong hat for the wrong occasion. Depending on the organization, in varying degrees you are responsible for the *development of the project plan.* This may include:

- Defining tasks, their sequence, and their duration
- Scheduling
- Resource planning (people, equipment, and materials)
- Organizational planning
- Cost estimating and budgeting
- Risk identification
- Quality planning
- Communication of planning

The project manager is responsible also for the *execution of the project plan,* which includes these tasks:

- Staffing
- Team building
- Contract administration
- Procurement
- Cost control
- Risk control
- Quality assurance
- Performance reporting
- Problem solving
- Change control

The *completion of the project plan* usually includes:

- Contract closures
- Administrative closures

As you work in Parts II through VI of this book, you find how to wear these many hats — often all at the same time.

Phases can happen simultaneously. Using the housebuilding example, the wallboard installers can do their work in the finishing phase while landscapers are doing their work in the exterior preparation phase. Also, certain elements of a phase can happen at the same time. The wallboard installers can do their work in the finishing stage while the kitchen cabinet installers are also doing their work in the finishing stage.

Resources

Resources are the people and materials who perform work related to your project. Microsoft Project associates resources with tasks. In Chapter 5, I show you how to enter resource information into your project.

Milestones

When you hear the word milestone, you probably think of a significant event. It's the same in Microsoft Project. A *milestone* marks specific places along your project timeline and denotes important events. These places usually are where a project begins or ends, or where some major stage of completion takes place. Milestones are not measurements of time. Instead, milestones are indicators of beginning or ending. For that reason, Microsoft Project assigns a zero-time duration to milestones.

Deliverables

The output of one phase becomes the input of the next phase and must be understood and acted upon. Each phase ends with a *deliverable* (output) that is the groundwork (input) for the beginning of the next phase. Examples of a deliverable may be a contract, an installed well, or an approved inspection. Sometimes, you can determine project phases by necessary deliverables. For example, if your company has moved to a new location, a new phone number list may be the deliverable for "move phone system" phase.

Communicating across phases

Progressive elaboration is the project management term for communicating a project's status sufficiently across the project's phases.The project manager has to communicate to the principals of a project in a manner that complements the unique technology and professional language of each.

For example, engineers communicate by using drawings and specifications in the design phase. People involved in the building phase must understand those drawings and specifications to proceed with building.

A project is often made up of clusters of activities (phases). A project phase ends successfully if it provides the basis for the subsequent phase to pick up and continue.

Breaking Down Phases into Tasks

I hate details. To me, details are crabgrass in the lawn of life. And this hatred of details makes me get warm and fuzzy about Microsoft Project. Whether or not I like it, the success of a project depends on the attention given to minutiae. In Microsoft Project, you control individual details of a project either as task information or resource information.

Identifying and managing the details of a project can be laborious and overwhelming. Fortunately, Microsoft Project is a powerful tool for identifying details, managing their relationship with other details, and tracking their evolution throughout a project. After you have assigned details as task information or resource information, you can use numerous Microsoft Project features to analyze and compare information.

After you define the phases of your project, you break down those phases into multiple *tasks*. Tasks are individual segments of work, each having a start and a finish, and each using specific resources.

Duration is the amount of time it takes to finish a task. Microsoft Project needs this information in order to track your project. You can tell Microsoft Project this information in increments of minutes, hours, days, or weeks.

Microsoft Project uses this information to help you keep track of task durations and determine whether you've got enough time to finish tasks on schedule. One of the helpful features of Microsoft Project is that it can alert you to scheduling inconsistencies. The design phase of a project has to be incorporated into the contract phase so that the design can be a deliverable to the contract phase. As you can see, Microsoft Project is a whiz at keeping track of these kinds of complexities.

Microsoft Project also helps you edit your duration estimates. But first, you need to estimate task durations.

Assembling Your Project Information

The best way to use Microsoft Project is to come prepared. Microsoft Project doesn't help you create project goals. The program doesn't help you identify phases or tasks, and it doesn't tell you what your resources are or what their schedules should be like. In this section, you prepare yourself for making the most of Microsoft Project.

Stated briefly, projects are a series of phases. This section helps you identify your project's phases, tasks, task duration, milestones, and resources. In Chapter 3, I show you how to start feeding your information to Microsoft Project.

Because of the nature of contracts, any inspections in a project may have to happen on fixed dates. Those dates can't be altered or the contractor involved will be penalized. You can manage these types of factors easily with Microsoft Project. You can track some tasks that happen sequentially, upon the completion of others. You can also assign and track other tasks that will happen at the same time.

Identifying resources

The identification, assignment, and management of resources are the trickiest parts of project management. Fortunately, Microsoft Project is well equipped to assist you with the challenge.

Remember that resources can be not only people, but also things. If something is necessary to perform a task, and if it's not automatically available, it can be included in the project plan. For example, someone on a sales staff has to reserve a conference room for an hour. The room is used for many purposes by a variety of staff and customers. In such a situation, the conference room is a managed resource.

Overallocation of resources is one of the most common problems in project management. As you allocate resources to tasks, you should double-check the availability of those resources and their commitment to other projects or operations.

In addition to resource overcommitment to multiple projects, resources can also be overallocated for a single project. You need to ensure that the contractor has allotted enough labor and equipment to reach a milestone. Don't forget that weather can be a factor in your reaching your milestones.

Planning effectively before your project starts

Effective planning for a project starts with having goals that are achievable. Clear goals, good planning, and adaptability are the high-octane fuel that keeps a project running smoothly and efficiently.

The following are some suggestions that outline a good approach to your project (see Figure 2-3) and prepare you for using Microsoft Project:

- ✔ **Scope out your project.** Define what your project is about, why it's important, and who is your target customer or audience.

- ✔ **Identify your stakeholders.** What people or organizations are involved in the project or will be affected by it?

- ✔ **Determine the standard of quality you want your project to meet.** Are there particular industry or government standards or regulations your project must meet? Everyone who has a stake in the project needs to agree on what is expected.

- ✔ **List constraints.** Are there time limitations on your project, or are key resources available during your project?

- ✔ **Determine whether the project fits your organization's style.** A project is never more important than the organization that supports it. But quite often, pressures within an organization can make a project tougher than anticipated.

Developing an Effective Project Plan		
Step	Question	Your Answer
1. Scoping it out	What is your project scope?	
	What is the importance or need of your project?	
	Who is your target customer, audience, or recipient?	
2. Identifying stakeholders	Who are the stakeholders for your project?	
3. Determining the quality	What are the explicit expectations about quality in your project?	
	Are there explicit expectations based on industry or government standards and regulations?	
	Are there any explicit policies?	
	What implicit expectations could affect your project?	

Figure 2-3:
These steps form a good self-assessment tool for planning a project.

Some organizations are function-based; they have structures grouped by specialty, such as marketing, design, and accounting. Function-based organizations are usually hierarchical. Each function has a boss, an assistant boss, and so on.

Other organizations are project-based. They exist to perform projects. Most organizations exist somewhere in between. The following questions help you determine where your organization fits between these ends of the continuum. Also, you identify important resources that can make or break your project.

- ✔ **Identify the source of authority for the project.**
- ✔ **Identify areas of your project that will require outside approval.**
- ✔ **Find out if a consensus exists about the goals of your project in your organization.**
- ✔ **Identify people unrelated to the project who feel that they are stakeholders and develop a plan to deal with their input.**
- ✔ **Identify potential risks.**
- ✔ **Set goals.**

Part II
Building a Project

The 5th Wave — By Rich Tennant

"HOW'S THAT FOR FAST SCROLLING?"

In this part . . .

After you define your project's scope and set the goals, you can create a schedule and start defining the relationships of the various project parts. In this part, using sample information or your own, you develop tasks, set durations, add resources, outline your project, clarify relationships, and set times.

Be careful; you may find yourself craving the company of other project managers so that you can talk Gantt charts and resource pools.

Chapter 3

Using Microsoft Project to Put the Pieces Together

*I*n this chapter, I tell you how to create a project schedule in Microsoft Project. The process is user-friendly and straightforward. If you occasionally do a "big shop" at a grocery store, you're ready to tackle this type of work. Before you shop, you probably create a list of what you need. If you're familiar with the store, you probably write down items on your shopping list in the order in which they're located in the store.

You approach your project in much the same way. However, instead of putting items in a cart, you enter tasks in a file. And instead of planning your shopping by aisles, you make sense of your tasks by placing them in phases, assigning time to devote to them, and divvying up responsibilities to get them done.

Starting a Project on Your Own Terms

Every time you start a new project in Microsoft Project, the slate is clean. The sun is shining, and you're not behind on anything. The world is yours to turn into one big project right now. You're probably opening Project because you want to plan your project, not start it. If you're lucky — really lucky — you have a little time between your next breath and when the project needs to actually begin. But until you tell Project something different, the program assumes your project is beginning today *<shudder>*. You need to figure out how to start a project on a future (or another) date.

Creating a new file from scratch (just like Betty Crocker!)

Starting a new project is simple. Just click the New button shown in the margin. The Project Information dialog box appears (Figure 3-1). Notice that in the figure the start, finish, and current dates are all the same (makes your stomach flutter, doesn't it?). To enter an actual start date for your project, follow these steps:

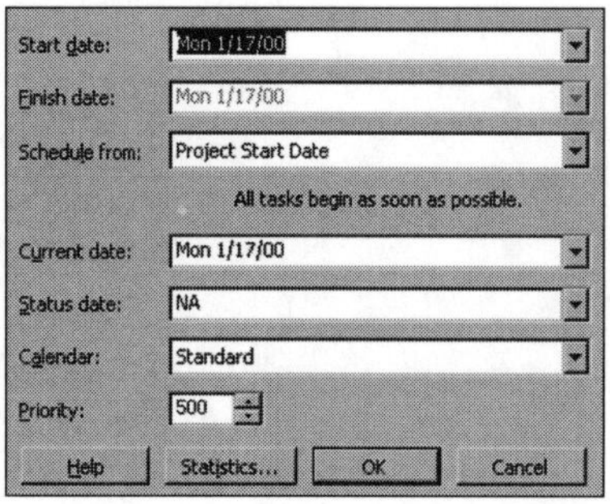

Figure 3-1:
In the Project Information dialog box, you set the date on which the project will begin.

Start date:	Mon 1/17/00	▼
Finish date:	Mon 1/17/00	▼
Schedule from:	Project Start Date	▼
	All tasks begin as soon as possible.	
Current date:	Mon 1/17/00	▼
Status date:	NA	▼
Calendar:	Standard	▼
Priority:	500	
Help	Statistics...	OK	Cancel

1. **Type a new date in the Start Date text box.**

   For instance, I typed **2/8/00**. Microsoft Project enters today's date by default. Well, no time like the present, I guess.

   Microsoft Project recognizes typed dates such as 2/8/00 and February 8, 2000. If you want, you can type 2/8. In this last case, Microsoft Project assumes you mean the current year. Or you can click the down arrow next to the text box and click a date on the calendar.

   The Schedule From text box says `Project Start Date` by default. This means the project schedule is based on the project start date. The project start date is usually not the same date as when you start building and first save your project file. Typically, a project start date is some time in the future. When you enter your anticipated project start date, that means your first project task will begin on that date. And you don't have to worry about entering a date in the Project Finish Date text box. Project changes this date automatically for you as you build your project.

2. **Click OK.**

   Project returns you to the opening screen and one subtle change takes place. The Gantt chart on the right of the screen jumps to your start date (see Figure 3-2).

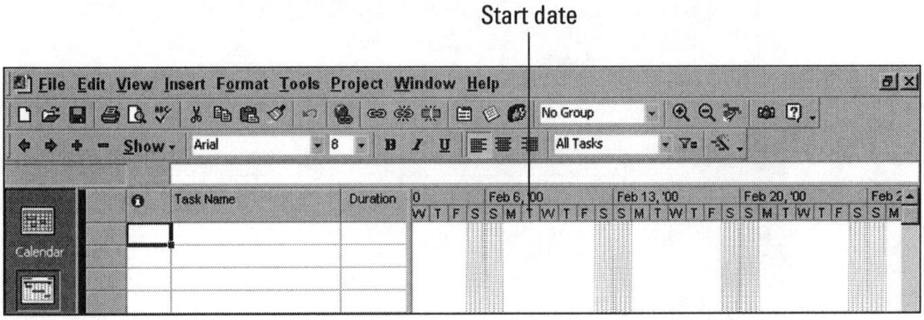

Start date

Figure 3-2:
Microsoft
Project
adjusts the
dates to
reflect your
start date.

Opening an existing project file

You may not be working on a new project, but rather on a preexisting project.
So you need to know how to open Project files. To open an existing Project
file, follow these steps:

1. **Click the Open button on the standard toolbar.**

   The Open dialog box sallies forth. By default, the Project displays the
   contents of the My Documents folder, where it saves all your projects by
   default.

2. **If the project that you want to open isn't in the My Documents folder,
   click the down arrow in the Look In box and navigate to another
   folder.**

   See Appendix C for instructions on finding the sample projects on the
   Microsoft Project 2000 For Dummies CD.

3. **Double-click the file that you want to open.**

   The Project file appears in the Gantt Chart view. See Chapter 7 for more
   information about Gantt Chart view.

   Figure 3-3 shows the results of opening the sample file Smith House 3.mpp
   file that's available on the CD-ROM. Feel free to practice with this file.

Entering Tasks and Phases

The first step in creating a schedule is to enter the project's tasks. Microsoft
Project's primary function is to help you keep track of the things left to
accomplish in your project, and the more tasks, the merrier. Major projects
can often be broken down into *phases*. Phases are tasks that you group
together in some way — usually because they are similar in nature or they
link together to define a manageable subset of the project.

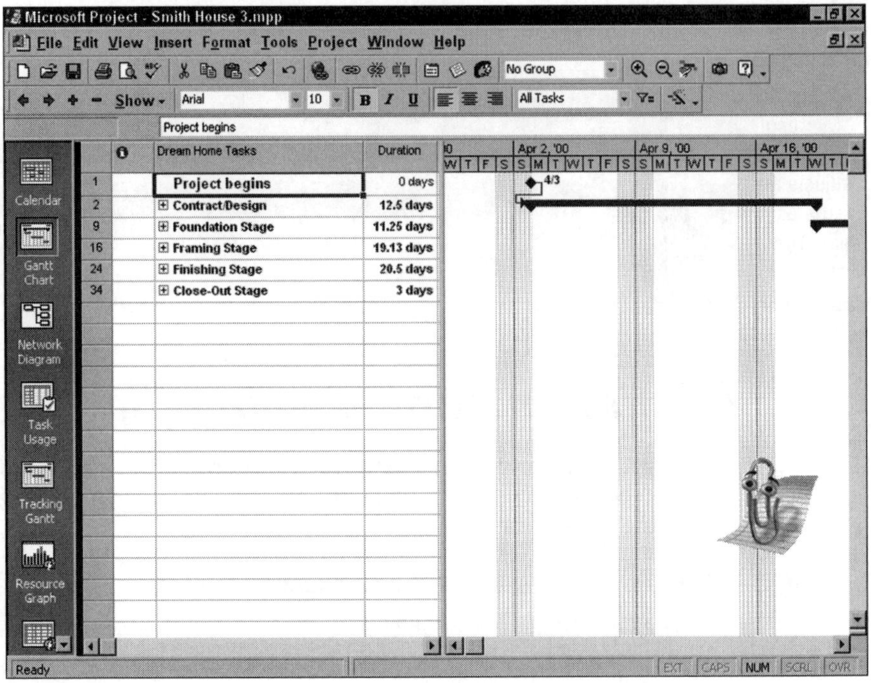

Figure 3-3:
The Smith
House 3
Project file
appears in
the Gantt
Chart view.

Suppose, for example, that you're planning a Throw a Party project. Within the project, you may need to include the all-important Clean Up This Pigsty phase. Subtasks of the Clean Up This Pigsty phase could be *dust, sweep, mop, vacuum,* and *throw away the (mostly) empty pizza boxes.*

In Microsoft Project, phases are *summary tasks,* which are merely run-of-the-mill tasks to which you make other tasks subordinate. (The trick to subordinating tasks is the Indent button, which I explain more about in the section titled "Filling phases with tasks" later in this chapter.) In essence, a summary task acts as a container for its subtasks. Summary tasks are useful because Project allows you to expand and collapse summary tasks to view the subtasks that the summary task represents. Also, the duration of a summary task is the sum of the durations of all its subtasks, which can help you see your project in terms of the big picture.

You can organize the tasks in your project into subtasks and summary tasks in two different ways — top down and bottom up.

✓ **Top down** refers to riding in a convertible. In Microsoft Project, however, this term refers to the process of listing the major parts of your project first and then filling those major parts with their various tasks. Use this method if you understand the organization of your project at the outset.

✔ **Bottom up** refers to listing all the tasks in your project first and then inserting summary tasks into the list and subordinating the tasks to subtasks. Use this method if you can think of the various things that you need to do, but an organization isn't immediately apparent.

In reality, you'll probably use a bit of both methods in the course of planning your project. But you're probably better off to start by thinking of your project in phases if you can, so that's the method that I concentrate on in this chapter.

Listing the project's phases

You can formulate your project schedule in two ways — by entering phases and then adding tasks below the summary tasks (phases); or by entering tasks and placing summary tasks above them. (The first approach is much easier to perform!)

Entering the phases of your project is a breeze; just follow these steps:

1. **Click in the Task Name column.**

2. **Type the phase task name in the Task Name column.**

3. **Press Enter.**

Figure 3-4 shows a partially-filled-in project file.

Figure 3-4:
When you start out, phases look just like tasks.

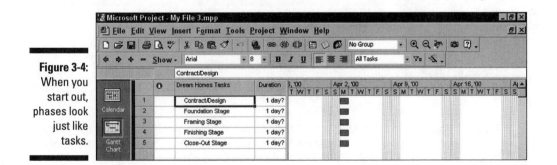

Filling phases with tasks

After you identify the phases of your project, you can add the subtasks (see Figure 3-5). When you enter subtasks, Microsoft Project will turn your phase task into a summary task.

To enter subtasks under phases, perform the following steps:

1. **Click the task name box below a phase.**

   The cell is probably filled with another phase, but don't worry.

2. **Press Insert on your keyboard.**

   The existing task drops down to the next row.

3. **Type the name of the task into the empty task name box.**

4. **Press Enter.**

   The new task appears like all the other tasks in the column.

5. **Click the new task to highlight it.**

6. **Click the Indent button on the Formatting toolbar (see Figure 3-5).**

   The new task indents. The task above the indented task changes in appearance. It is now a summary task. The summary task bar in the Gantt chart changes from blue to black and changes in shape with downward arrows that indicate the beginning and end of the summary task.

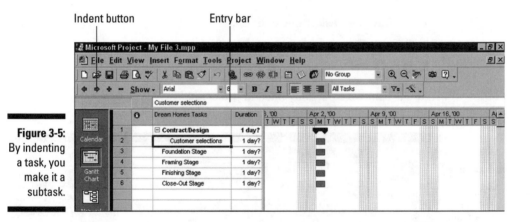

Figure 3-5:
By indenting
a task, you
make it a
subtask.

If you make a mistake typing a task name, simply select what you typed and retype the correct information in the entry bar below the formatting toolbar (refer to Figure 3-5). The entry bar displays the contents of the active cell. When everything appears the way you want it, click the green check mark button. If you don't want to make the change, click the red X button. That will cancel the change.

The number to the left of each task is its ID. This number has two functions. It indicates the order of a task and is the unique identifier of the task. Because each task has its own ID, you can have multiple tasks with the same name.

The idea of thinking about phase tasks can really help you in dividing your project into manageable chunks and help you with reporting the progress of your project. Table 3-1 shows the breakdown of phases and subtasks in the project of building your dream home.

Phase tasks are summary tasks when they have subtasks. All really refer to the same thing in Project, tasks. The only difference is in your judicious use of the Indent and Outdent buttons.

Table 3-1	Phases and Subphases of a Construction Project
Phase	*Subphase*
Foundation Phase	Excavation
	Landscaping
	Footing/foundation
	Inspection
Framing Phase	Wood framing
	Roofing
	Plumbing lines
	Furnace and A/C
	Electrical wiring
	Inspection
Finishing Phase	Wallboard
	Stairway
	Painting
	Trim
Finishing Phase	Landscaping
	Customer walkthrough
	Punch list corrections
	Final inspection
Close-Out Phase	Contract closure
	Administrative closure

Customizing column names

A cool way to customize your project is by renaming the columns in the Gantt table on the left of the Gantt Chart view. Use these steps to customize columns:

1. **Double-click the name of the column that you want to change.**

   The Column Definition dialog box appears, as shown in the figure to the right.

2. **In the Title text box, type a new name for the column.**

3. **Click OK.**

I'm partial to calling tasks in my Smith Home project *Dream Home Tasks,* for example. I kinda like the ring of it. So by performing these steps on the Task Name column, I get what I wish for.

Notice in Table 3-1 that *inspection* appears more than once (as shown in Figure 3-6). How does Project keep the different inspections straight? That's what the task ID numbers are for. Each task has its own unique ID, so Project never mixes them up (hmmm. . . I wonder if Project can manage my sock drawer?).

You can demote as many levels as you want. A quick way to demote a task is by using the mouse. Position the mouse cursor over the first letter of the task's name. The cursor turns into a right-left arrow. While holding down the left mouse button, drag the task to the right to demote it or to the left to promote it.

Showing and hiding subtasks

A subtask is a task existing within a phase task (known as a summary task). One of the advantages of having a summary task acting as a container for the subtasks is that you can hide the subtasks. Hiding subtasks can make a long list of project tasks much easier to manage. Refer to Figure 3-2, which shows a gray column of nonsequential numbers at the left of the figure. The numbers are not in order because some of the tasks are hidden. The hidden tasks are *subtasks*.

To see the subtasks, choose Show⇨All Subtasks. Whoa! Where did all this information come from? Actually, it was there all the time, just waiting for you to access it (see Figure 3-7).

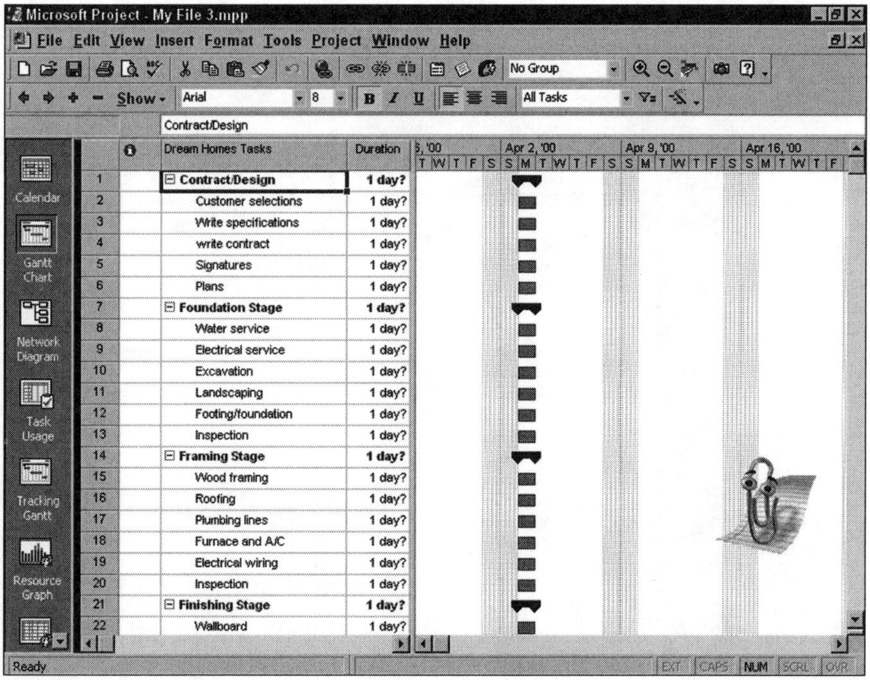

Figure 3-6:
This schedule includes more than one inspection, but each task has its own ID.

Adjusting the width of the task column

A task's name doesn't have to fit completely in the task name cell. The full name still exists even if you can't see all of it. But for outlining and reporting, the schedule looks better if all of the text fits in a cell. I explain outlining and reporting in Chapter 19.

To make task names fit, you can either shorten the names or enlarge the task column to fit the longest task name.

To make all the tasks fit, you can do one of four things:

✔ Drag the border between the Task Name and Duration column headings to the right.

✔ Double-click the Task Name heading. The Column Definition dialog box appears. For Width, enter a number larger than the current 24 (up to 128 characters).

✔ Double-click the Task Name heading. In the Column Definition dialog box, choose Best Fit. The column is automatically sized based on the length of the task name.

✔ Double-click the border between the Task Name and Duration column headings. Doing so automatically sets the width to the length of the longest task.

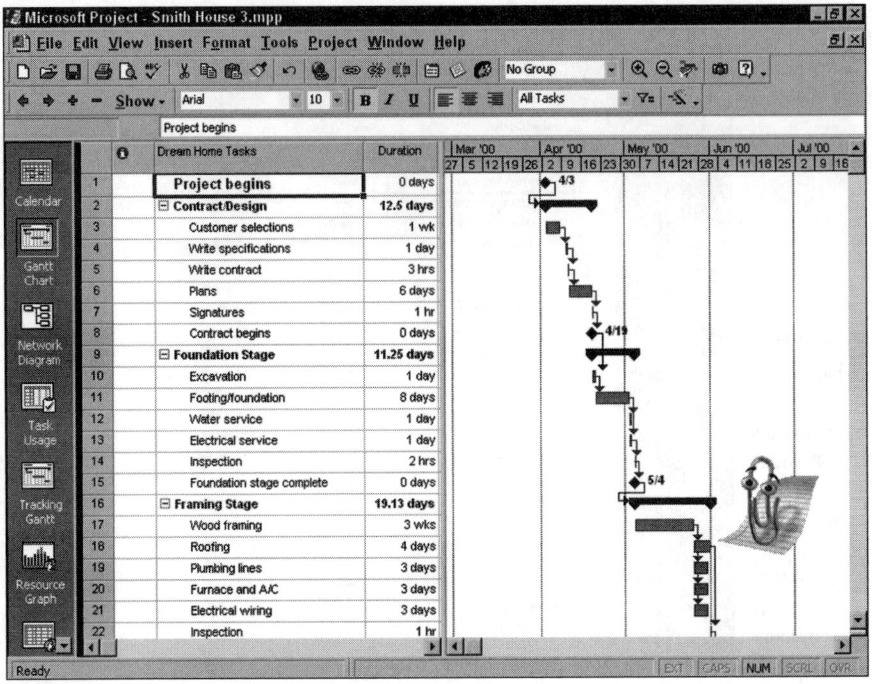

Figure 3-7:
The Gantt
chart fills
with task
information.

Figure 3-7 shows a project that comprises summary tasks and subtasks. To see how the project appears in other views, click buttons on the view bar. After you're done looking at other views, click the Gantt Chart view again.

Deleting summary tasks

Is one of your summary tasks less brilliant than it first appeared? Have circumstances changed and you need to cluster a few groups of subtasks under a single summary task? You can delete a summary task — carefully! Use the following steps to delete a task:

1. **Select the summary task.**

2. **Press the Delete key.**

   The Planning wizard appears (see Figure 3-8), warning you that what you selected is a summary task and that deleting it will delete its subtasks as well. Pretty sharp, huh?

3. **You can continue and delete the summary task by clicking OK or click cancel to retreat.**

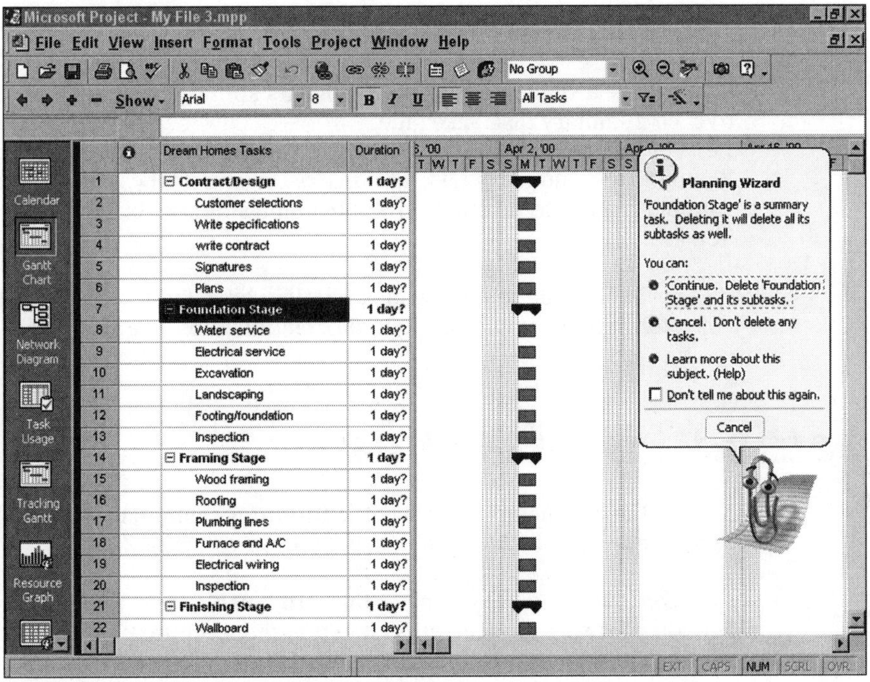

Figure 3-8:
The
Planning
Wizard
gives you
the option of
clicking
Cancel to
avoid delet-
ing a sum-
mary task.

Project still offers you another opportunity to undo your deletion. You can undo a deletion by selecting Edit➪Undo (Ctrl+Z). The Undo function is only available for your last action.

The Planning Wizard gives you good advice as you become familiar with Microsoft Project, so you may want to ensure that it's activated until you have a project or three under your belt. On the other hand, you may decide at some point that you don't want it telling you what to do anymore. You can toggle the Wizard on and off by choosing Tools➪Options and then selecting or deselecting the Advice from Planning Wizard check box and its three subordinate check boxes.

To delete a summary task without affecting any subtasks, you promote the subtasks beneath the summary task to tasks before deleting anything. A summary task without subtasks becomes a regular old task. Promote subtasks by selecting them and clicking the Outdent button on the formatting toolbar.

Moving summary tasks

If you move a summary task, you move its subtasks as well. Subtasks stick to their summary tasks like glue.

If you move a summary task into an existing summary group, the moved summary task and its children will become subtasks of the subtasks. Oh, my head!

You probably need to modify task relationships if you've already linked tasks. For information about changing task relationships, see Chapter 4.

Setting Task Duration

Next to the task name column is the Duration column. By default, Microsoft Project assigns a task length in the duration column.

Duration is the amount of time it takes to finish a task. You can't have a schedule for your project without estimating each task's duration. This section shows you how to enter duration into Microsoft Project.

In Microsoft Project, you can use the following durations:

- ✔ m (minutes)
- ✔ h (hours)
- ✔ d (days)
- ✔ w (weeks)
- ✔ 0 (milestones)

To find out more about milestones, see the section, "Inserting milestones," later in this chapter.

By default, Microsoft Project assigns five days to a workweek and eight hours to a workday.

You enter durations in the same way you enter task names. Simply select the cell you want to type in and type. Press Enter, and the next cell is highlighted automatically. Type the following durations next to their respective tasks (see Figure 3-9). (If you can't see the Duration column to the right of the Task Name column, drag the vertical bar separating the Gantt table and the Gantt chart to the right.)

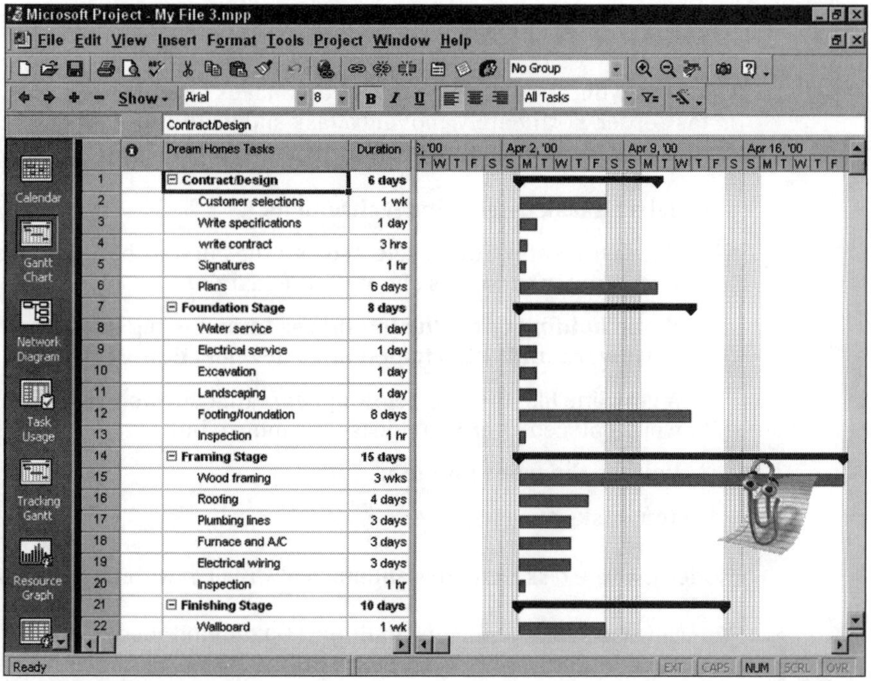

Figure 3-9:
The sum-
mary tasks
now show
the longest
duration of
any of their
subtasks.

Editing Tasks

One of the nicest features of Microsoft Project is how easily you can make
changes. Adding, deleting, and moving tasks is a piece of cake. Even late into
your project, the program can keep up with your changes and alert you to
their effects on other aspects of your project.

You may be at the beginning of your project and yet need to make a few
changes. For example, suppose that while reviewing your plan for construct-
ing your dream home (Smith House 3.mpp), you notice the following:

- ✔ The design phase takes place after the contracts are signed. Normally,
  design plans are part of the contract. You need to move the contract task.

- ✔ Water service and electrical service can be put in only after the foundation has been erected or poured. You need to move this small group of
  tasks.

- ✔ The landscaping task is listed twice. Sometimes there may be a good
  reason to list a task twice, but not this time. All landscaping work would
  be ruined in the early stages of construction. You need to delete one
  landscaping task and change the other task's duration.

- ✔ You need to add some tasks with zero duration, specifically, milestones.

Moving a task

Once in a while, you'll notice that a task makes more sense somewhere else in task order. Fortunately, moving a task and its duration is simple. To move a task, follow these steps:

1. **Select a task by clicking its ID number.**

    The task's entire row is selected and the cursor changes to the north-west pointer cursor, as shown in the margin.

2. **While holding down the left mouse button, drag the cursor upward or downward until it's situated at its new location.**

   A gray line like the one below appears that shows you where the task will be placed after you release the mouse button.

3. **Release the mouse button.**

   Your tasks change places.

Notice that the task durations automatically realign with the new task positions.

 You can also select and move multiple tasks simultaneously, but the tasks must be contiguous. To select the multiple tasks click the first task, press and hold the Shift key, and then click the last task you want to move. Move the group of tasks by clicking any task number within the highlighted group and dragging to the new location.

Deleting a task

If you need to delete a task and adjust the durations of the remaining tasks, follow these steps:

1. **Select a task on the task pad.**

   You can click anywhere on the task.

2. **Press the Delete key.**

   That task is gone. The tasks that followed now ripple up into their new positions.

If you make a mistake or change your mind, you can undo your most recent action by clicking the Undo button on the standard toolbar. Fwoop! Unlike other Microsoft Office products such as Word, you can only undo your last action. After that, the Undo function becomes a Redo function. So make your decision quickly.

Save your project often as you go along. When you're happy with something you've done, don't wait — save! Doing so protects your work in the event of a power outage or a Windows crash. The shortcut key for saving is Ctrl+S. Use it often!

Inserting tasks into an existing project

Inserting a task or tasks into an existing project is easy. Just click an existing task and press the Insert key (or choose Insert➪New Task). Space is inserted for your new task at that point, and the former occupant of the cell moves to the next cell down. Enter the information for the new task in that space.

Inserting milestones

A *milestone* is a significant event in a project that you use to assess your progress. Often, milestones occur at the conclusion of a summary task. Sometimes milestones are a place for changing some project team members.

◆ Any task in Microsoft Project that has a duration of 0 is automatically displayed as a milestone. To insert a milestone, you click in the cell where you want to insert the milestone, and press the Insert key. The task that currently holds that place will trickle down one task line (as will all subsequent tasks). Then enter a task with a duration of 0. Microsoft Project displays the milestone symbol on that day, as shown in the margin.

Although milestones usually serve as a signal of a significant point in a phase or project, milestones can also be actual tasks. An example might be the breaking of a bottle of champagne on a ship's prow during a launching ceremony. The breaking of the bottle is a milestone but it's also a task with resources connected to it. You make a task a milestone by selecting the Mark Task as Milestone check box in the Advanced tab of the Task Information dialog box. I discuss this dialog box in Chapter 4.

If you want a bit of practice with milestones, insert these other milestones into the sample project Smith House 3.mpp, all with a duration of 0d:

✔ Insert a milestone at the very beginning called Project Begins, as shown in Figure 3-10.

✔ After Signatures, insert a milestone called Contract begins.

✔ After Inspection in the Foundation Phase, insert a milestone called Foundation stage complete.

> ✔ After Inspection in the Framing Stage, insert a milestone called Framing stage complete.
>
> ✔ After Final inspection in the Finishing Stage, insert a milestone called Finishing stage complete.
>
> ✔ After Administrative closure, enter a milestone called Project complete.

If you're using the sample project, don't be bothered by the fact that your milestones have the same date as the project start date. You can change those later.

Linking Tasks

After you enter tasks and their durations, the next step is usually to link tasks. Linking tasks is a procedure where Microsoft Project assigns relationships between tasks.

By using the default link, you ensure that a task doesn't begin until previous tasks are finished. It's called a *finish-to-start* link. (To find out about other types of links, check out Chapter 4.)

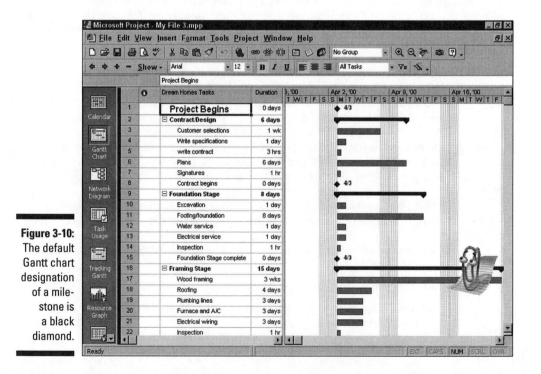

Figure 3-10: The default Gantt chart designation of a milestone is a black diamond.

You can link only two tasks or all of them. To link all the tasks on the Gantt chart, follow these steps:

1. **While holding down the mouse button, select a task.**

2. **Drag the cursor through all the tasks you want to link.**

3. **Click the Link Tasks button on the standard toolbar.**

   The tasks in the Gantt chart also move to the right showing that they occur sequentially. By default, Project inserts a finish-to-start dependency, although you can change the dependency type if you like. (I cover changing dependency types in Chapter 4.) Lines with arrowheads show the linkage of tasks.

Practicing with task linking

To get comfortable with task linking, open up Smith Home 3.mpp. As you scan the project, you notice that all the project's tasks are set to start on the same date. The painters are going to have trouble getting to the second floor of a house that hasn't been designed yet. Hmm. Something is missing. Although the task durations are all relatively accurate, the overall project has no layout in time. To fix this problem, follow these steps:

1. **While holding down the mouse button, select Task 1.**

2. **Drag the cursor through all the tasks.**

3. **Click the Link Tasks button on the standard toolbar.**

   Now the Gantt chart comes alive. Tasks are linked in the finish-to-start relationship and stretch out beyond the screen's width (unless you have a monitor shaped like a two by four).

4. **Press the Page Up key until you return to the first task.**

The Gantt chart looks much different now.

5. **Press the Page Down key once or twice until you see the last few tasks.**

6. **Select the final task cell entitled** Project Complete.

7. **Click the Go To Selected Task button on the standard toolbar.**

After linking tasks, you should do a reality check. In this example, we have troubles. The project, in its current state, will finish on August 2, the contractual finish date. "Great!" you may say, but what about the possibility of an occasional thundershower raining on your parade?

Unless you know some weather dances, you need to do some project management magic to shorten the project's length. But like all other forms of magic, project management is really a craft. You need to know a number of disappearing tricks to make the Smith Home project realistically shorter. That's what this chapter and Chapters 4, 5, and 14 are about — optimizing work through quality time management.

Unlinking tasks

One of the magic feats you need to know is how to unlink tasks. Sometimes you'll need to unlink tasks so that you can reorganize task relationships. To unlink tasks, follow these steps:

1. **Click the first task.**

2. **Click the Go To Selected Task button on the standard toolbar to see your task duration in the Gantt Chart.**

3. **While holding down the mouse button, select the first task.**

4. **Drag the cursor down through the tasks you want to unlink.**

5. **Click the Unlink Tasks button on the standard toolbar.**

   The project returns to its previous unlinked condition.

Understanding dependency types

Microsoft Project has four kinds of task dependency:

- **Finish-to-start (FS)** relationships are the default Microsoft Project task relationship. It means that Task A must finish before Task B can begin. When you create a link, the default relationship is finish-to-start.

- **Start-to-start (SS)** relationships mean that Task B can't start until Task A does. An example of this is heating a store-bought pizza. Task A heats the oven. Task B puts the pizza in the oven.

- **Finish-to-finish (FF)** relationships mean that Task B cannot finish before Task A does. An example is a credit card sale. Task A delivers the product to the customer. Task B gets the customer to sign the credit slip.

- **Start-to-finish (SF)** relationships mean that Task B can't finish until Task A starts. An example of this is a temporary electrical generator that can't stop until power is turned on to a permanent electrical system.

I tell you in Chapter 4 how to change from the default finish to start to another type of dependency.

Chapter 4

Task Relationships

Microsoft Project is all about relationships — it's a master of whodunits (or whosgoingtodoits). As the project manager, you are the storyteller. You get to choose the twists and turns and control the outcome. The story's players, the tasks, are dependent on other tasks beginning or ending. The end of one task (a predecessor) may signal the start of a new task. The Predecessors! What a title! You'll sell a million. Can I come to your book signing?

The success of your project depends largely on the care you put into relating your tasks. Sometimes the players are constrained by circumstances beyond their control. This chapter tells you how to establish various task relationships and constraints in your project.

You're welcome to use your own real-life project as you check out task relationships in this chapter. Or if you'd like, you can use a practice file I've created. The practice file in this chapter is based on the Smith Home project file that I introduce in Chapter 3. You can pick up the file where it begins this chapter by opening Smith House 4.MPP on the CD in the back of this book. For instructions on using the practice files on the CD, see Appendix C.

Introducing Task Control Central: The Task Information Box

One of the quickest and easiest ways to insert the information that applies to a particular task is by using the Task Information dialog box. This box is a centralized collection of options for adding specific information to a task throughout the life of a project. To open the Task Information dialog box, use one of the following methods:

- Double-click a task.
- Highlight a task and press Shift+F2.
- Select a task and then click the Task Information button on the Standard toolbar.
- Choose Project⇨Task Information.

The General tab

The General tab provides you the flexibility to change the name or duration of a task, to set start and finish dates, and a lot more (see Figure 4-1). The following list explains the options available on the General tab of the Task Information dialog box:

- **Estimated:** The Estimated check box gives you the option of indicating that you aren't yet prepared to assign a fixed duration for the task. Selecting the Estimated check box adds a ? character after the duration in the task sheet.

- **Percent Complete:** You can enter a number between 0 and 100 into the Percent Complete text box to indicate how close your task is to completion (expressed, of course, as a percentage).

An easier way to enter the percentage-complete information is by displaying the Tracking toolbar (View⇨Toolbars⇨Tracking) in the Gantt Chart view of your project, as I explain in Chapter 16. This method allows you to select 25%, 50%, 75%, or 100% at the click of a button. Clicking one of these buttons updates the information in the Percent Complete text box in the Task Information dialog box as well, so you can always find out the latest information about the status of your task there.

- **Priority:** Each task's priority is set to 500 by default in the Priority spinner box. Your most important task can have a priority of 1000, and your least important task can be as low a 0 — so 500 is a middle-of-the road task. The reason for setting priorities for tasks is to act as a tie-breaker when your resources can't accomplish everything. For example, Jane has more tasks than she has time to perform them (isn't that always the way ?).

When Project tries to automatically level resource allocation, Jane keeps her high-priority tasks and the lower priority tasks go to other resources, are delayed, or split into doing a bit now and the rest later. Tasks with a priority of 1000 are not leveled by Microsoft Project. See Chapter 13 for more information about leveling resources in your projects.

✔ **Hide task bar:** Selecting the Hide Task Bar check box hides (but doesn't delete) a task bar on the Gantt chart.

✔ **Roll up Gantt bar:** Selecting the Roll Up Gantt Bar to Summary check box moves a task so that it resides on a summary bar rather than appearing sequentially on the timeline of the Gantt chart.

TIP

The Name and Duration text boxes and the Estimated check box appear in all the tabs of the Task Information dialog box.

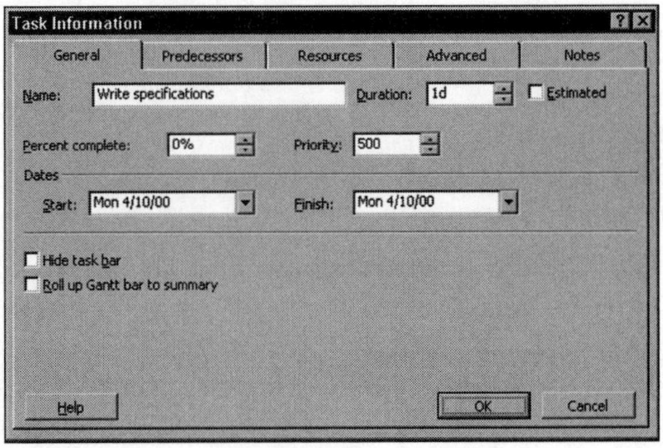

Figure 4-1:
The General tab of the Task Information dialog box.

The Predecessors tab

The Predecessors tab gives you the opportunity to indicate which tasks precede a task, the type of relationship the predecessor has with the task, and to what extent the task's start date will lag in its dependency on the predecessor (see Figure 4-2).

Double-click in the ID column and enter the ID number for the task's predecessor, or double-click in the Task Name column and click the down arrow to choose the task's predecessor from a list. You can select as many predecessors as you like.

In determining the relationship between the predecessor and task, Microsoft Project has four kinds of task relationships: finish-to-start, start-to-start, finish-to-finish, and start-to-finish:

ON THE CD

Sorting out task relationships

Some task relationships in the Smith Home 4.MPP home-building project aren't the default finish-to-start relationship. Specifically, you need to change some relationship types in the Finishing Stage of the project.

The Wallboard task (ID 25) and the Stairway task (ID 26) should start at the same time. They should have a start-to-start (SS) relationship.

The Painting task (ID 27) should also have a start-to-start (SS) relationship with the Wallboard task (ID 25), but it should lag by four days. That way, the wallboard crew can finish a portion of the house so that the painter can begin priming and applying the first coat.

The carpenter can begin doing the finish woodwork as soon as the paint dries. When one-third

of the Painting task (ID 27) is completed, the Trim task (ID 28) should begin. This is also a start-to-start (SS) relationship.

The Landscaping task should coincide with the completion of the Painting task. This is a finish-to-finish (FF) relationship.

The Customer walkthrough task (ID 30) should follow the completion of the Painting task (ID 27) and should have a two-day lag. This is a finish-to-start (FS) and a lag.

This may seem like a lot, but it's not. Juggling each of these conditions is normal in a project plan and is easy to perform (and understand) in Microsoft Project. Scout's honor.

✔ **Finish-to-start (FS) relationships** are the default Microsoft Project task relationship. It means that Task A must finish before Task B can begin. When you create a link, the default relationship is finish-to-start.

✔ **Start-to-start (SS) relationships** mean that Task B can't start until Task A does. An example of this is heating a store-bought pizza. Task A heats the oven. Task B puts the pizza in the oven.

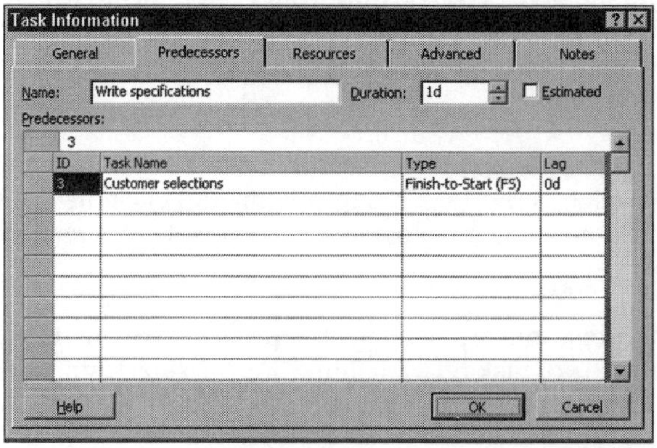

Figure 4-2:
The Predecessors tab of the Task Information dialog box.

- **Finish-to-finish (FF) relationships** mean that Task B can't finish before Task A does. A credit card transaction is a good example. Task A delivers the product to the customer. Task B gets the customer to sign the credit slip.

- **Start-to-finish (SF) relationships** mean that Task B can't finish until Task A starts. An example of this is a temporary electrical generator that can't stop until power is returned to a permanent electrical system.

You can also change a task relationship by double-clicking a link in the Gantt chart. Double-click anywhere on a link between tasks. The Task Dependency dialog box appears. The dialog box identifies the link from Task A to Task B. The Type box enables you to select a task relationship. The Lag box enables you to enter lag (or lead) time.

The Resources tab

You can use the Task Information dialog box to add or modify resources for a task. You do this in the Resource tab. I tell you all about adding or modifying resources in Chapter 5.

The Advanced tab

The Advanced tab contains some detailed constraint selections and some other choices that relate to special task details (see Figure 4-3). The following list explains the options available under the Advanced tab:

- **Deadline:** The Deadline box provides you the option to set a deadline for a task. This date prompts an indicator to appear if the task finishes after the deadline.

- **Constraint type:** A *constraint* is a limit you place on the start or finish of a task. Some tasks have to begin or end on certain dates. This may be due to the availability of a key consultant or limited access to an important piece of equipment. Other tasks can start as soon as their predecessors finish. In either case, priorities govern the beginning and end of every task.

  All linked tasks have constraints. In Microsoft Project, the default constraint is the As Soon As Possible constraint. Of course, all tasks don't relate this way — one ending and then the next immediately beginning. You need to apply constraints that best fit the reality of your project. In fact, Microsoft Project uses eight kinds of constraints, as shown in Table 4-1.

✔ **Task type:** You select Fixed Units, Fixed Duration, or Fixed Work with Fixed Units being the default task type. With Fixed Units, adding resources shortens a task. With Fixed Duration, adding resources decreases units of work. Fixed Work functions the same way as Fixed Units, except that it can't be effort driven.

✔ **Effort Driven check box:** Effort-driven tasks are resource-driven rather than task-driven. For a task that's effort-driven, adding resources cuts down the amount of time necessary: If you add four people to a job that would take one person four days, four people can do the job in one day.

✔ **Calendar:** You can select a calendar other than the default calendar for task completion. I discuss the significance of calendars in Chapter 5.

✔ **WBS code:** The WBS code (Work Breakdown Structure code) is an alphanumeric code for representing a task's place in the hierarchical structure of a project.

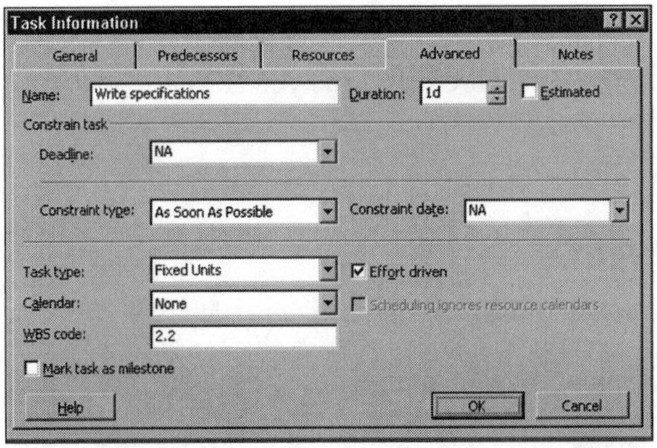

Figure 4-3:
The
Advanced
tab of the
Task
Information
dialog box.

Table 4-1	Constraints and Their Effects
Constraint	*Description*
As Late As Possible (ALAP)	The task must start as late as possible without impeding the start date of subsequent tasks. This constraint has no actual constraint date.
As Soon As Possible (ASAP)	The task must start as early as possible. This constraint has no actual constraint date. This is the Microsoft Project default constraint for tasks.
Finish No Earlier Than (FNET)	The task must end no sooner than a certain constraint date.
Finish No Later Than (FNLT)	The task must finish no later than a certain constraint date.

Constraint	Description
Must Finish On (MFO)	The task must finish on a certain date. The date is anchored in the schedule.
Must Start On (MSO)	The task must start on a certain date. The date is anchored in the schedule.
Start No Earlier Than (SNET)	The task must start on or after your constraint date.
Start No Later Than (SNLT)	The task must start on or before your constraint date.

The Notes tab

The Notes tab provides you the opportunity to write information you may need to keep for a specific task. The Notes tab works much like a text editor. When you complete your task note and click OK, an indicator appears next to the task alerting you to the existence of the note.

Getting some practice with the Task Information dialog box

Although using the Task Information dialog box isn't the only way to edit details of a task, using the dialog box is definitely one of Microsoft Project's fastest and easiest ways to get the job done. The Task Information dialog box functions as a kind of task control central. In this example, you use the Task Information dialog box to change a task start date for an existing project.

1. **Double-click the task for which you want to change the start date to display the Task Information dialog box.**

   In the Smith Home 4.mpp example, select the Signatures task. In this example, Microsoft Project assigns the default ASAP constraint when it links all the tasks in the home building project. Some remodeling is in order — not of the house, but of some task constraints:

   • The ASAP default set the signing of the contract on April 19. It actually is scheduled on May 1.

   • The contract begins at the signing of the contract, but the actual scheduled beginning of the work is July 8.

2. **Click the General tab.**

3. **Highlight the Start text box and type a new date in the text box or use the down arrow to the right of text box and select a date.**

   In this example, type **5/1**.

   The project start date is April 3, 2000. So, if the current year is not 2000, enter **2000**.

4. **Click OK.**

   A Planning Wizard dialog box appears (see Figure 4-4), alerting you that you're about to modify the relationship of a task and its predecessor.

   If the Planning Wizard doesn't appear, click Undo on the standard toolbar. Then choose Tools⇒Options. Click the General tab and then select the Advice from Planning Wizard check box. Make sure all the advice check boxes are checked. Click OK and repeat Steps 1 through 4.

5. **Select the second option, the one that moves the task and keeps the link.**

6. **Click OK.**

   You've changed a constraint from ASAP to SNET (Start No Earlier Than).

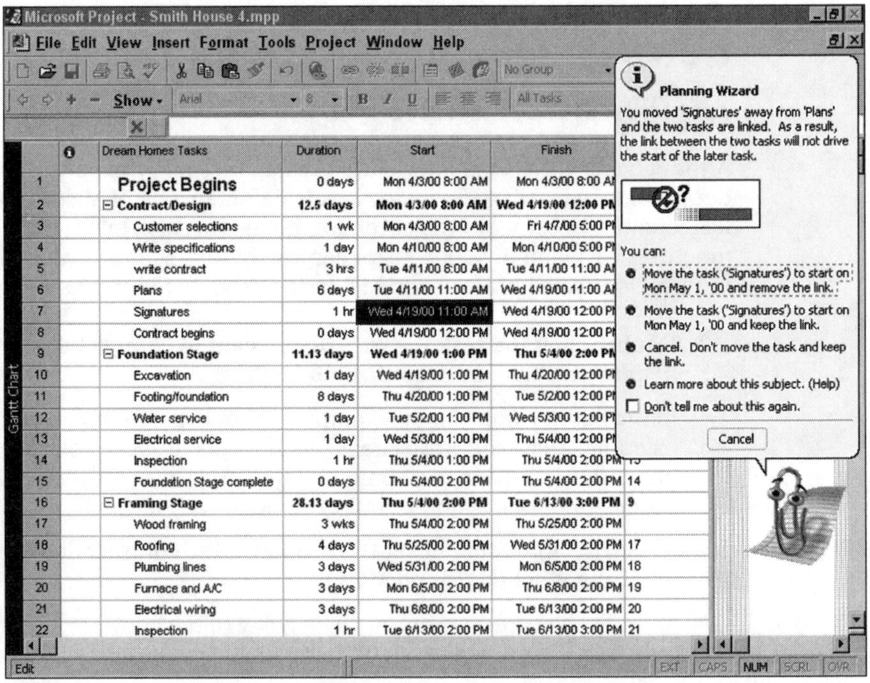

Figure 4-4:
The Planning Wizard asks whether you want to maintain a link even though you have changed a constraint.

Displaying dates and times in the Gantt table

To take full advantage of the Gantt table's reporting capability, you need to change how Microsoft Project displays dates and times. Showing a day/date is Microsoft Project's default method. But you need to see time of day as well. To change the way Microsoft Project displays days and dates, follow these steps:

1. Select Tools⇨Options.

2. Click the View tab.

3. In the Date format box, select the day/date/time format (Mon 1/31/00 12:33 PM).

4. Click OK.

The Gantt table shows your project plans in a table format.

Who knows what lurks behind the Gantt chart? To see more of the Gantt table, use these steps:

1. Select the vertical separator bar between the Gantt table and the Gantt chart.

2. Drag the bar to the right until it reveals all the columns, including Resource Names.

   Two columns, the Start column and the Finish column, may be full of hash marks.

3. Double-click the right edge of each column heading to expand the column's width and change the hash marks to dates.

Notice that the indicator (i) column now contains a constraints indicator icon. If you place your cursor over the icon, a tool tip appears telling you that the task is now Start No Earlier Than as well as the constraint date.

Working with Combination Views

A *combination view* contains two views about information. The lower view, or pane, shows detailed information about the task or resource that is highlighted in the upper pane. Combination views are a way to double the details of task and resource information on your screen. A lot of people find the view helpful because you can keep the big picture in one window and work on details in the other. Microsoft Project offers a number of combination views — four for the Gantt chart. Here are the Gantt Chart combination views:

✔ **Gantt Chart view (top)/Task view (bottom):** In this combination, the bottom pane shows information about the task you select in the Gantt Chart view.

✔ **Gantt Chart view (top)/Resource view (bottom):** In this combination, the bottom pane shows information about the resource(s) assigned to the task you select in the Gantt Chart view. Chapter 10 explains Resource view in more detail.

> ✔ **Task view (top)/Gantt Chart view (bottom):** In this combination, the bottom pane shows information about the task you select in Task view.
>
> ✔ **Resource view (top)/Gantt Chart view (bottom):** In this combination, the bottom pane shows information about the tasks associated with the resource you select in the resource view.

A good way to get the bead on combination views is to practice with them a little. In this example, you may need to arrange the Gantt Chart view so that Task Sheet only shows the Task Name and Duration columns. Do so by choosing Window⇨Split. Your screen should now look something like Figure 4-5.

Welcome to a combination view! This combination view shows you the Gantt Chart view in the top pane and the Task form in the bottom pane. This isn't exactly a view from Pike's Peak, but it's about the best that Microsoft Project has to offer.

To remove a split view, choose Window⇨Remove Split or double-click the horizontal split-screen separator. The screen returns to a full Gantt chart. Scroll the Gantt chart so that the Finishing Stage summary task is near the top-left corner of the chart.

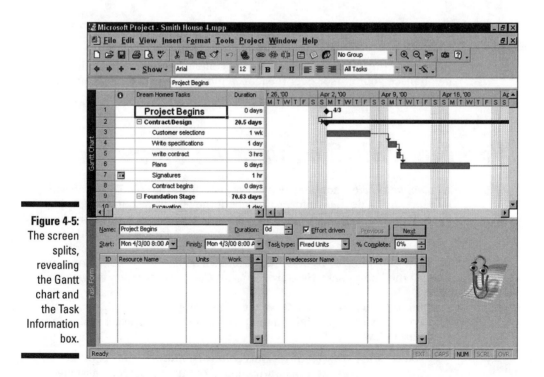

Figure 4-5:
The screen splits, revealing the Gantt chart and the Task Information box.

Saving a custom combination view

You can make up your own combination view and save it for future use. Microsoft Project provides a way for you to select your own choice of the upper and lower panes. And you can make as many custom combination views as you would like. To do so:

1. **Select View⊏>More Views to open the More Views dialog box.**

2. **Click the New button.**

   A dialog box appears asking whether you want a new single view or combination view.

3. **Select the Combination View radio button and then click OK.**

   The View Definition dialog box appears.

4. **In the Name text box, enter a name for your custom view.**

5. **Using the down arrow next to the Top text box, select a view for the top pane of your custom combination view.**

6. **Using the down arrow next to the Bottom text box, select a view for the bottom pane of your custom combination view.**

7. **If you would like your new view to appear in the View menu, select the Show in Menu check box.**

8. **Click OK to close the View Definition dialog box.**

You can also easily split and remove the split by right-clicking anywhere in the Gantt Chart of the Gantt Chart view and toggling between Split and Remove Split.

Practicing with combination views

Other than making your eyeballs cross (vertically), combination views are easy to use and they can greatly increase your efficiency in building a project or modifying an existing one. Using the Smith House 4 example in a combination view, you can hone your project management skills.

You can manipulate each of the two panes and their sections. For example, to view a combination of perspectives on one piece of information, do the following:

1. **Select a task.**

   If you want to follow along with the example, select the Signatures task.

 2. **Click the Goto Selected Task button on the standard toolbar.**

3. **Click the Zoom In button on the standard toolbar a few times to see the bihourly timescale.**

   4. **If necessary, click the Goto Selected Task button again to line up the view with the task view.**

   You can zoom out again to the weeks timescale to return to the default weeks/days timescale.

In this example, you use the Task form in a combination view to change a duration of a task and a task relationship. In the Gantt table, highlight one of the tasks. Then if necessary, in the task form, click the Next button until the Excavation task is highlighted and Excavation appears in the Name box of the Task form.

The Start date for the Excavation task is wrong. Excavation is the first task after the contract has been signed. As the schedule is currently written, the excavation is slated to begin right after lunch on the same day as the contract signing. Realistically, the excavation contractor will need a three-day lead time.

To change the excavation contractor's lead time, you need to change the constraints on the Excavation task.

The standard Task form doesn't offer a constraint option. One of the nice features of combination views is that you can change one of the panes while leaving the other pane alone. In this case, you need to change the bottom pane to show a task form that includes constraint. You need to change to the Task Details form. To change the bottom pane, do the following:

   1. **Choose View⇨More Views to change to the Task Details form.**

   A list box appears.

   2. **Scroll through the list until you find Task Details Form and double-click it.**

   The Task Details form, shown in Figure 4-6, replaces the standard Task form.

After you change from the Task form to the Task Details form, you can modify constraint.

   1. **Under Constraint, click the down arrow.**

   A list box appears.

   2. **Select Start No Earlier Than.**

   3. **In the Date box under Constraint, type a new date. In this example, type** 5/4.

   If the current year isn't 2000, type the year 2000 also, such as **5/4/00**.

   4. **Click OK.**

   Notice that the start and finish dates for the task have changed in the Task Details form. Also notice that the Gantt chart has moved the Excavation date to Thursday, May 4 (see Figure 4-7).

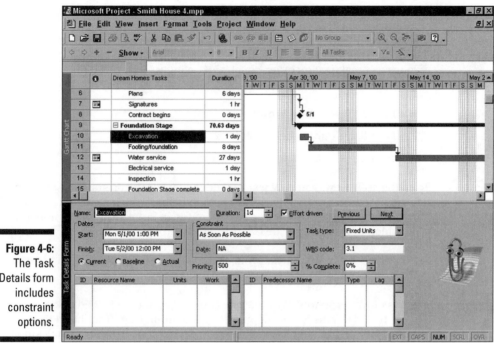

Figure 4-6:
The Task Details form includes constraint options.

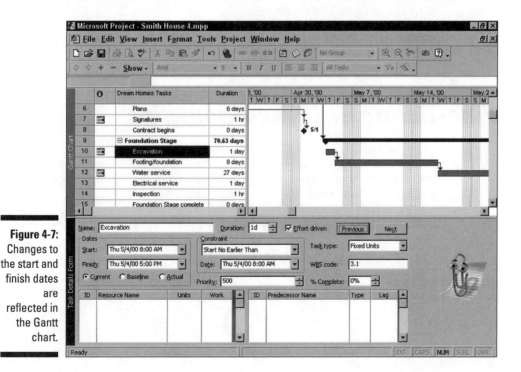

Figure 4-7:
Changes to the start and finish dates are reflected in the Gantt chart.

From the Task Details form, click Previous until you reach the Signatures task. Notice that the constraint change you made to Signatures is recorded in the list box under Constraints. Click Next until you're back to the Excavation task.

If you aren't making any other constraint changes, go back to the standard Task form:

1. **Choose View➪More Views.**

2. **In the list, double-click Task form.**

   You're back to the standard Task form.

From the split view, you may want to judge your project's status in relation to the estimated completion date. Click anywhere in the Gantt chart. The vertical bar on the far left of the window is highlighted in color rather than appearing gray, which indicates that the Gantt window is the active view.

Press Page Down until you see your final task. Select the Project complete task.

The Task form probably says that the project finish date is Wednesday, August 16, 2000. This is unacceptable. The customer contract has a firm move-in date of no later than August 2. You have some project management to do to meet this deadline. One of the ways you can do some time managing is by changing task relationships.

Press Page Up until the Excavation task appears again. Then click anywhere in the Task form to make it active.

Fine-Tuning Task Relationships

Projects seldom proceed in a completely linear manner. More often than not, many tasks take place at the same time. As a project manager, you need to find ways to schedule and manage tasks that take place at the same time. To change how tasks relate to other tasks, follow these steps:

1. **Click the Previous or Next button until you reach the Water service task.**

   The Task form shows that the predecessor of Water service is Footing/foundation, ID 11. This is okay.

2. **Click Next.**

   You should be at Electrical service. Its predecessor is Water service, ID 12. To make Electrical service occur concurrently with Water service, the Electrical service and the Water service must share the same predecessor.

To change a predecessor, use the following steps:

1. **Select the ID column in the Task form and type a new number.**

   In the Smith Home 4.MPP example, change the Electrical service predecessor by selecting the ID column in the Task form and typing **11**.

2. **Click OK.**

   Notice that the predecessor name has changed to Footing/foundation.

To see the effect of the change:

1. **Click anywhere in the Gantt chart to activate the Gantt window to view the result.**

2. **With the changed task highlighted, click the Goto Selected Task button on the standard toolbar. In this example, highlight Electrical service (see Figure 4-8).**

Notice that the Gantt chart now assigns the same predecessor to Water service and Electric service. Both start on the same day. Because both tasks have the same duration, they also end on the same day.

Lag time and lead time

Sometimes you need to make room in a project (and maybe in your life, if you're like me) to allow for some time flexibility. You achieve time flexibility between dependent tasks by adding *lag time,* which is a bit of wiggle room before the beginning of the next task. By adding lag time to a successor task, you tell that task to begin later. For example, in a start to start relationship, the start of the successor task lags behind the start of the predecessor task. In a finish to start relationship, the start of the successor task lags behind the finish of the predecessor task.

Lead time is the opposite of lag time. A simple way to understand lead time is to think of a finish to start relationship between two tasks. In this relationship the successor task begins as soon as the predecessor task finishes. By adding lead time to the successor, you start the successor task before the predecessor task is finished. So, for example, you can have a 1d lead time for a successor task. This means that the successor task will begin one day before the predecessor finishes.

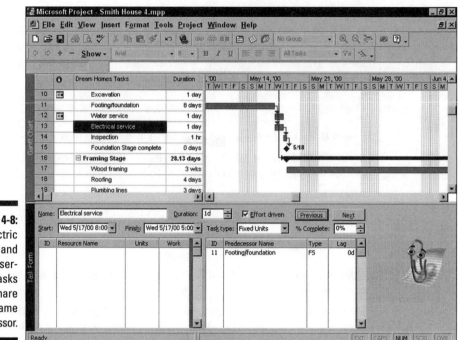

Lag time is expressed positively and lead time is expressed negatively. Both lag and time can be in increments of minutes, hours, days, weeks, or months. Or, you can express lag time and lead time in percentages.

In the Smith Home.MPP example, in the Task Details Form, you can see that the Finish date and time for the Electrical service task is Wednesday, May 17, at 5:00 p.m. Click the Next button to arrive at the Inspection task. Its Start date is Thursday, May 18, at 8:00 a.m. This is the next workday and the next work hour. You need to add some lag time to this task relationship.

Follow these steps to change the lag time between a task and its predecessor:

1. **Select the Lag column and type a unit of time.**

    • To create lag time enter a positive number and a unit of time, such as 1d.

    • To create lead time, enter a negative number and a unit of time, such as -1d or enter a percentage, such as -33%.

    In the Smith Home 4.MPP example, type **1d** in the lag column for predecessor of the Inspection task. This creates a one-day lag.

2. **Click OK.**

In the home example, notice that the Lag column now says 1d and that the start date has changed to Friday (see Figure 4-9). Also notice that the Gantt chart has changed to reflect the lag. In addition, because the Inspection task is a subtask of the Foundation Stage summary task, the summary bar has elongated. Way to go, you ol' project manager! Since you've made some elbow room, maybe you and your buddies will have time for a couple of cold ones down at the corner lagoon.

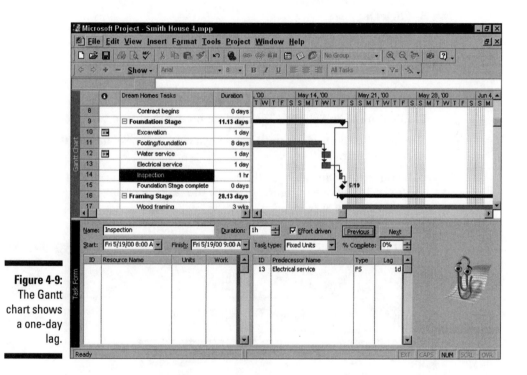

Figure 4-9: The Gantt chart shows a one-day lag.

Sharing predecessors

Sharing predecessors is a good way to shorten a project because it enables you to schedule more than one task to occur at the same time. For example, roofing, plumbing, furnace and A/C, and wiring tasks can take place simultaneously because all four tasks are dependent on a single predecessor — construction of the structure's wood frame. To share predecessors, follow these steps:

1. **In the Task Details Form, click the Previous or Next button until you reach the task.**

   In Smith Home 4.MPP, go to the Roofing task.

2. **Change the task's predecessor by selecting the ID column and typing the new ID in the column.**

   In our example, type **17**.

3. **Click OK.**

   Repeat Steps 1 through 3 for the remaining tasks — plumbing, furnace and A/C, and wiring.

4. **Click a task in the Gantt chart.**

   For this example, select the Electrical wiring task.

5. **Click the Goto Selected Task button on the standard toolbar.**

6. **Scroll the Gantt chart until you can see all the tasks having the same predecessor.**

   If you're following along with the example, your screen should appear similar to the one in Figure 4-10 with the tasks occuring parallel in time rather than in series.

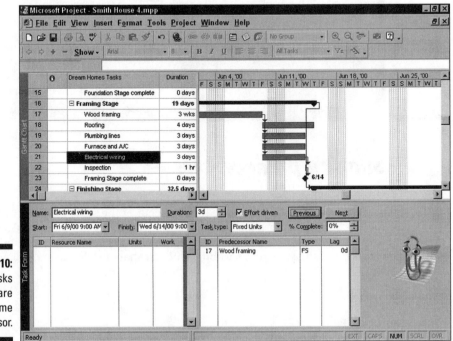

Figure 4-10: Four tasks share the same predecessor.

Sometimes you correct one problem but create another. For example, in Figure 4-10, the four tasks all have the same predecessor, but the inspection task (Task 22) appears as if it's going to take place before the roofing (Task 18) is complete. The reason is that Inspection has Task 21, electrical wiring, as its predecessor. The problem is that the Electrical wiring task's duration is shorter than the Roofing task. Inspection can't occur until all Framing Stage construction subtasks are complete.

Sheesh. Does it feel like you're trying to rub out an ink spot? It's really not that bad. As you edit your project, changes sometimes require other changes. In that case, you have to change the Inspection task predecessor and provide a one-day lag as you did before the Foundation Stage inspection.

Fixing a glitch also may include retaining consistency with similar tasks in other parts of the project. For example, you may need to add lag time in a project to allow for a phone call to schedule an inspection.

To fix the problems in the Smith House.4MPP file that you see in Figure 4-10 and add a day of lag time, follow these steps:

1. **Click the Next button in the Task form until you come to the ID for Task 22, the Inspection task.**

2. **Type 18 in the Predecessor ID column to change the predecessor from the Inspection task to the Roofing task.**

   Roofing is the longest of the stacked tasks.

3. **Select the Lag column and type 1d to allow a bit of time to call the inspector.**

4. **Click OK.**

Your example project should now look like Figure 4-11, which seems to make much better sense.

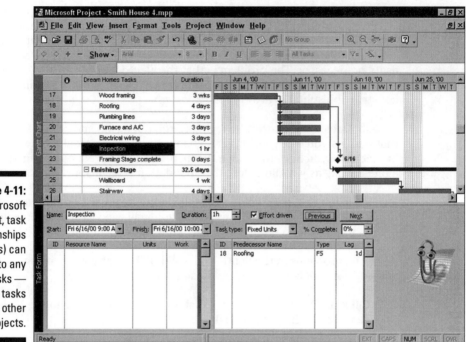

Figure 4-11:
In Microsoft
Project, task
relationships
(links) can
relate to any
tasks —
even tasks
in other
projects.

Chapter 5

Delegating Resources to Tasks

● ●

In This Chapter

▶ Identifying people and things as resources

▶ Predicting what resources you need

▶ Connecting resources to tasks

▶ Putting the details into resources

▶ Managing time with multiple calendars

▶ Using the Task Form as an assignment shortcut

● ●

*1*deally, you want your project to be so well planned that it could run on AutoProjectManager. (That word hasn't made its way into the dictionary yet!) Unfortunately, you have to deal with a little problem called reality. People overbook their commitments, materials arrive late, and equipment breaks down. Still, nothing changes the fact that you have to meet your project goals on time and on budget. Aaaah, the life of the project manager.

Staying on goal and on budget isn't as tough as it may appear, though. Don't throw out your AutoProjectManager manual just yet. Maybe this seems radical, but how about planning for people overbooking, materials arriving late, and equipment breaking down? How about making these eventualities part of your project schedule? Microsoft Project 2000 helps you. Microsoft Project is designed for the well-intentioned but imperfect world of project management. You can set your goals with lots of room to fudge the dates.

You can use a practice file that I developed to help you get accustomed to attaching resources to projects. The example in this chapter is based on the practice project (Smith Home project) that's also used in Chapters 3 and 4. In those chapters, you develop a schedule and relate tasks to one another. The practice file for this chapter is called Smith House 5.mpp. See Appendix C for information on opening the practice files on the CD.

Resources are People and Things

A good place to start is to define what Microsoft Project considers resources. *Resources* are equipment and the people who perform work on your project. However, resources aren't *every* piece of equipment and *every* person who performs work on your project.

For instance, ensuring that every member of the project team has a desk and a chair may be outside the scope of your project management responsibilities. That may be part of the operational givens of the organization that initiate the project. In contrast, if you and your project team need to meet in a conference room every Monday morning at 8:30, that conference room may be one of the resources of your project. You may need to manage the room's availability.

The same is true of people. It may be an operational given that the shipping department provides the people power to handle all incoming and outgoing mail and parcels. If you have a mass mailing that must go out on a certain date, however, the shipping department personnel become a project resource. The proper scheduling of and communication about that mailing is a project management responsibility.

The art of resource planning is a beauty to behold when performed well — and ugly to the bone when performed poorly.

Predicting Your Resource Needs

How you determine and manage the quality, quantity, and availability of resources separates you from the wanna-be project managers. Making the right resource decisions isn't as scary as it may seem. Consider the following factors before you identify and allocate resources for your project:

- ✔ **Remember your goal:** A new project manager may be tempted to spend hours developing a dynamite list of goals and objectives that sits on a desk somewhere and never applies to the project. As you assign resources, they should relate directly to your goals, objectives, and project scope. If they don't, beware! Back up, take a deep breath, meet with your project team, and get on track immediately.

- ✔ **Tie the right resources to tasks:** Ensuring a successful marriage of resources to the project is much easier if you specifically assign resources to individual tasks or groups of tasks. Microsoft Project recognizes only resources tied to tasks.

✔ **Create a detailed resource pool:** A *resource pool* is the sum of people and equipment you have available for your project. Some resources are unlimited in their availability; others are specific as to when and to what degree they can be utilized. Some carry no direct cost to your project, some are a fixed cost, and others are available a la carte. Prepare the list accordingly.

✔ **Know your limitations:** When it comes to resources, you need to know about company policy regarding rentals, consulting fees, equipment purchases, and the like. Be sure that you or another project team member can quote company policy on any matter relevant to your resource planning. Of course, avoid any assumptions or half-implied approvals. The more you get approvals explicitly endorsed, the greater the likelihood of project success.

A real-life blunder illustrates my point. A friend of mine managed a multi-million-dollar video production project that involved stakeholders in Los Angeles, Indianapolis, and Washington, D.C. The project deadlines were tight, and approval for all production phases required signatures from all three stakeholders. Therefore, overnight delivery of materials was almost a daily occurrence. At the conclusion of the highly successful project, my friend received a negative performance appraisal because he had violated his company's policy regarding overnight deliveries.

✔ **Consider the cost of resources:** You can't separate resources from their cost. (See Chapter 13 for more about tracking resources and cost.) Microsoft Project makes it possible for you to work on both simultaneously. Microsoft Project enables you to:

- Determine whether the resource cost accrues up front, throughout the work, or at the end of the project.

- Set hourly and overtime rates.

- Indicate flat per-visit charges.

- Establish that a resource is working on a contractual fixed cost.

Resource-Driven and Fixed-Duration Tasks

Microsoft Project assumes that you're working with resource-driven tasks unless you tell it otherwise. If you increase the amount of resources assigned to a *resource-driven task,* the task will be shorter in duration. For example, if it takes two people six hours to unload boxes of oranges from a truck, four people could do it in three hours. In contrast, a *fixed-duration task* is unaffected by resources. For example, signing a mortgage takes an hour. If 15 people were in the room, it would still take an hour.

The first time you assign resources and their units to a task, Microsoft Project assumes that the resource assignment equals the duration you first estimated. After you assign a resource and unit designation, the task becomes a resource-driven task by default. Therefore, if you change the units, the task duration changes automatically.

To change a task type from resource-driven to fixed-duration, double-click the task. The Task Information dialog box appears. Click the Advanced tab and deselect the Effort Driven check box next to the Task Type text box. Click OK to close the Task Information dialog box.

Hitching Resources to Tasks

Before you go through all the trouble of assigning resources to tasks, you may ask yourself whether you really need to do so. Some projects don't need that kind of specificity. If you don't associate resources to tasks, Microsoft Project does its schedule calculations by using the project's task duration and task relationship information. (See Chapter 4 for more about task relationships.)

In most cases, assigning resources to tasks is helpful. Microsoft Project is a trooper, tracking and automatically updating even the most complex resource and cost relationships. By assigning resources to tasks, you can:

- **Keep an eye on costs.**
- **Determine whether too many or too few resources are allocated to a task.**
- **Find out when resources are scheduled to be in two places at one time.**
- **Track the stages of completion of a task by various resources.**
- **Understand and report with accuracy.**

Assigning resources to tasks

In Microsoft Project, the easiest way to hitch resources to tasks is by using the Assign Resources dialog box which you open by clicking the Assign Resources button on the Standard toolbar. The Assign Resources dialog box provides you a way to connect a resource or resources to a task. You perform this connection by selecting from a resource list. The Assign Resources dialog box has two columns: *Name* and *Units*.

Working with the Name column

Name is the title you assign to a resource. To assign resources in Microsoft Project, follow these steps:

1. **Select a task.**

   For example, select the Customer Selections task.

2. **Click the Assign Resources button on the Standard toolbar.**

   The Assign Resources dialog box appears.

3. **Type a resource name in the Name box.**

   The resource can be a fellow staff member or a contract employee or anyone else who you identify as a person performing the task. The resource name can be a person's name, his or her title, a shirt size, or anything else you want to use as the identifying title for the resource list.

4. **Press Enter.**

So far, you created a resource, but you haven't assigned it to the task. Microsoft Project first wants you to determine the unit assignment of the resource.

Working with the Units column

Units refers to the quantity of resource units you need for a selected task. Microsoft Project's default unit assignment is 1. This means 1 unit (person or equipment) is assigned for 100 percent of its time per day throughout a task's duration. For example, by entering 0.25, you tell Microsoft Project that a person devotes one-fourth of his or her time to the project. To enter time units in Microsoft Project, follow these steps:

1. **Type a decimal fraction of 100 percent in the Units box.**

2. **Press Enter.**

Three changes occur, as shown in Figure 5-1:

- ✔ A check mark appears next to the resource name in the Assign Resources dialog box. The check mark indicates a resource assignment.

- ✔ The resource name appears next to the taskbar on the Gantt chart.

- ✔ The unit allocation appears next to the resource name on the Gantt chart.

Unit allocation

Resource name

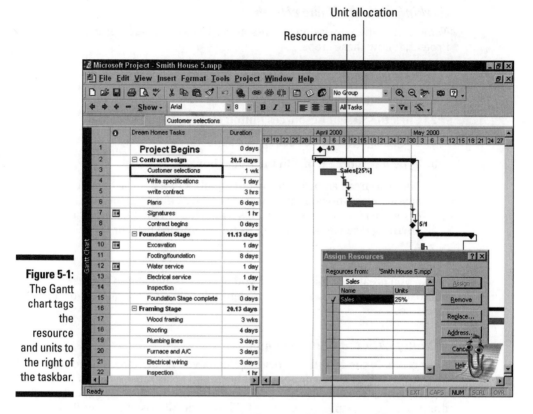

Figure 5-1:
The Gantt chart tags the resource and units to the right of the taskbar.

Check mark

Creating a resource pool

Creating a resource pool enables you to identify the resources available for your project and assign them to tasks. To put together a resource pool, use the following steps:

1. **Highlight a task in the Gantt table.**

2. **Click the Assign Resources button on the Standard toolbar.**

3. **In the Name column, type a resource name.**

4. **Press Enter.**

5. **Repeat Steps 1 through 4 until you enter all of your resources.**

For practice, use the Smith Home example and follow Steps 1 through 5 to add the tasks in the following list below the Sales resource. When you finish, your project should look similar to Figure 5-2.

Resources to add to your resource pool

Specifications

Counsel

Drafting

Excavation Contractor

Water Utility

Electric Utility

Building Inspector

Framing Crew

Plumbing Contractor

Mechanical Contractor

Electrical Contractor

Wallboard Crew

Paint Crew

Finish Carpenters

Project Manager

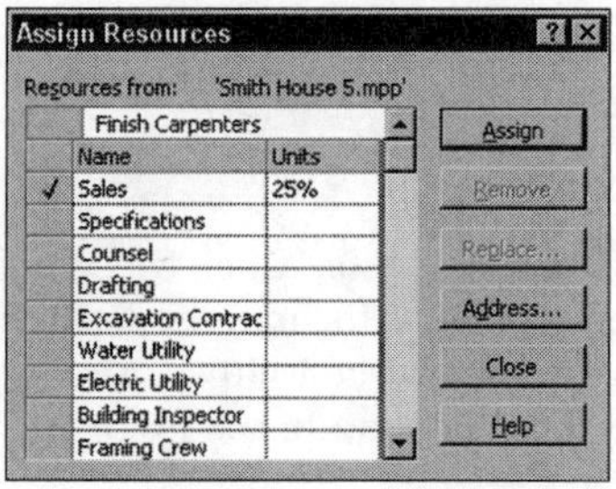

Figure 5-2:
The check
mark shows
the Sales
resource is
assigned to
a task.

Assign Resources	? ✕
Resources from: 'Smith House 5.mpp'	

	Finish Carpenters	▲	Assign
	Name	Units	Remove
✓	Sales	25%	
	Specifications		Replace...
	Counsel		
	Drafting		Address...
	Excavation Contrac		
	Water Utility		Close
	Electric Utility		
	Building Inspector		Help
	Framing Crew	▼	

A smart way to enter resources is by title rather than by a person's name and by specialty rather than by a company name. This gives you some leeway for changes in personnel and contracts.

Creating a resource pool is a major step in resource allocation. After you finish this important step, save your project file. Because you're still likely to be in the planning section of your project, you should save the project without a baseline.

Getting detailed about your resources

Microsoft Project can manage as many project details as you want to give it. You may want to enter resource information about people whose salaries aren't directly related to your project's budget. Or you may want to program into Microsoft Project hourly worker data that directly relates to your project's budget. Still other resources may include working for a fixed amount.

To open the Resource Information dialog box, as shown in Figure 5-3, simply click the Assign Resources button and then double-click a resource name.

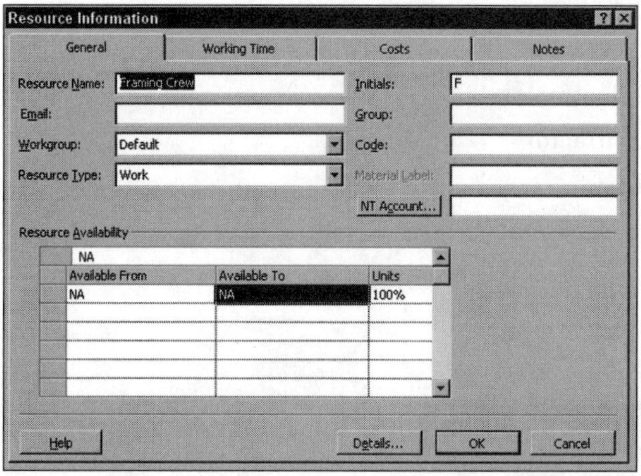

Figure 5-3:
Enter a little or a lot of information in the Resource information dialog box.

The Resource Information dialog box has four tabs. Click these tabs to show a group of fields where you can enter specific information about your resources. Information you enter about a resource follows it no matter where the resource is assigned. The tabs and fields include the following (see Figures 5-4 and 5-5):

✔ **General tab:** The General tab contains the following information:

- **Resource Name:** All resources are identified by their name or their initials.

- **Initials:** A substitute for the Name field. This saves you some keystrokes when you're assigning resources.

- **Group:** The name of a resource group. Any resource using this group name will be part of the group. (For example, you may put water and electric service in a group called Utilities.) Then you can sort by the group name.

- **Code:** An alphanumeric code for the resource. This is a helpful tool for accounting. For example, some companies use cost codes as a way of tracking expenses.

- **Resource Availability:** The total number of units available for a project. This number can range from 0 to 100. Microsoft Project uses this number to calculate whether you have enough resources for a task or multiple, simultaneous tasks. (If your unit designation appears as a percentage, select Tools⇨Options. Click the Schedule tab, and then change the Show Assignment Units as: list box to Decimal.)

✔ **Working tab:** The Working tab contains the Base Calendar. Microsoft Project offers three flavors of base calendars: Standard, Night Shift, and 24 Hours. These three calendars are based on default settings. For example, the Standard work calendar is Monday through Friday, from 8 a.m. to 5 p.m. with one hour for lunch and no holidays.

✔ **Costs tab:** The Costs tab contains the following information:

- **Standard Rate:** The cost for regular work. Microsoft Project's default multiplier in this box is hours. If you type 15, for example, Microsoft Project assumes that you mean $15/hour. Possible time units are minutes (m), hours (h), days (d), and weeks (w).

- **Overtime Rate:** The cost for overtime work. Use this if the resource expects an overtime rate for overtime work. As with Standard Rate, enter an amount followed by a time unit abbreviation.

- **Per Use Cost:** The cost per use fee, for example, a building inspector's fee of $65 per visit.

- **Cost Accrual:** When the cost for the resource actually occurs. The three choices are Start (incur total actual cost as the tasks using this resource start), Prorated (incur actual costs as the tasks using this resource progress), and End (incur total actual cost as the tasks using this resource end). Microsoft Project defaults to an Accrue at Prorated cost unless you specify otherwise.

Using the example, open the Resource Information dialog box for the Framing Crew and assign the following details:

Option	Value
Initials	FC
Group	Carpenters
Max units available	16
Standard Rate	10
Overtime Rate	15

The General and Costs tabs of the Resource Information dialog box should now look like Figures 5-4 and 5-5, respectively. Click OK. The Resource Information dialog box automatically interprets rates as a per-hour amount unless you use m for minute, d for day, or w for week.

Click OK after you're finished looking at the dialog box.

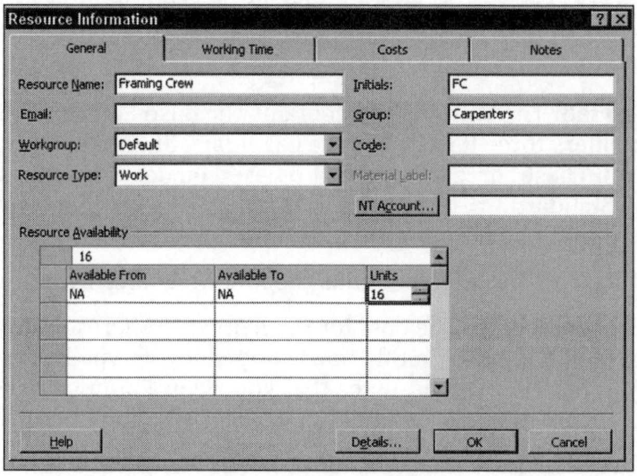

Figure 5-4:
The General tab of the Resource Information dialog box.

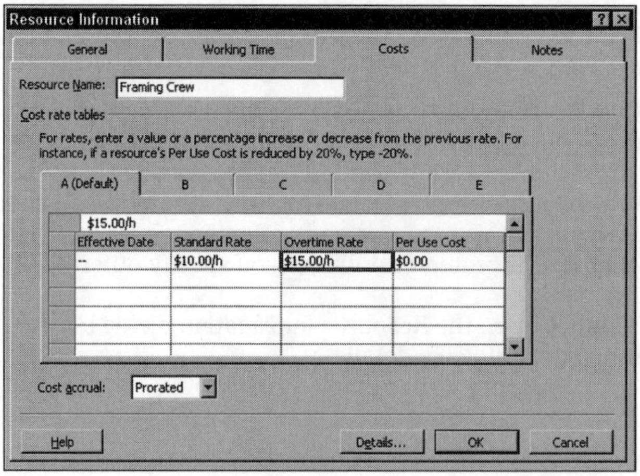

Figure 5-5:
The Costs tab of the Resource Information dialog box.

Dragging a resource

Dragging resources from the Assign Resources dialog box to a task in the Gantt table is an easy way to assign resources from the resource pool. To drag a resource, follow these steps:

1. **Select a resource from the resource pool.**

   In this example, scroll the Gantt chart to the top. Then, select Specifications from the resource pool.

2. **Move the cursor to the leftmost column of the Assign Resources dialog box.**

   The cursor changes into a face.

3. **Click and drag the cursor over the task.**

   In this example, drag the cursor over the Write specifications task.

4. **Release the mouse button.**

Notice that in Figure 5-6, the Specifications resource is now checked. A unit of 1 is associated with the resource for that task. In addition, the Gantt chart lists the resource name.

Figure 5-6:
The Specific-ations resource is checked, indicating that the resource has been assigned to a task.

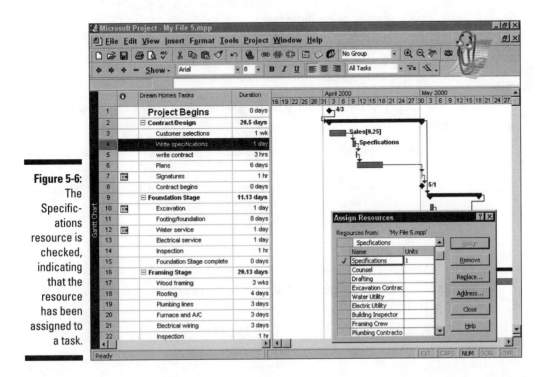

The drag feature automatically assigns a unit of 1 to the resource. After you assign the resource, change the task units to modify the task duration. So if you're planning an initial unit assignment of something other than 1.0, don't use the drag feature. Instead, enter a unit value in the Units column of the Assign Resources dialog box and click the Assign button.

Assigning a resource to multiple tasks

By using the resource pool, you can assign a resource to several tasks at the same time. If the tasks are grouped sequentially, select the first task, hold down the Shift key, and select the last task in the sequence. Release the Shift key. All the tasks in the sequence should be highlighted.

If the tasks aren't grouped sequentially, select the first task, hold down the Ctrl key, and select the tasks you want. After you select the final task, release the Ctrl key. All the nonsequential tasks you selected are highlighted.

After you select the tasks, select a resource from the resource pool. If you want, you can add a unit assignment. When you're satisfied with your selections, click the Assign key.

Note that you can also assign multiple resources to a single task, and assign multiple resources to multiple tasks.

As an example, use the home building example to assign two resources to three tasks. It just so happens that the project manager and the building inspector must both perform the inspection task.

Make some preliminary changes to the Gantt Chart view to see your work more easily:

1. **Scroll through the Gantt chart until the first task is the topmost visible task.**

   In this example, scroll through the Gantt Chart until Task 14, the first Inspection task, is the topmost visible task.

2. **Select the first task.**

   In this example, select Task 14.

3. **Click the Goto Selected Task button on the standard toolbar.**

4. **Click the Zoom Out (or Zoom In) button until the timescale is months and weeks.**

5. **Drag the Assign Resources dialog box to the upper-right corner of the screen.**

   This gives you a fuller view of the Gantt chart to assign resources to multiple tasks.

To assign a resource to multiple tasks:

1. **Select a task if it isn't selected.**

   In the example, select the first Inspection task, Task 14.

2. **Hold down the Ctrl key and select additional tasks. Then release the Ctrl key.**

   In the example, hold down the Ctrl key and select the other two Inspection tasks, Tasks 22 and 32. Then release the Ctrl key.

3. **In the Assign Resources dialog box, select the first resource.**

   In the example, in the Assign Resources dialog box, select Building Inspector.

4. **Hold down the Ctrl key, scroll the resource pool to the next resource and select it. Then release the Ctrl key.**

   In the example, hold down the Ctrl key, scroll to the bottom of the resource pool, and select Project Manager. Then release the Ctrl key.

5. **Click the Assign button in the Assign Resources dialog box.**

   Assigning multiple resources to a task doesn't affect the task's duration (see Figure 5-7). But changing units in a multiple resource assignment, as well as in a single resource assignment, changes the task's duration unless the task is a fixed-duration task.

 To restore the Gantt chart to the normal time scale, click the Zoom In button until Project reaches its normal time scale.

Adding and removing resources from tasks

The success or failure of a project is based on the timely completion of tasks. But tasks can't be completed on time without sufficient resources. Too often, projects come to a screeching halt because of changes in resource availability. Your job as project manager is to ensure that your project survives changes by making accurate assessments and timely modifications to the project plan. Changing resource assignments can be simple or tricky depending on when in the project you make changes. Changing resource assignments early is a piece of hot fudge ice cream cake.

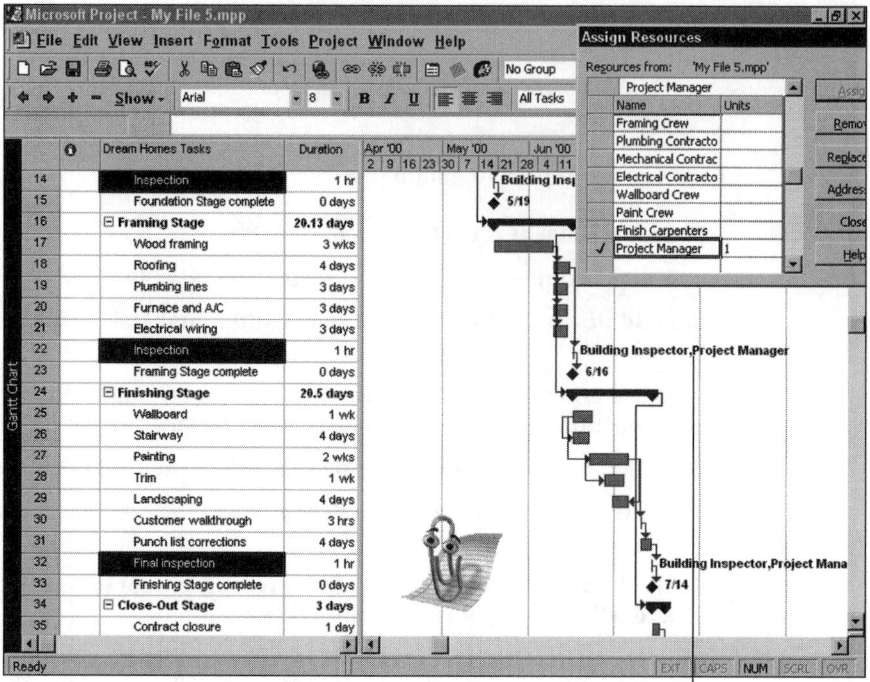

Figure 5-7:
Multiple
resources
are
assigned to
a task.

Multiple resources assigned

You can practice changing a few things in the Smith home example. First, an important person is missing from the resource pool, namely the project foreman. Second, the project foreman rather than the project manager should perform the inspection tasks with the building inspector.

To add or remove resources, follow these steps:

1. **Select the tasks whose resources you want remove or add.**

   In the Smith Home example, you can select the three Inspection tasks (if they aren't still selected). To do so, select the first Inspection task, Task 14. Hold down the Ctrl key and select the other two Inspection tasks, Tasks 22 and 32. Then release the Ctrl key.

2. **Click the Assign Resources button on the standard toolbar.**

3. **In the first empty Name box, type the resource name.**

   In the Smith Home example, type **Project Foreman** in the first empty box.

4. **Select a resource and click the Replace button.**

   The Replace With dialog box appears.

   In the Smith Home example, select Project Manager as the resource.

5. **Select a another resource and click OK.**

   In the Smith Home example, select Project Foreman.

6. **Close the Assign Resources dialog box.**

The three inspection tasks change to show the removal of the project manager and the addition of the project foreman to each task.

Deleting a resource from the pool

Deleting a resource from the resource pool requires that you work in the Resource Sheet view. This view is especially helpful in summarizing details about all resources. You can also use the Resource Sheet view to make changes to resources. To change to the Resource Sheet view:

1. **Open the view bar by right-clicking the far-left vertical bar and selecting View Bar from the shortcut menu.**

2. **Open the resource sheet from the view bar or choose View⇨Resource Sheet.**

   The screen should now look like Figure 5-8.

In the home building example, the Plumbing task and the Furnace task will now be performed by a single contractor. Therefore, you must delete a resource and modify a resource name.

To delete items from the resource pool, follow these steps:

1. **From the Resource Sheet view, select a resource.**

   In the example, select Resource 10, Plumbing Contractor.

2. **Press the Delete key.**

   The Plumbing Contractor resource is deleted and all the subsequent resources ripple up, changing Mechanical Contractor from Resource 11 to Resource 10.

To modify a resource using the Resource Sheet view, follow these steps:

1. **Select a resource.**

2. **Type a new name in the Resource Name box.**

A new, combined resource replaces two previously distinct resources. After you look over the resource sheet, change back to the Gantt Chart view by clicking the Gantt Chart button on the view bar.

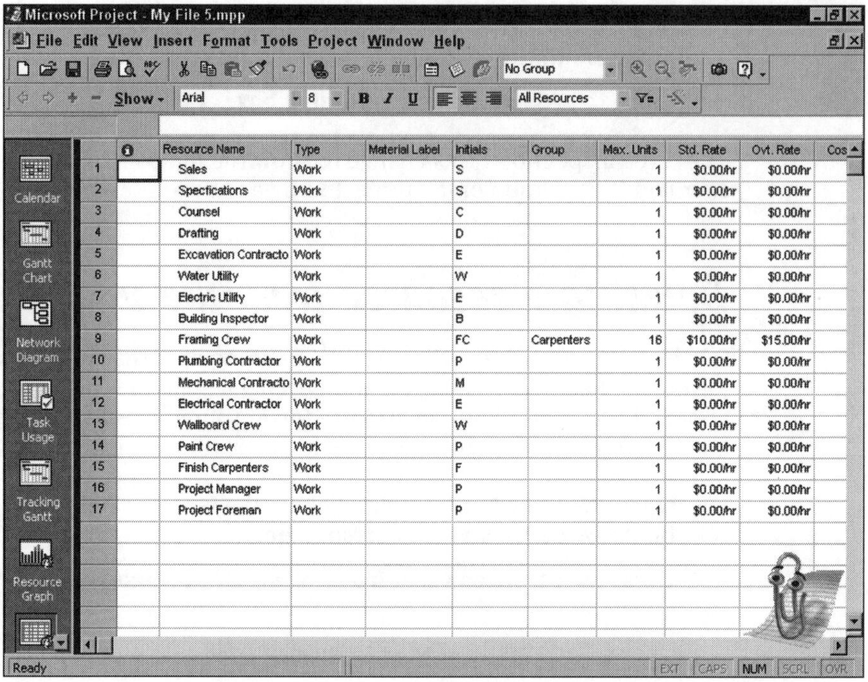

	Resource Name	Type	Material Label	Initials	Group	Max. Units	Std. Rate	Ovt. Rate
1	Sales	Work		S		1	$0.00/hr	$0.00/hr
2	Specfications	Work		S		1	$0.00/hr	$0.00/hr
3	Counsel	Work		C		1	$0.00/hr	$0.00/hr
4	Drafting	Work		D		1	$0.00/hr	$0.00/hr
5	Excavation Contracto	Work		E		1	$0.00/hr	$0.00/hr
6	Water Utility	Work		W		1	$0.00/hr	$0.00/hr
7	Electric Utility	Work		E		1	$0.00/hr	$0.00/hr
8	Building Inspector	Work		B		1	$0.00/hr	$0.00/hr
9	Framing Crew	Work		FC	Carpenters	16	$10.00/hr	$15.00/hr
10	Plumbing Contractor	Work		P		1	$0.00/hr	$0.00/hr
11	Mechanical Contracto	Work		M		1	$0.00/hr	$0.00/hr
12	Electrical Contractor	Work		E		1	$0.00/hr	$0.00/hr
13	Wallboard Crew	Work		W		1	$0.00/hr	$0.00/hr
14	Paint Crew	Work		P		1	$0.00/hr	$0.00/hr
15	Finish Carpenters	Work		F		1	$0.00/hr	$0.00/hr
16	Project Manager	Work		P		1	$0.00/hr	$0.00/hr
17	Project Foreman	Work		P		1	$0.00/hr	$0.00/hr

Figure 5-8: The resource sheet displays information about each resource.

Using and Customizing Work Schedules

Microsoft Project uses two kinds of calendars: project calendars and resource calendars. A *project calendar* (also called a standard calendar) is the default calendar that applies to all tasks and resources. This calendar measures duration by assigning Monday through Friday as working days and by assigning 8 a.m. to 5 p.m. as working hours, with one hour off for lunch at noon. By default, the project calendar excludes holidays. What a grump!

You can change any part of a project calendar or all of it. You can make it so that any day of the week with a *y* in its name is a day off. Or you can schedule a siesta from noon to 3 p.m. It's up to you and your understanding, totally-cool boss.

A *resource calendar* can march to the beat of a different drummer. A resource calendar is a calendar that you can customize to match the availability and work times of a specific resource. For example, you can create a resource calendar that schedules painting after wallboarding, because painters hate dust.

Modifying the project calendar

Modifying your project's calendar is no more difficult or uncommon than making changes to the calendar beside your phone. The only difference is that this calendar isn't hanging on your kitchen wall. Well, this calendar doesn't have an ad for Franklin Funeral Parlor either. Pity.

To modify the project calendar, follow these steps:

1. **Choose Tools ⇨Change Working Time.**

   The Change Working Time dialog box appears, as shown in Figure 5-9.

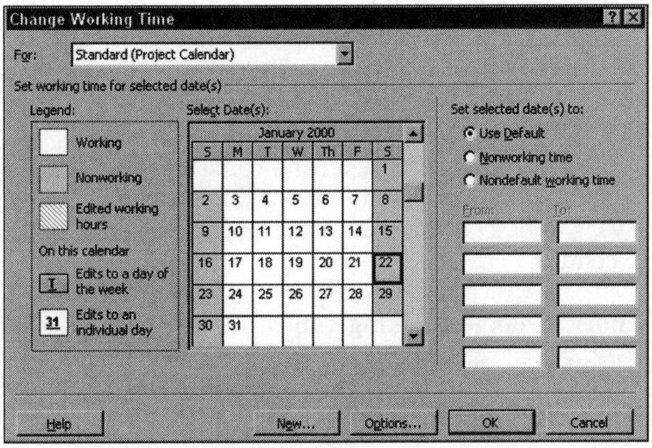

Figure 5-9:
Shaded days represent default nonworking days.

2. **Manipulate the scroll bar until you come to the month you want to modify.**

3. **Select the day you want to change to a nonworking day.**

4. **Under Set Selected Date(s) to, select the Nonworking Time option.**

5. **Repeat Steps 1 through 4 for other nonworking times.**

6. **Click OK.**

If you want, you can use the GoTo Selected Task button to peruse your work. In the Smith Home example, select task 27, the Painting task, and click the Go To Selected Task button on the Standard toolbar. The Gantt chart indicates that Tuesday, July 4, 2000 is a nonworking day. The day is grayed in the chart. The changes to the project calendar have adjusted all tasks after May 29 to be one day later and all tasks after July 4 to be two days later than they were prior to your changing the project calendar. Benevolent project managers are such martyrs!

Gray is a rotten color for a nonworking day! Chapter 7 covers how to customize the look of your Gantt chart. May all your nonworking days be sunny and sky blue!

Creating a new calendar

Sometimes you need another calendar to complement the project calendar. Fortunately, understanding and using multiple calendars is easy in Microsoft Project. And, unlike trying to coordinate a home and an office calendar, you can stay away from time conflicts by using Microsoft Project.

Suppose, for example, that construction workers involved in your project arrive at work at 7 a.m., take a half-hour lunch, and end their workday in mid-afternoon. In contrast, office workers who perform other project-related duties arrive at work at 8 a.m., take an hour-long lunch, and leave at 5 p.m. — the default calendar settings.

To resolve this, you need to create a second calendar. You create it by first duplicating the project calendar and then making changes. This way, dates such as holidays, will be carried over to the new calendar. Simple, right? To create a new calendar:

1. **Choose Tools⇨Change Working Time.**

   The Change Working Time dialog box appears.

2. **Click the New button.**

   The Create New Base Calendar dialog box appears.

3. **Type a name for the base calendar in the Name box.**

   In this example, type **Construction Hours Calendar.**

4. **Make sure that the second option (Make a Copy of) is selected, and that it reads Make a Copy of Standard Calendar, as shown in Figure 5-10.**

   Anything you did to the standard calendar is carried over to the Construction Hours calendar.

5. **Click OK.**

You don't replace the standard calendar when you create a new calendar. All resources base their working hours and days on the standard calendar, until directed otherwise.

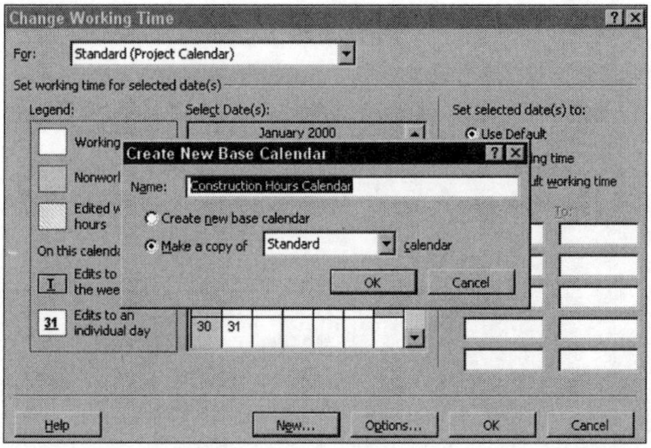

Figure 5-10:
The Create
New Base
Calendar
dialog box.

Next, to change the working hours for the Construction Hours calendar,
follow these steps:

1. **Select the columns for working days by clicking M (Monday) and
   dragging horizontally to F (Friday).**

2. **In the Set Selected Dates To panel, select the Nondefault Working
   Time option.**

3. **In the From and To boxes, type the new morning working time.**

   In the example, type **7 am** in the From box and **11 am** in the To box.

4. **On the next line of the From and To areas, type a new after-lunch
   work-time information.**

   In the example, type **11:30 am** in the From box and **3:30 pm** in the To
   box. If you follow the example, your screen should look like Figure 5-11.

5. **Click OK.**

The last step is to apply this calendar to all appropriate resources. An easy
way to do this is by using the Resource Sheet view. To assign the new base
calendar to the appropriate resources, use the following steps:

1. **Select Resource Sheet View on the view bar.**

   Notice that resource names appear.

   In the example, resource names are listed 1 through 16. Notice in particular that Excavation Contractor is in Row 5.

2. **Scroll to the right until you see the Base Calendar column.**

Figure 5-11:
Use the
Change
Working
Time dialog
box to
create a
custom
work
schedule
that
includes
changes
made in the
standard
calendar.

Change Working Time

For: Construction Hours Calendar

Set working time for selected date(s)

| Legend: | Select Date(s): | Set selected date(s) to: |

○ Use Default
○ Nonworking time
● Nondefault working time

January 2000

S	M	T	W	Th	F	S
						1
2	3	4	5	6	7	8
9	10	11	12	13	14	15
16	17	18	19	20	21	22
23	24	25	26	27	28	29
30	31					

Working
Nonworking
Edited working hours
On this calendar
Edits to a day of the week
Edits to an individual day

From: To:
7:00 AM | 11:00 AM
11:30 AM | 3:30 PM

Help   New...   Options...   OK   Close

3. **Select a cell in the Base Calendar column.**

A down arrow appears.

In the example, select Row 5 in the Base Calendar column (the Excavation Contractor).

4. **Click the down arrow.**

Four choices appear, as shown in Figure 5-12.

5. **Select the base calendar you want to assign to this resource.**

In the example, select the Construction Hours Calendar. The Construction Hours Calendar replaces Standard in the Base Calendar cell for Resource 5, the Excavation Contractor.

If you want, you can double-click the vertical line separating the headings for the Base Calendar and Code columns. This causes the Base Calendar to expand, showing the full name for the Construction Hours Calendar.

6. **Follow Steps 2 through 5 to assign a new base calendar to other resources.**

In the example, assign the Construction Hours Calendar to resource rows 6, 7, 9–13, and 16. The results should look like Figure 5-13.

Now that you know how to modify the standard calendar and now that you've created an additional base calendar, creating a resource calendar will ever after be easy. I cover creating a resource calendar in the following section.

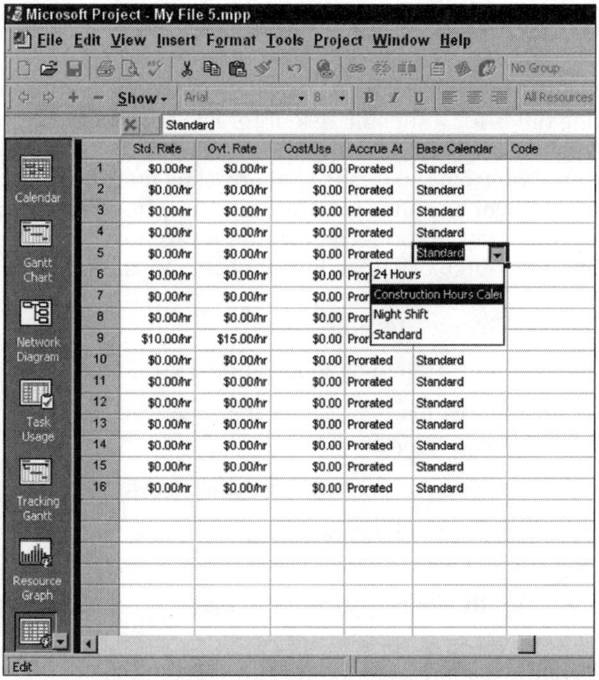

Figure 5-12:
The text box
lists the
base calen-
dars for the
project.
Three
calendars
are defaults,
and the
Construction
Hours
Calendar is
the one you
created.

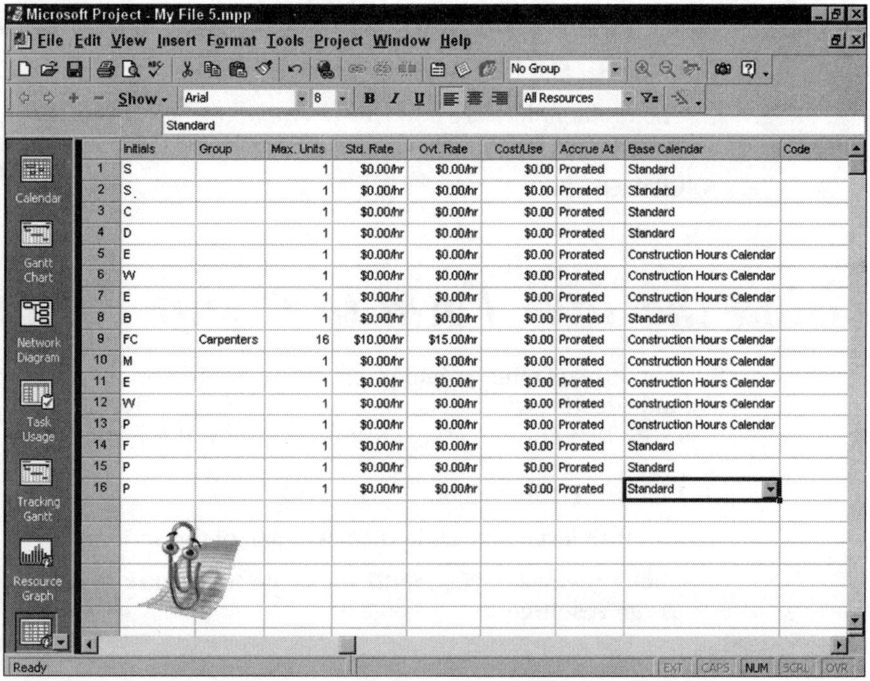

Figure 5-13:
The
Resource
Sheet
shows the
changes.
Microsoft
Project
automati-
cally
records
these
changes to
any view
that displays
work times.

Creating a resource calendar

A resource calendar is different from a base calendar in that it keeps working and nonworking times for a specific resource. The best view for creating a resource calendar is Gantt Chart view, which you can access by choosing the Gantt Chart view icon from the view bar at any time. In the example project for this chapter, you get a chance to create a special holiday for your under-appreciated drywall crew. National Screw Gun Awareness Week, here we come! To create a resource calendar, follow these steps:

1. **Choose Tools⇨Change Working Time.**

   The Change Working Time dialog box appears.

2. **In the For drop-down list box, select the resource for which you want to create a resource calendar.**

   In the example project, select the Wallboard Crew resource.

   Notice that the default color of working days for a resource calendar are a hatched, light shade of gray.

3. **Scroll to the month where you want to make the working time change.**

   In the example, scroll to June, 2000. The week beginning June 11 is the beginning of the wallboard workers' national holiday.

4. **Drag across the time you want to change.**

   In the example, drag the whole week beginning June 11 to highlight it.

5. **In the Set Selected Dates To panel, select the Nonworking Time option.**

   The wallboarders are now free to attend the Screw Gun Olympics. Fortunately, your schedule didn't need them that week anyway.

6. **Click OK.**

Using the Task Form to Assign Resources

Microsoft Project often provides umpteen ways to accomplish something. An easy and effective way to assign resources to tasks is by using the Task form. To use the Task Form to assign resources, follow these steps:

1. **Choose Window⇨Split.**

   The Task form appears in the lower half of the screen.

2. **Click Previous or Next until you come to the task to which you want to assign resources.**

In the example, click the Previous button or the Next button until you come to Task 5, Write contract.

3. **Select the space below the Resource Names column title.**

A highlighted box appears. In addition, a down arrow appears to the right.

4. **Click the down arrow to the right of the box.**

A list of the resources in the resource pool appears, as shown in Figure 5-14.

5. **Select the resource.**

In the example, select Counsel. The resource now appears below Resource Names.

6. **Click OK.**

The resource is assigned to the task.

You can enter as many resources as you want in the Resource Names column. They all become assigned to that particular task. When you're back in the single view, you can still see the resource assignments by highlighting the task and clicking the Goto Selected Task button on the standard toolbar.

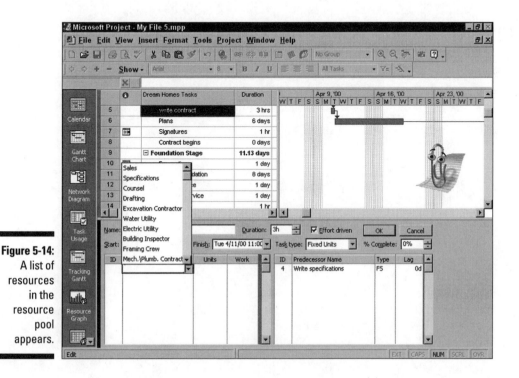

Figure 5-14:
A list of resources in the resource pool appears.

Save your work every time you accomplish something (such as assigning resources to tasks).

Part III
Analyzing a Project

The 5th Wave   By Rich Tennant

"WHAT DO YOU MEAN IT SORT OF IS AND ISN'T COMPATIBLE?"

In this part . . .

How many project managers does it take to change a light bulb? Sorry, that's operations. Okay. How many light bulbs does it take to change a project manager? Now, that's a good question. A project manager often needs all kinds of light shed on a subject before there's enough clarity to make a change. In project management, you add light to a subject by changing views.

In this part, you learn how to view charts, tables, and graphs. You use and customize the Gantt Chart view, Network Diagram view, the Calendar view, and the Resource view. And you find out about filters.

Chapter 6

Viewing Your Project from All Sides

● ●

In This Chapter

▶ Getting multiple views of a project

▶ Using views to keep track of resources

▶ Managing small projects in Calendar view

▶ Tracking a project by flow chart

● ●

*I*n the foggy stages of a project, the project manager, like a pilot, wants ready access to a map and an intelligent navigator. Microsoft Project competently keeps you on the right path by providing views.

Views are to project management what flying by instruments is to a pilot. One perspective can't give you all the information you need. One reading may indicate that you're right on schedule with a whole slew of resources. But another reading may show that the resources are headed into a maze of conflicting tasks.

A *view* is a display of project information. Microsoft Project has two major classifications of views: task views and resource views. This chapter is about task views. To find out about resource views, check out Chapter 10.

Using Views to Look at a Project

After you're up and running with a project, you can begin to take advantage of Project's letting you access your project information in a variety of ways. This chapter helps you understand how to access views of your project.

Microsoft assumes that you most likely want to see the Gantt Chart view when you open Microsoft Project (Figure 6-1). The assumption is probably true. Nine times out of ten, you'll probably find yourself doing most of your project management tasks in the Gantt Chart view. But sometime you may want to step away from the crowd and change Microsoft Project defaults to reflect your own project view preference. Project has a lot of views to choose from. To name a few, you could open Project in a Calendar view, a Network Diagram (flowchart) view, or in Resource Graph view (a graphical representation of available and used resources).

Feel free to use a file I've created to practice with views titled Chapter 6.mpp. The practice file in this chapter is based on the Smith Home project file that I introduce in Chapter 3. See Appendix C for more information on copying the practice files from the CD. When the file opens, you see something similar to Figure 6-1.

To designate a view other than the Gantt Chart view as the default view, select Tools⇨Options. The Options dialog box appears. Click the View tab. Click the down arrow next to the Default View text box. Select the view you want as your new default view. Click OK to close the Options dialog box. The new default view appears the next time you open a Project file.

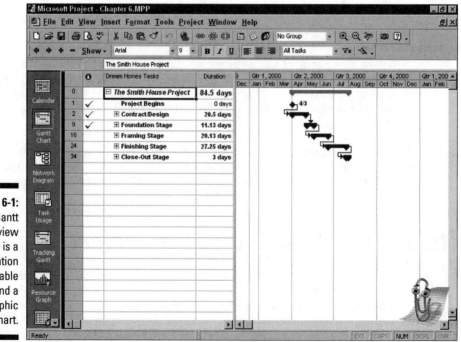

Figure 6-1: The Gantt Chart view is a combination of a table and a graphic chart.

Focusing on the Gantt Chart View

The Gantt Chart view textually and graphically shows you important information about your project. Microsoft Project presents this view as the default because the Gantt chart presents just about everything you need for building and managing your project.

Entering information in a task table

Microsoft Project calls the left side of the Gantt Chart view the Task Entry table. This table is a compilation of task management operations presented to you in columns and rows much like a spreadsheet. And, as with a spreadsheet, you enter and remove task information from individual cells as you build your project. Hidden inside each of the cells are project formulas that cause your text entry to affect relationships with other cells and with the entire project. You build and modify your project by entering information about tasks, resources, time, and relationships.

Microsoft Project offers you lots of task tables, which I describe in the following sections. Use these steps to see the available tables in Microsoft Project:

1. **Choose View⇨Table: Entry.**

   The Task Table list appears, as shown in Figure 6-2. Notice that the Entry table is checked because it's the one currently being used. In the Task Table list, Microsoft Project offers you the most commonly selected tables. You can click the More Tables option to see a complete table list.

2. **Choose More Tables.**

   The More Tables dialog box appears (Figure 6-3). Notice that you can select either Task or Resource tables. If you want to see resource tables, click the Resource radio button.

Entry table

The Entry table is the table that you normally use to enter task names, add duration, link tasks, and assign resources. The table is chock-full of information and organizational tools. Much of what the table has to show you is also graphically represented by the Gantt chart. To fully expose the Entry table, follow these steps:

1. **Place your cursor over the vertical bar between the table and the chart.**

2. **Drag the vertical line all the way to the right.**

   If you're in 800 x 600 resolution, you can see almost the entire table.

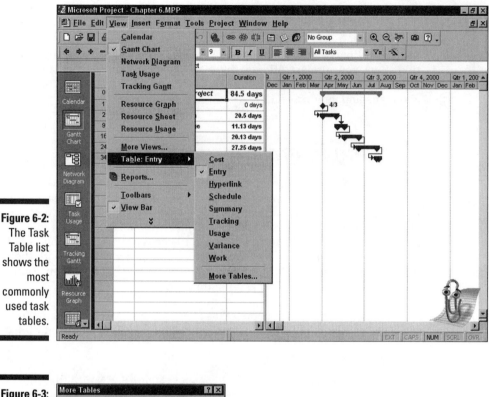

Figure 6-2:
The Task
Table list
shows the
most
commonly
used task
tables.

Figure 6-3:
The More
Tables
dialog box
lists all
task and
resource
tables.

You can adjust your monitor's resolution by right-clicking in the open area of Window's desktop and by clicking Properties. The Display Properties dialog box appears. Click the Settings tab. Depending on your computer's video card, you can adjust the number of pixels (picture elements) from low resolution (640 x 480) to high resolution (1024 x 768) and higher.

3. **To Hide the view bar on the left, right-click the view bar and click View Bar.**

You have expanded the view about as far as you can. The view may look great except that you may have some columns showing hash marks (#). These little critters appear in place of information in a cell when the width of the information — such as a date — exceeds the width of the column. A narrow column may show *February 28, 2000* as ######.

4. **To remove hash marks, double-click the vertical line separating column headings.**

   The columns expand to show all the text in each field. The Entry table now looks like Figure 6-4.

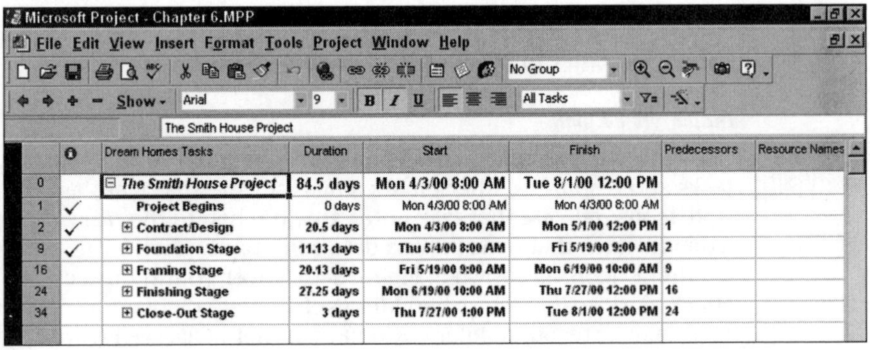

Figure 6-4:
The fully-exposed Task Entry table shows columns of basic information about the project.

Microsoft Project cleverly organizes the Entry table so that you're not over-saturated with information all at one time. You can organize the Entry table information by using any or all of the following organizational tools and options:

- ✔ **Project Summary Task option**
- ✔ **Indicators Column option**
- ✔ **Phase Expansion and Contraction tool**
- ✔ **Outline Numbering option**
- ✔ **Individual cell height**

Project summary task

The sum of your project's individual summary tasks equals the duration of the Project summary task. Project summary task gives you an overall perspective of the length of your entire project. To access the Project summary task option, follow these steps:

1. **Select Tools⇨Options.**

   The Options dialog box appears.

2. **Click the View tab.**

3. **In the Outline Options For panel, select the Project Summary Task check box.**

4. Click OK.

The Options dialog box disappears and the Project summary task appears in the task name column.

To finish your creation of the Project summary task, give it a name as you would any other task by following these steps:

1. Click the Summary task cell.

2. Type a Summary task name.

3. Press Enter to accept your Summary task name.

Indicators column

The Indicators column displays various icons that reveal information about tasks and resources. Check mark icons indicate that tasks are completed. Note icons indicate that task notes are attached to the tasks. The Calendars icon indicates that tasks have a date constraint. (Notice the column containing the "i" icon, as shown in Figure 6-4.) Hover your mouse cursor over the check mark beside a task and Microsoft Project displays a text box that contains task or resource information about that task (see Figure 6-5).

You can hide the Indicators column by right-clicking the column head and selecting Hide Column from the context menu that appears.

Figure 6-5:
Microsoft
Project
automatically
adds infor-
mation
icons in the
Indicators
column.

	0	Dream Homes Tasks	Duration	Start	Finish	Predecessors	Resource Names
0		⊟ *The Smith House Project*	84.5 days	Mon 4/3/00 8:00 AM	Tue 8/1/00 12:00 PM		
1	✓	**Project Begins**	0 days	Mon 4/3/00 8:00 AM	Mon 4/3/00 8:00 AM		
2	✓	⊞ **Contract/Design**	20.5 days	Mon 4/3/00 8:00 AM	Mon 5/1/00 12:00 PM	1	
9	✓	⊞ **Foundation Stage**	11.13 days	Thu 5/4/00 8:00 AM	Fri 5/19/00 9:00 AM	2	
16		⊞	13 days	Fri 5/19/00 9:00 AM	Mon 6/19/00 10:00 AM	9	
24		⊞	25 days	Mon 6/19/00 10:00 AM	Thu 7/27/00 12:00 PM	16	
34		⊞ Close-Out Stage	3 days	Thu 7/27/00 1:00 PM	Tue 8/1/00 12:00 PM	24	

✓ This task was completed on Fri 5/19/00 9:00 AM.

Expanding and contracting project phases

In Microsoft Project, you can see your entire project by using an expanded view or see individual phases of your project by contracting your view. To expand a Project file:

1. Click the Show button on the formatting toolbar.

A drop-down list box appears.

2. **Select All Subtasks.**

   The project expands fully, revealing all tasks.

Using the preceding steps, you can also contract a portion or all of a Project file. For example, to contract a Project file to hide all subtasks:

1. **Click the Show button on the formatting toolbar.**

   A drop-down list box appears.

2. **Select Outline Level 1.**

   The project contracts to hide all subtasks under their summary tasks.

Outline numbering

Microsoft Project offers you the option of adding outline numbering to your tasks and removing the plus and minus symbols from summary tasks. The Outline numbering option numbers tasks in the following structure: 3.1; 3.2; 3.3; 3.4. This is unlike the outline structure you used for your high school term paper: A.1.a., for example.

The Outline option aligns tasks according to a project management system called Work Breakdown Structure (WBS). In this system, tasks are organized to facilitate detailed reporting and tracking of costs. Each additional indent of a subtask is an increasingly detailed breakdown of project work.

Before you activate outline numbering, you may want to fully expand the practice file. By expanding the practice file fully, you can see the full effect of the outline numbering system.

To activate the outline option and to deactivate the outline symbols, follow these steps:

1. **Choose Tools➪Options.**

   The Options dialog box appears.

2. **Click the View tab.**

3. **Deselect the Show Outline Symbol check box.**

4. **Select the Show Outline Number check box.**

5. **Click OK.**

The tasks and subtasks are now associated with outline numbers, as shown in Figure 6-6. The outline numbers reflect the number of a summary task, the numbers of related subtasks, and the level of hierarchy within the summary task. The task number differs from a task ID. For example, task ID 10 in outline numbering may be 3.1, which means it's the first subtask of summary task 3.

Microsoft Project - Chapter 6.MPP

File Edit View Insert Format Tools Project Window Help

No Group

The Smith House Project

	O	Dream Homes Tasks	Duration	Start	Finish	Predecessors	Resource Names
0		*The Smith House Project*	**84.5 days**	**Mon 4/3/00 8:00 AM**	**Tue 8/1/00 12:00 PM**		
1	✓	**1 Project Begins**	0 days	Mon 4/3/00 8:00 AM	Mon 4/3/00 8:00 AM		
2	✓	**2 Contract/Design**	**20.5 days**	**Mon 4/3/00 8:00 AM**	**Mon 5/1/00 12:00 PM**	1	
3	✓	2.1 Customer selections	1 wk	Mon 4/3/00 8:00 AM	Fri 4/7/00 5:00 PM		Sales[0.25]
4	✓	2.2 Write specifications	1 day	Mon 4/10/00 8:00 AM	Mon 4/10/00 5:00 PM	3	Specfications
5	✓	2.3 write contract	3 hrs	Tue 4/11/00 8:00 AM	Tue 4/11/00 11:00 AM	4	Counsel
6	✓	2.4 Plans	6 days	Tue 4/11/00 11:00 AM	Wed 4/19/00 11:00 AM	5	
7	✓	2.5 Signatures	1 hr	Mon 5/1/00 11:00 AM	Mon 5/1/00 12:00 PM	6	
8	✓	2.6 Contract begins	0 days	Mon 5/1/00 12:00 PM	Mon 5/1/00 12:00 PM	7	
9	✓	**3 Foundation Stage**	**11.13 days**	**Thu 5/4/00 8:00 AM**	**Fri 5/19/00 9:00 AM**	2	
10	✓	3.1 Excavation	1 day	Thu 5/4/00 8:00 AM	Thu 5/4/00 5:00 PM		
11	✓	3.2 Footing/foundation	8 days	Fri 5/5/00 8:00 AM	Tue 5/16/00 5:00 PM	10	
12	✓	3.3 Water service	1 day	Wed 5/17/00 8:00 AM	Wed 5/17/00 5:00 PM	11	
13	✓	3.4 Electrical service	1 day	Wed 5/17/00 8:00 AM	Wed 5/17/00 5:00 PM	11	
14	✓	3.5 Inspection	1 hr	Fri 5/19/00 8:00 AM	Fri 5/19/00 9:00 AM	13FS+1 day	Building Inspecto
15	✓	3.6 Foundation Stage comple	0 days	Fri 5/19/00 9:00 AM	Fri 5/19/00 9:00 AM	14	
16		**4 Framing Stage**	**20.13 days**	**Fri 5/19/00 9:00 AM**	**Mon 6/19/00 10:00 AM**	9	
17	✓	4.1 Wood framing	3 wks	Fri 5/19/00 9:00 AM	Mon 6/12/00 9:00 AM		Fra...ng Crew[7]
18		4.2 Roofing	4 days	Mon 6/12/00 9:00 AM	Fri 6/16/00 9:00 AM	17	F...
19		4.3 Plumbing lines	3 days	Mon 6/12/00 9:00 AM	Thu 6/15/00 9:00 AM	17	Me... Cor
20		4.4 Furnace and A/C	3 days	Mon 6/12/00 9:00 AM	Thu 6/15/00 9:00 AM	17	... Cor
21		4.5 Electrical wiring	3 days	Mon 6/12/00 9:00 AM	Thu 6/15/00 9:00 AM	17	Elec... ontrac

Ready

EXT CAPS NUM SCRL OVR

Figure 6-6: Outline numbers remain visible until you clear the Show Outline Number check box in the Options dialog box.

Individual cell height

Entering a long task name was a problem in earlier versions of Microsoft Project. Entering long task names in reports meant printing extra pages to accommodate the names. If you wanted to make a task more than one row in height, you had to make all the rows the same height. Microsoft Project 2000 enables you to make an individual long-name cell more than one row in height. To make a cell more than one row in height, use these steps:

1. **Place the mouse between rows in the task ID column (the number column).**

   The cursor changes from a plus to the row height cursor.

2. **Drag the row line down until it touches the next row line.**

3. **Release the mouse.**

   The long task name now should appear in two rows.

If the task name is still too long, repeat Steps 1 through 3 to increase row height. Also, you can use the same procedure in reverse to reduce row height.

Cost table

Another task table available in the Gantt Chart view is the Cost table. The *Cost table* is very similar in appearance and functionality to a spreadsheet. This is one of the more dynamic task tables. Throughout the life of a project, the Cost table keeps track of task costs, calculates comparisons with your original estimates, and apprises you of the remainder of your budget. To access the Cost table, choose <u>V</u>iew⇨Ta<u>b</u>le:⇨<u>C</u>ost. The Cost table, shown in Figure 6-7, appears, providing information on the cost of the project's tasks.

Based on the predicted duration and the per-hour fee for each unit of a necessary resource, Microsoft Project can predict the total labor cost of a task. Microsoft Project tracks actual costs and how much money remains for other tasks.

For example, in the Smith Home 6.mpp project, Task 18, the roofing task, shows an estimated cost of $1,600. The actual cost so far is $800, and $800 remains. Task 10 is a *fixed cost*. Fixed costs are often set based on contractual agreements — in this case a contract with the excavation contractor. Costs are discussed in detail in Chapter 12.

	Task Name	Fixed Cost	Fixed Cost Accrual	Total Cost	Baseline	Variance	Actual	Remaining
0	**The Smith House Project**	**$0.00**	**Prorated**	**$35,100.00**	**$35,100.00**	**$0.00**	**$18,700.00**	
1	**1 Project Begins**	$0.00	Prorated	$0.00	$0.00	$0.00	$0.00	
2	**2 Contract/Design**	**$0.00**	**Prorated**	**$500.00**	**$500.00**	**$0.00**	**$500.00**	.00
3	2.1 Customer selection	$0.00	Prorated	$0.00	$0.00	$0.00	$0.00	$0.00
4	2.2 Write specifications	$0.00	Prorated	$0.00	$0.00	$0.00	$0.00	$0.00
5	2.3 write contract	$500.00	End	$500.00	$500.00	$0.00	$500.00	$0.00
6	2.4 Plans	$0.00	Prorated	$0.00	$0.00	$0.00	$0.00	$0.00
7	2.5 Signatures	$0.00	Prorated	$0.00	$0.00	$0.00	$0.00	$0.00
8	2.6 Contract begins	$0.00	Prorated	$0.00	$0.00	$0.00	$0.00	$0.00
9	**3 Foundation Stage**	**$0.00**	**Prorated**	**$9,000.00**	**$9,000.00**	**$0.00**	**$9,000.00**	**$0.00**
10	3.1 Excavation	$2,000.00	End	$2,000.00	$2,000.00	$0.00	$2,000.00	$0.00
11	3.2 Footing/foundation	$6,000.00	End	$6,000.00	$6,000.00	$0.00	$6,000.00	$0.00
12	3.3 Water service	$400.00	Start	$400.00	$400.00	$0.00	$400.00	$0.00
13	3.4 Electrical service	$500.00	Start	$500.00	$500.00	$0.00	$500.00	$0.00
14	3.5 Inspection	$100.00	End	$100.00	$100.00	$0.00	$100.00	$0.00
15	3.6 Foundation Stage c	$0.00	Prorated	$0.00	$0.00	$0.00	$0.00	$0.00
16	**4 Framing Stage**	**$0.00**	**Prorated**	**$19,700.00**	**$19,700.00**	**$0.00**	**$9,200.00**	**$10,500.00**
17	4.1 Wood framing	$0.00	Prorated	$8,400.00	$8,400.00	$0.00	$8,400.00	$0.00
18	4.2 Roofing	$0.00	Prorated	$1,600.00	$1,600.00	$0.00	$800.00	$800.00
19	4.3 Plumbing lines	$1,800.00	End	$1,800.00	$1,800.00	$0.00	$0.00	$1,800.00
20	4.4 Furnace and A/C	$5,700.00	End	$5,700.00	$5,700.00	$0.00	$0.00	$5,700.00
21	4.5 Electrical wiring	$2,100.00	End	$2,100.00	$2,100.00	$0.00	$0.00	$2,100.00

Figure 6-7: Fixed costs can be based on contractual agreement.

The baseline column (refer to Figure 6-7) represents a kind of snapshot of your project that you take when your planning is complete but before the project actually begins. After you begin your project, Microsoft Project tracks your costs, deadlines, and how much of available resources you've used by comparing these components to the baseline. The baseline is what you track your project against. Chapter 16 covers baselines in detail.

Summary table

The Summary table tracks the progress of a project on a task-by-task basis. To access it, choose View⇨Table:⇨Summary. In Figure 6-8, notice that Microsoft Project tracks the progress of a task category in the %Comp. column. The Framing Stage category is 71 percent complete, while its subtasks show stages of completion ranging from 0 percent to 100 percent complete.

Schedule table

The Schedule table shows scheduled start and finish dates for tasks. To access it, choose View⇨Table:⇨Schedule. It also shows the latest dates that tasks can start and finish without messing up the schedule. The difference between the planned start and finish and the latest start and finish is shown in the two slack columns shown in Figure 6-9. *Free slack* is how much slack Microsoft Project allows a task before it conflicts with a successor task. *Total slack* is how much slack the task has until it delays the completion of the project.

Figure 6-8:
The %
Comp.
Column
displays the
sum of all
work to be
performed
by all
resources
for each
individual
category
and its
subtasks.

	Task Name	Duration	Start	Finish	% Comp.	Cost	Work
3	2.1 Customer selection	1 wk	Mon 4/3/00 8:00 AM	Fri 4/7/00 5:00 PM	100%	$0.00	10 hrs
4	2.2 Write specifications	1 day	Mon 4/10/00 8:00 AM	Mon 4/10/00 5:00 PM	100%	$0.00	8 hrs
5	2.3 write contract	3 hrs	Tue 4/11/00 8:00 AM	Tue 4/11/00 11:00 AM	100%	$500.00	3 hrs
6	2.4 Plans	6 days	Tue 4/11/00 11:00 AM	Wed 4/19/00 11:00 AM	100%	$0.00	0 hrs
7	2.5 Signatures	1 hr	Mon 5/1/00 11:00 AM	Mon 5/1/00 12:00 PM	100%	$0.00	0 hrs
8	2.6 Contract begins	0 days	Mon 5/1/00 12:00 PM	Mon 5/1/00 12:00 PM	100%	$0.00	0 hrs
9	**3 Foundation Stage**	**11.13 days**	**Thu 5/4/00 8:00 AM**	**Fri 5/19/00 9:00 AM**	**100%**	**$9,000.00**	**2 hrs**
10	3.1 Excavation	1 day	Thu 5/4/00 8:00 AM	Thu 5/4/00 5:00 PM	100%	$2,000.00	0 hrs
11	3.2 Footing/foundation	8 days	Fri 5/5/00 8:00 AM	Tue 5/16/00 5:00 PM	100%	$6,000.00	0 hrs
12	3.3 Water service	1 day	Wed 5/17/00 8:00 AM	Wed 5/17/00 5:00 PM	100%	$400.00	0 hrs
13	3.4 Electrical service	1 day	Wed 5/17/00 8:00 AM	Wed 5/17/00 5:00 PM	100%	$500.00	0 hrs
14	3.5 Inspection	1 hr	Fri 5/19/00 8:00 AM	Fri 5/19/00 9:00 AM	100%	$100.00	2 hrs
15	3.6 Foundation Stage c	0 days	Fri 5/19/00 9:00 AM	Fri 5/19/00 9:00 AM	100%	$0.00	0 hrs
16	**4 Framing Stage**	**20.13 days**	**Fri 5/19/00 9:00 AM**	**Mon 6/19/00 10:00 AM**	**71%**	**$19,700.00**	**1,074 hrs**
17	4.1 Wood framing	3 wks	Fri 5/19/00 9:00 AM	Mon 6/12/00 9:00 AM	100%	$8,400.00	840 hrs
18	4.2 Roofing	4 days	Mon 6/12/00 9:00 AM	Fri 6/16/00 9:00 AM	50%	$1,600.00	160 hrs
19	4.3 Plumbing lines	3 days	Mon 6/12/00 9:00 AM	Thu 6/15/00 9:00 AM	0%	$1,800.00	24 hrs
20	4.4 Furnace and A/C	3 days	Mon 6/12/00 9:00 AM	Thu 6/15/00 9:00 AM	25%	$5,700.00	24 hrs
21	4.5 Electrical wiring	3 days	Mon 6/12/00 9:00 AM	Thu 6/15/00 9:00 AM	75%	$2,100.00	24 hrs
22	4.6 Inspection	1 hr	Mon 6/19/00 9:00 AM	Mon 6/19/00 10:00 AM	0%	$100.00	2 hrs
23	4.7 Framing Stage com	0 days	Mon 6/19/00 10:00 AM	Mon 6/19/00 10:00 AM	0%	$0.00	0 hrs
24	**5 Finishing Stage**	**27.25 days**	**Mon 6/19/00 10:00 AM**	**Thu 7/27/00 12:00 PM**	**0%**	**$5,900.00**	**279.2 hrs**

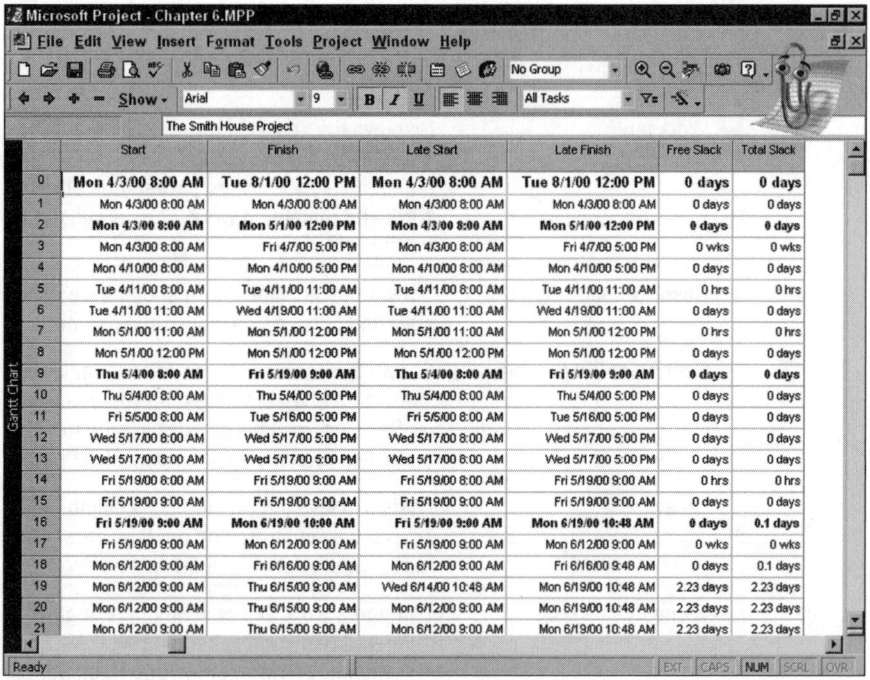

Figure 6-9:
Late Start
and Late
Finish
dates are
Microsoft
Project
estimates of
how late a
task may
start and
finish
without
compromis-
ing the
schedule.

Other tables

Microsoft Project gives you eight other task tables in the Gantt Chart view, as described in Table 6-1. If you can't see them by selecting View➪Table, try selecting View➪Table:➪More Tables.

Table 6-1	More Task Tables
Table	**What It Does**
Tracking table	Shows actual information about the progress of a project's tasks. You can keep apprised of the schedule and the money being spent. Information includes the actual start and finish dates, the percentage of completion, the actual and remaining duration, the actual cost, and the actual amount of work performed.
Variance table	Shows how the actual start and finish dates vary from the planned (baseline) start and finish dates in terms of task duration. The default measurement for this table is days.

(continued)

Table 6-1 *(continued)*

Table	What It Does
Work table	Displays the variance between estimated work and actual work for individual tasks (similar to the Variance table). It also shows the percentage of completed work and remaining work. The default measurement for this table is hours.
Baseline table	Shows the baseline information for each task's duration, start and finish dates, hours of work, and cost.
Constraint Dates table	Shows the constraint type of each task. Unless you specify otherwise, Microsoft Project assigns a default As Soon As Possible constraint type to all tasks. The table also lists any specific constraint dates.
Delay table	Assists in leveling resources. Leveling (see Chapter 13) is a way of stretching out task durations to lessen resource allocation at a given time.
Earned Value table	Compares work and cost amounts, including cost of budgeted work and scheduled work. Scheduled data is sometimes different than budgeted data because it can be based on updated information. The column abbreviations include: BCWS (Budgeted Cost of Work Scheduled); BCWP (Budgeted Cost of Work Performed); ACWP (Actual Cost of Work Performed); SV (Earned Value Schedule Variance); CV (Earned Value Cost Variance); BAC (Budgeted at Completion); and FAC (Forecast at Completion).
Export	Transfers a Microsoft Project file to another application, such as a spreadsheet.

See Chapter 13 to find out how to create your own customized table in Microsoft Project.

You may want return to the Entry table by selecting View➪Table:➪Entry. Then, drag the vertical view bar to the left until it rests on the right edge of the Duration column. Also, reopen the view bar by right-clicking the far left edge of the screen and clicking the View Bar option.

If the Indicators column has disappeared, right-click the heading of the Task Name column. Choose Insert Column from the context menu. The Column Definition dialog box appears. Click the down arrow to the right of the Field Name text box and click Indicators. Then click OK. The Indicators column reappears.

Henry Gantt, you're my kind of guy

You may have wondered why the Gantt chart is the place where Microsoft Project begins. And where does the name Gantt come from?

Henry Laurence Gantt (1861-1919) was well known in his day as a pioneer in industrial and scientific management. He was one of the first people to emphasize the importance of maintaining working conditions that would cause favorable psychological effects on workers.

Henry's altruism may be notable. But what gets him mentioned in Trivial Pursuit and *Jeopardy!* games is his invention of a graphical way to depict work over time — the Gantt chart.

Reading Gantt charts

On the right side of the Gantt Chart view is a graphic chart. The chart is comprised of a series of horizontal bars inlaid in a table and spanning measurements of time. Each bar is a task that's directly related to the corresponding table row to its left. Project information that you enter into each row of the left-hand table manipulates the characteristics of the graphic bar, as well as affects the bar's relationship to other bars in the chart. Frequently (but not always) you see names next to the bars. These names are the resources assigned to the task. The resource assignments were also performed in the chart on the right.

Getting information from a Gantt chart

The Gantt chart gives you four kinds of information about your project simultaneously: time, task progress, task relationships, and resource assignments to tasks.

Time

On the Gantt chart, you can zoom in to see whether individual tasks are staying on schedule or you can zoom out to get the bigger picture of your project's timetable.

Change the time view to weeks and days by clicking the Zoom In button three times. If tasks aren't visible, click the Go To Selected Task button to show Task 1. The Project file should now look like Figure 6-10.

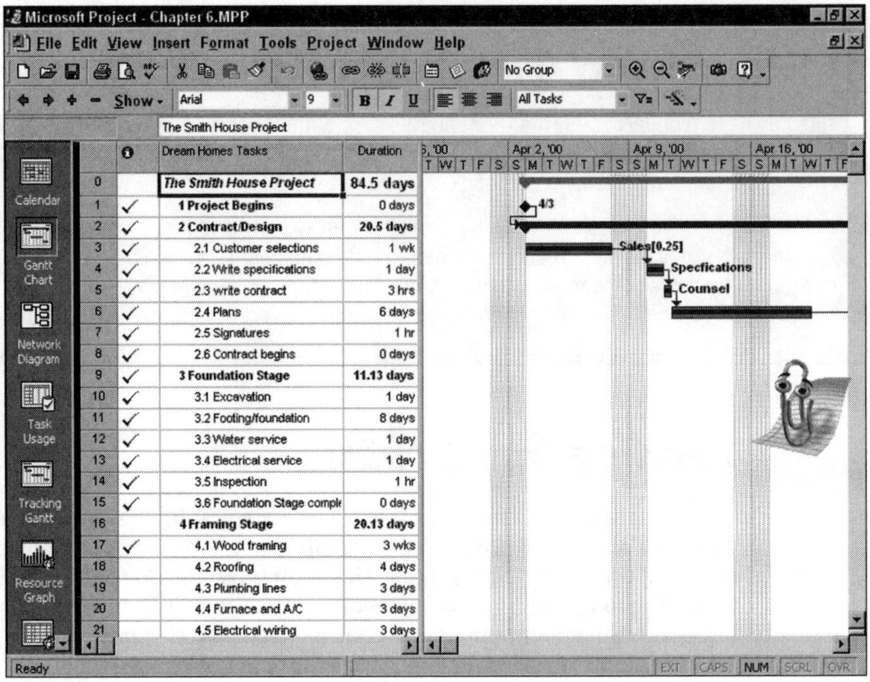

Figure 6-10:
The
timescale of
the Gantt
chart is in
weeks over
days.

In the Gantt chart, you can visually determine when a task should begin and end by comparing the task's front and back edges to dates and times on the timescale.

Task progress

Microsoft Project denotes a completed project by displaying a solid black line through the horizontal task bar. Pause your mouse over the black line in the task. An information box appears, telling you that the task is completed, and other information about the task (see Figure 6-11). If the black line extends only part of the way through the task, the task isn't finished. Pause your mouse over the black line in the task. An information box appears, telling you that the task is only partially complete. I discuss task progress in detail in Chapter 17.

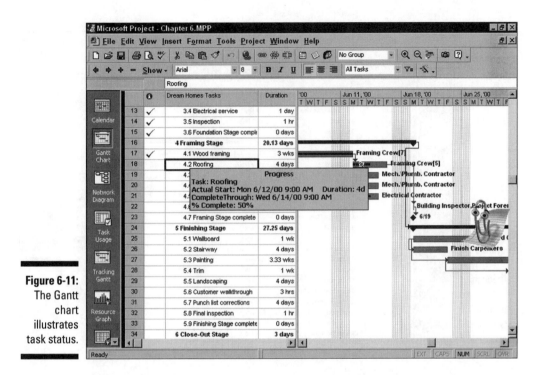

Figure 6-11:
The Gantt
chart
illustrates
task status.

Task relationships

The status of each of the tasks in some way affects the status of other tasks. For example, you can't install plumbing in a house unless the wood framing has been sufficiently completed. The Gantt chart communicates task relationships by using arrowed lines.

Place your mouse over the arrowed line between two tasks. An information box appears, telling you that the task you chose has a Finish-to-Start (FS) relationship with the task that precedes it (see Figure 6-12). Chapter 4 describes the kinds of task relationships.

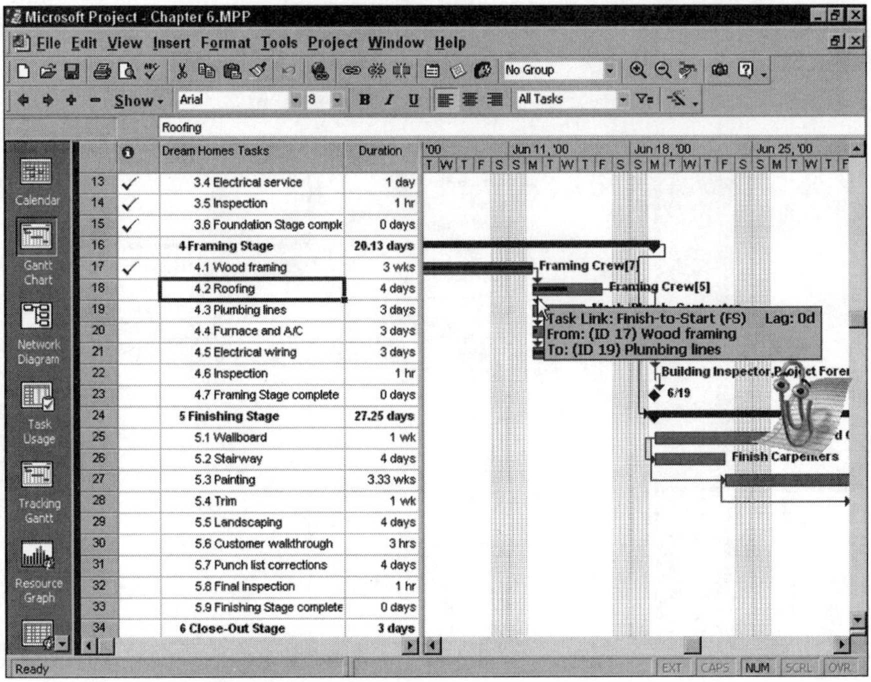

Figure 6-12:
Task
relationships
are
represented
by arrowed
lines.

Resource assignments to tasks

Resource assignments tell you who's doing what in relation to your project, with whom, and when. Microsoft Project tells you how many units (people or things) are devoted to a particular task.

Tracking Gantt view

No, tracking Gantt isn't a search for Henry. Rather, it's a useful method for getting a quick visual overview of the status of tasks in comparison to their baselines. To access the Tracking Gantt view, click the Tracking Gantt button in the view bar. The Tracking Gantt view appears.

You can display the Tracking table (refer to Table 6-1) simultaneously by choosing View⇨Table:⇨Tracking. Looking at your project through these views enables you to keep watch over critical project elements at a glance (see Figure 6-13). See Chapter 17 for more about Tracking Gantt.

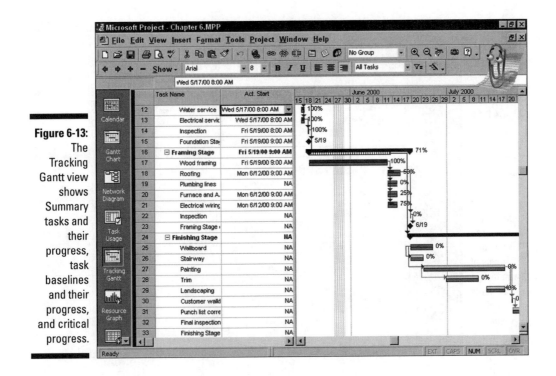

Figure 6-13:
The
Tracking
Gantt view
shows
Summary
tasks and
their
progress,
task
baselines
and their
progress,
and critical
progress.

Using the Gantt Chart Wizard

If you want to generate your own views, Microsoft Project is ready to help. Just click the Gantt Chart Wizard button on the Formatting toolbar. The Gantt Chart Wizard appears and walks you step-by-step through the process of creating your own custom view. You can choose your own Gantt bar colors, patterns, and end shapes. You can make unique summary task bars. And you can use unique patterns and shapes for milestones. Beyond the value of being different for difference's sake, customized Gantt Chart views can be helpful when you've got a bunch of projects. Each individual project can have its own look.

Tracking Resources in Task Usage View

The Task Usage view lists in one quick visual reference the task and its associated resources; the amount of work each resource has performed over time; and duration and start/finish dates. (See Figure 6-14.) The table portion of the view is mostly task information; the chart portion of the view is mostly resource information. In Chapter 11, you can find out how to use this view with special filters.

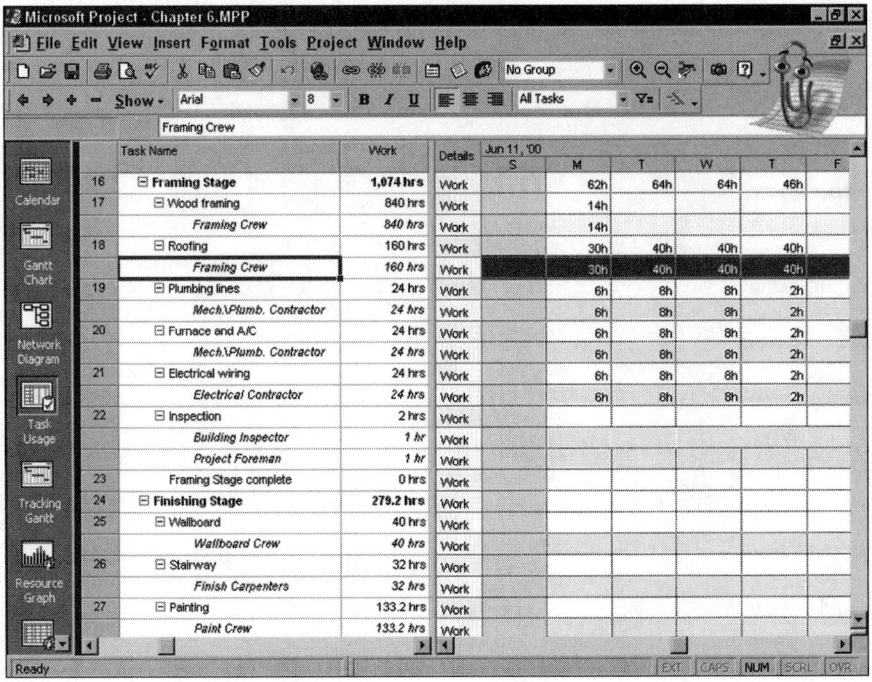

Figure 6-14:
The Task
Usage View
addresses
the need for
a visual
represent-
ation of the
resource
work and
costs of
each task in
increments
of time,
such as
hours.

Looking at Schedules in Calendar View

The Calendar view is a helpful communications tool for printing schedules
and can be a primary means of managing small projects. The default
Calendar view in Microsoft Project is a monthly calendar that displays tasks
in bar form, as shown in Figure 6-15.

The length of a bar indicates a task's duration. You can access the Calendar
view by selecting the Calendar View icon on the View bar. Chapter 9 covers
the Calendar view in detail.

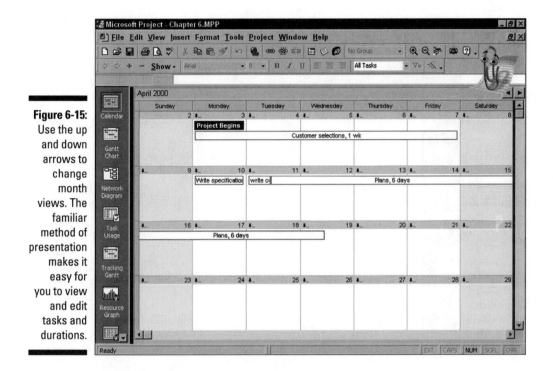

Figure 6-15:
Use the up
and down
arrows to
change
month
views. The
familiar
method of
presentation
makes it
easy for
you to view
and edit
tasks and
durations.

Creating a Flow Chart with Network Diagram View

An altogether different way to build and manage a project is by using the Network Diagram view. With the Network Diagram view, you can build or edit your project tasks and task relationships as a flow chart. Each task is contained in a box, also known as a *node*. The line connecting two nodes depicts the relationship of the two tasks. One diagonal line through a task indicates that it has begun. Two diagonal lines means that the task is completed.

To access this view, click the Network Diagram view in the View bar. The Network Diagram view appears, as shown in Figure 6-16. (See Chapter 8 for more details about the Network Diagram view.)

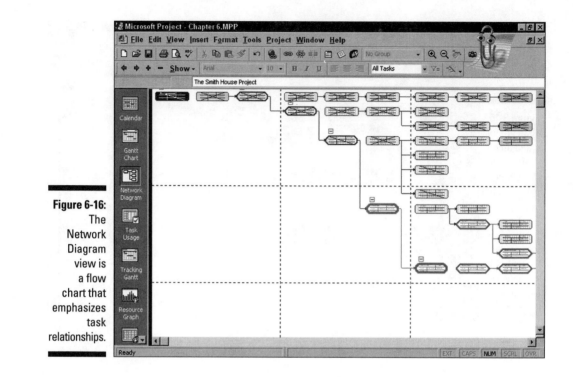

Figure 6-16:
The
Network
Diagram
view is
a flow
chart that
emphasizes
task
relationships.

Chapter 7

Using the Gantt Chart for All It's Worth

In This Chapter

▶ Adjusting the timescale in your Gantt chart

▶ Changing the face of your Gantt chart

▶ Finding facts about tasks

▶ Making a good-looking chart

▶ Copying graphics in Microsoft Project

*E*arly in the 19th century, Henry Gantt introduced a new way to show information in a bar chart and spreadsheet fashion. Voilà! The man was immortalized. Now, whenever project managers discuss their work, they indirectly pay homage to him. Just as Henry Gantt's creation was a winner, you can win accolades for customizing the Gantt chart to flawlessly guide your project.

A *Gantt chart* is a way of displaying project task information graphically. Gantt bars provide information about task duration, start and finish dates, and relationships of one task to another. Gantt bars rest on a timescale. The position of Gantt bars on the timescale in relationship to each other is a way of simultaneously seeing the whole project and pieces of the project within the dimension of time. In this chapter, you find out the neat little Gantt chart options just waiting for you in Microsoft Project, and you discover how to modify the chart to emphasize and segregate various kinds of information. Old Henry may have been the first to fiddle with this kind of chart, but you're going to make the Gantt chart sing.

In this chapter, I show you how to customize the look of the Gantt chart to better match your project needs. I've put together a practice file that you can use while getting used to the Gantt tools. The file is called Award Program 7.mpp. See Appendix C for more information about using the practice files on the CD-ROM.

Getting Time on Your Side

In project management (and in life), time management is never easy. Microsoft Project can't solve all your time challenges, but at least it can tell you whether time is helping or hurting your project. One of the time tools Microsoft Project provides is the *timescale*.

The timescale is the horizontal bar at the top of the Gantt chart that shows time in major and minor increments. In Figure 7-1, the timescale breaks down into *major* increments that appear on the top row of the bar and *minor* increments that appear on the bottom row. In Figure 7-1, the major timescale is weeks and the minor timescale is days.

If you want to enter specific dates for your project into the timescale, use the following steps:

1. **Double-click the timescale area of the Gantt chart.**

   The Timescale dialog box appears, as shown in Figure 7-2.

2. **Click the Timescale tab, if it isn't already visible.**

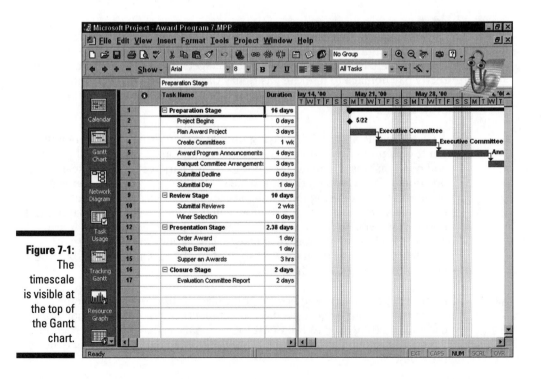

Figure 7-1:
The timescale is visible at the top of the Gantt chart.

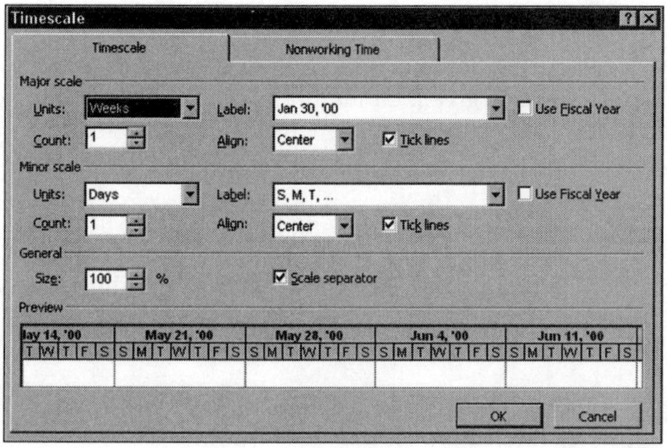

Figure 7-2:
The
Timescale
dialog box
offers set-
tings for
working and
nonworking
time.

The default setting of the timescale is weeks in the major scale and days in the minor scale. Notice the default manner of depicting time in the major and minor scales. The major timescale time lists month, day, and year. The minor timescale time lists an abbreviation for days. Back in the third grade, my music teacher told me that notes on the major scale make you happy and notes on the minor scale make you sad. Using that analogy on the Gantt Chart timescale, the major timescale lets you sort of stand back and glibly peruse the project. The minor timescale forces you up close so that you can sweat a little bit about how the project details are doing.

The Count box under both Major Scale and Minor Scale enables you to depict measurements of time sequentially or by skipping. *Skipping* is achieved when you change the count from 1 to some other number. For example, if the major setting is months (January, February, March), you can show every other month (January, March, May) by changing the count to 2. After checking out the settings in the Timescale dialog box, you can click OK to save your changes or click Cancel to maintain the default settings.

Changing the Look of Your Gantt Chart

Microsoft Project offers general text editing features and specialized formatting functions. Use these to polish your Gantt chart for on-screen readability, aesthetics, and reporting.

Using spell checker

One of the fastest ways to give a bad impression is by misspelling or misusing a word. Microsoft Project doesn't offer help with word selection, but it does provide a spell checker.

To use the spell checker, click the Spelling button on the Standard toolbar, or press F7. The Spelling dialog box appears, as shown in Figure 7-3. The location of the word as a task or a resource is shown in the Found In box. Perform the corrections as needed.

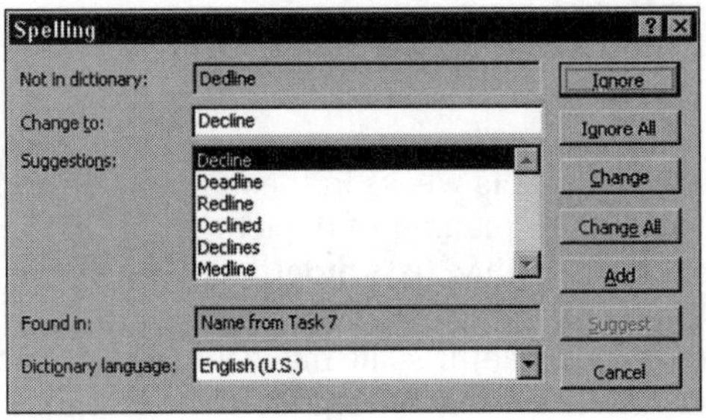

Figure 7-3:
The spell
checker dis-
plays the
word it
deems mis-
spelled.

Spelling	? X
Not in dictionary:	Dedline	Ignore
Change to:	Decline	Ignore All
Suggestions:	Decline / Deadline / Redline / Declined / Declines / Medline	Change
		Change All
		Add
Found in:	Name from Task 7	Suggest
Dictionary language:	English (U.S.)	Cancel

Just as in any word processing application, Microsoft Project's spell checker doesn't catch everything. If a task name contains the article *an* that should be the conjunction *and,* you have to correct that spelling the old-fashioned way: Highlight the task and change the text in the entry bar.

Customizing text

What's black and white and read all over? The traditional answer is a newspaper. With Microsoft Project, it never has to be a Gantt chart. The Formatting toolbar is the ticket for making changes to fonts, font sizes, and colors. Those kinds of changes make the chart easy to read and visually pleasing.

To change the font style of your Gantt chart, follow these steps:

1. **In the Filter list box on the formatting toolbar, select the tasks you want to change.**

   In Figure 7-4, summary tasks are now the only tasks listed. (Chapter 11 discusses the Summary Task filter and other filters in detail.)

2. **Highlight the tasks by clicking the first one and dragging the mouse cursor through the final task.**

   The tasks are highlighted.

3. **In the Font list box on the formatting toolbar, select a font.**

4. **In the Font Size list box on the formatting toolbar, select a size.**

   If you select 12-point, the font size of the tasks changes to 12-point, as shown in Figure 7-5.

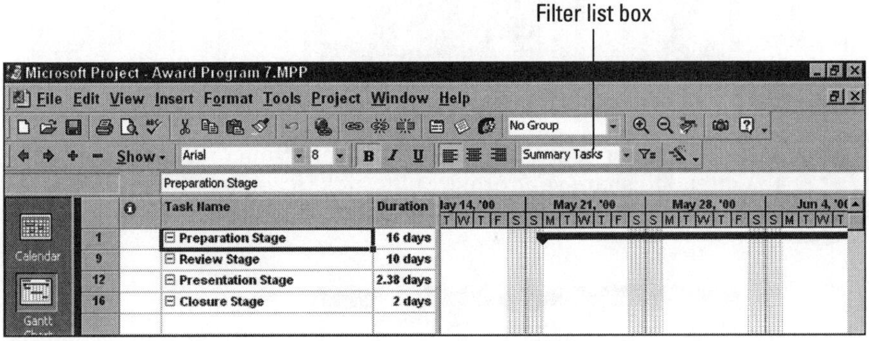

Filter list box

Figure 7-4:
The Summary Tasks filter isolates and displays only summary tasks, hiding subtasks and milestones.

How about if you want to change a summary task color, too? Not a problem, Ganttologist. To change the text color of a task, use the following steps:

1. **Highlight all the tasks you want to change (if they're not already highlighted) by dragging the mouse cursor through the tasks.**

2. **Right-click in the highlighted area.**

3. **In the shortcut menu, select Font.**

   The Font dialog box appears (see Figure 7-6). The dialog box should already show that the selected tasks have changed from 8-point Arial to 12-point Times New Roman.

4. **In the Color list box, select a color and then click OK.**

5. **In the Filter list box on the formatting toolbar, select Summary Tasks.**

   The summary tasks are highlighted in a new color.

Font Size list box

Font list box

Figure 7-5:
The
Formatting
toolbar has
some of the
features
commonly
found in a
word
processor.

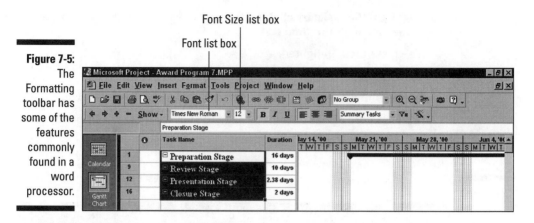

The number of available fonts may vary from one computer to the next. If you intend to share your project file, stick to commonly used fonts so that you can be sure about how your project will look on another computer.

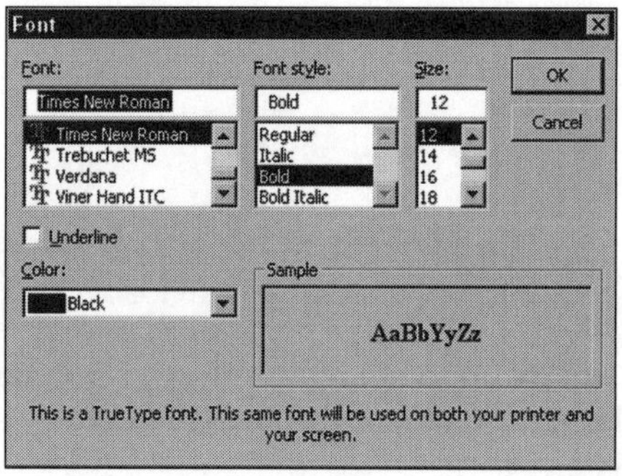

Figure 7-6:
You can
change font
style, size,
and color in
the Font
dialog box.

Adding notes

Sometimes you may need to write yourself or someone else a note about a task, a resource, or the entire project. To write a note about a particular task in the Gantt Chart view, you can use the Task Notes button on the Standard toolbar. Follow these steps to write a note about a task:

1. **Select any task.**

2. **Click the Task Notes button on the standard toolbar.**

   The Task Information dialog box appears, set to the Notes tab, as shown in Figure 7-7.

3. **In the Notes section, type your message.**

4. Click OK.

A note indicator appears next to the task number.

TIP

You can view the note at any time by hovering your cursor over the note indicator or by selecting the task and then clicking the Task Notes button.

To delete a note, highlight the task and choose Edit⇔Clear⇔Notes.

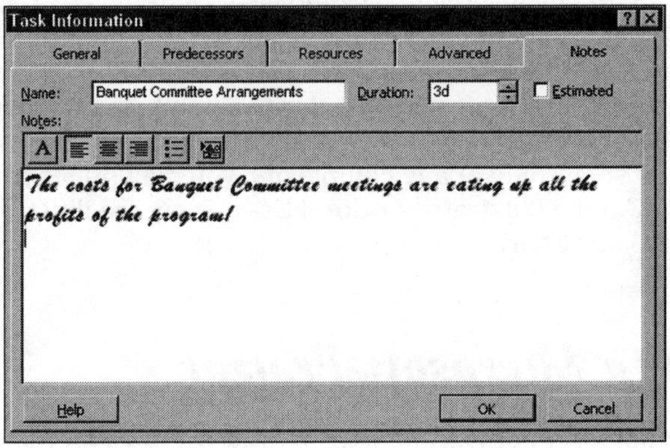

Figure 7-7:
Enter task
details
such as
resources,
predeces-
sors, and
start and
finish dates.

Task Information
| General | Predecessors | Resources | Advanced | Notes |

Name: Banquet Committee Arrangements Duration: 3d ☐ Estimated

Notes:

The costs for Banquet Committee meetings are eating up all the profits of the program!

Help   OK   Cancel

Revealing Information about Tasks

You can use your mouse to solicit information from or change information in the Gantt chart. Click the mouse and hold it in the middle of a task bar. Do the same for a summary task and then for a milestone. An information box appears, reporting the start and finish times of each task. These kinds of readouts are helpful when you're scanning the various stages of a project. By dragging the task duration bar right or left, you can move the entire task duration to new start and finish dates. To use your mouse to read a task information box and to move a task, perform the following steps:

1. Position your cursor over a task.

A task information box appears, providing you with information about the start and finish dates of the task.

2. Move a task with your mouse by clicking the task and dragging either to the left or to the right.

When you drag a task, a Planning Wizard may appear, warning you that you are about to break a link by making this move.

Drawing and Copying on the Gantt Chart

When you were in elementary school, drawing was a good thing and copying could get you into a heap of trouble. In Microsoft Project, drawing is at best a problem and copying is a good thing. If you want to draw something in Microsoft Project, prepare to be unimpressed. The program's copying capability from or into Microsoft Project receives a passing grade, however.

You may be wondering why someone would want to draw on a Gantt Chart. Some examples might be that you can draw lines to various tasks and have the lines converge on a text box with information about those tasks. Or you can draw a simple illustration or map to clarify a point. Some companies like to "stamp" their Gantt charts with a company logo or a professional seal. If you want to draw something of any complexity, you may prefer to use a draw program such as Adobe Illustrator or Corel Draw, copy the illustration, and paste it into the Gantt Chart.

Drawing in Microsoft Project

You can use a limited set of drawing tools to draw in the Gantt chart. To access the drawing toolbar, right-click anywhere on the toolbar and choose Drawing from the drop-down list. The Drawing toolbar has the following tools:

- ✔ By clicking the Line tool, you can draw a line from any location to any other location on the Gantt Chart. After you've drawn a line, you click on it and move the line.

- ✔ The Arrow tool functions the same as the Line tool except that the line you draw ends with an arrowhead.

- ✔ Click the Box tool to draw a box on the Gantt Chart. With the box tool selected, click and drag on the Gantt Chart to form a box. After you have the approximate size and shape of the box, release your mouse. A box appears. When the box is highlighted, it has eight nodes. The nodes in the middle of lines allow you to lengthen or shorten any side. The nodes in the corners allow you to diagonally reshape the box. By clicking the box anywhere but on a node, you can drag the box to any location on the Gantt Chart.

- ✔ The Oval tool works in the same manner as the Box tool to create ovals. By holding down the Shift key as you draw, you will make a circle.

- ✔ The Arc tool provides you the ability to create curved lines on the Gantt Chart. After clicking the tool, click and drag anywhere on the Gantt Chart. The initial location where you clicked acts as an anchor as you draw the arc. One drawback of the Arc tool is that Project deals with the area within the arc as a solid object. As a result, an arc crossing nonworking time or any other shaded area on a Gantt Chart looks sort of weird.

✔ Use the Polygon tool to draw a straight-sided shape with as many corners as you wish. To complete the polygon, click the starting point. After you have created the polygon, adjust its size, shape, and location like any other box.

✔ Draw with the Text Box tool like any other box. After you have created the text box, you can keystroke text of any length. By right-clicking in the text box, you can paste text from a word processing program.

✔ Click Cycle Fill Color to fill a highlighted box, oval, polygon, or text box with background color. By continuing to click the Cycle Fill Color tool, you cycle through a limited selection of color options.

✔ By clicking the Attach to Task button, you are given options for attaching a highlighted box, oval, polygon, arc, or text box to the beginning or end of a task bar on the Gantt chart. The Format Drawing dialog box appears, enabling you to specify the task ID to which you want to attach the object.

Copying graphics into Microsoft Project

Graphics can spruce up your Gantt chart to make it more visually interesting, or they can display your company's logo or confidentiality information. If you have a graphics program, you can create an image and then copy it to the Windows clipboard. Then you simply use the Paste Special command in Microsoft Project to insert the graphic in the Gantt chart.

For example, you can put a graphic in the Award Program's Gantt chart. To do so, use the standard Paint program that comes with Windows 95, 98, or Windows 2000. If you have a favorite graphics program, feel free to use it instead.

To add the graphic into the Gantt Chart, follow these steps:

1. **Choose Start⊏⟩Programs⊏⟩Accessories⊏⟩Paint.**

   The Paint application appears, as shown in Figure 7-8. Although somewhat limited in image-editing capabilities, Paint is good for copying and pasting graphics.

2. **Choose File⊏⟩Open to display the Open dialog box.**

3. **Navigate to the appropriate folder on your hard drive.**

   In this example, navigate to the folder that contains the CD sample files for this book. See Appendix C for details.

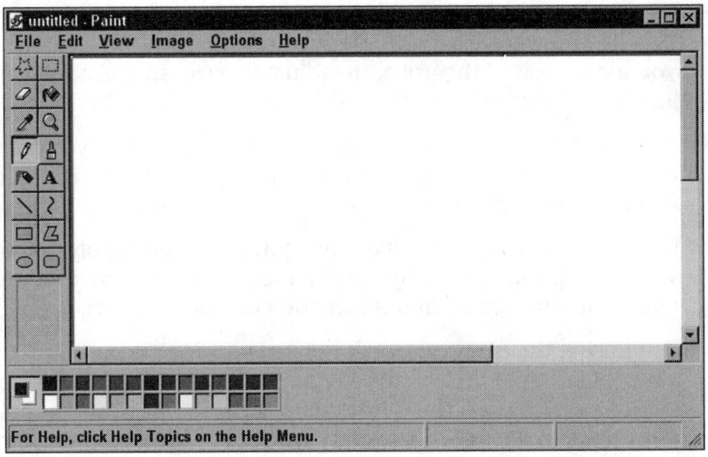

Figure 7-8:
The Paint
application
recognizes
only BMP
and PCX
extensions.

4. **Double-click the graphic file to open it.**

   In this example, double-click award.bmp. The award graphic appears in the Paint application.

5. **Click the graphic to select it (or, in Paint, you can choose Edit⇨ Select All).**

6. **Choose Edit⇨Copy (or a similar command in your favorite graphics program).**

7. **Switch Microsoft Project by clicking its task button on the task bar and click in the Project window to activate it.**

8. **Choose Edit⇨Paste Special.**

   The Paste Special dialog box appears.

9. **Select the Bitmap Image option and click OK.**

   The graphic is pasted into your project. You can drag it around to position it or double-click on the graphic to edit it.

Copying from Microsoft Project

You can make a portion of your project file into a picture to copy it to another application such as Word. You can also make a portion of a project file into a GIF file for publishing on the World Wide Web. If you want to copy a portion of your project file, click the Copy Picture button on the Standard toolbar. The Copy Picture dialog box appears. The dialog box gives you the choices of rendering a copy for your printer, for another application, or as a saved GIF file.

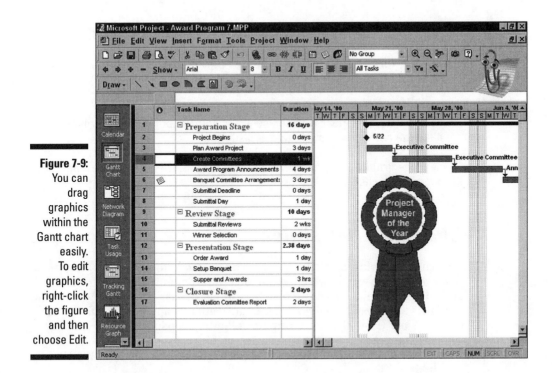

Figure 7-9:
You can
drag
graphics
within the
Gantt chart
easily.
To edit
graphics,
right-click
the figure
and then
choose Edit.

Customizing the Look of the Gantt Chart

Microsoft Project enables you to change the way your Gantt chart looks without modifying the information you've entered. Doing so won't put you on the inside track for winning an art award, but it will make working with task information less of a task.

Changing gridlines

Gridlines are the horizontal and vertical lines that appear in the Gantt Chart view and in some other views. Changing the number and the look of gridlines may make reading your Gantt chart easier. To make changes to gridlines, use the following steps:

1. **Right-click in one of the white areas of the Gantt chart (not the Gantt table).**

   A list box appears.

2. **Choose <u>G</u>ridlines.**

   The Gridlines dialog box appears.

3. **With Gantt Rows highlighted, click the Normal Type box's down arrow. Select a line type.**

4. **In the Normal Color box, select the color you want for the Gantt row lines.**

5. **Click OK.**

   The gridlines appear with the selected color. Don't worry; if you don't like the color, you can change it easily.

To clear the gridlines, repeat Steps 1 through 3 and then select the blank box at the top of the list.

Changing bar styles

Changing bar styles has nothing to do with the trend toward microbreweries. A *bar style* is the way in which you depict duration in the Gantt chart. Sometimes it's helpful to customize a Gantt bar design. Don't worry, changing the Gantt bar doesn't affect your task information in any way. To modify bar styles in your Gantt chart, perform the following steps:

1. **Right-click in one of the white areas of the Gantt chart (not the Gantt table).**

2. **In the list box, select Bar Styles.**

   The Bar Styles dialog box appears.

3. **Select a name from the Names list.**

   For example, you can use the Bars selections to change the Start shape, the Middle bar, and the End shape of all summary bars in the Gantt chart.

Making individual bar style changes

Sometimes it's neat to modify individual elements of the bar chart. For instance, making individual summary bars different colors or patterns may make identifying the stages of a project easier.

To change the color or pattern of a summary bar, follow these steps:

1. **Right-click a summary bar.**

2. **Choose Format Bar.**

The Format Bar dialog box appears.

3. **Choose the Bar Shape tab.**

4. **Change the start, middle, or end of the bar by changing its shape, type/pattern, or color.**

   For example, change the middle bar color to a unique color, shape, or pattern. You can change anything else you want, too.

5. **Click OK.**

6. **Repeat Steps 1 through 5 as many times as you want to make changes.**

Making other cosmetic changes

Your days off from work can finally be sky blue if you want! By right-clicking in the general chart area, you can change the color and look of nonworking time. Double-clicking a particular area or element causes a dialog box to appear, allowing you to change the look of that specific feature.

Changing links

Double-clicking a link between tasks on the Gantt chart enables you to change more than the look of the chart. By double-clicking a link, you can modify your project's schedule.

For example, if you've scheduled a committee meeting on your project the day after the committee is formed, it's unlikely that all of your members will be there. To figure in extra time for project information to trickle up or down in your organization or to tend to details, you need to create lag time. (For more about lag time, see Chapter 4.) To build lag time into your project, follow these steps:

1. **Double-click the link between tasks on the Gantt chart.**

   The link's Task Dependency dialog box appears.

2. **In the Lag box, change the lag time from its existing setting to a longer time increment. (See Figure 7-10.)**

3. **Click OK.**

   All projects that follow your chosen task move up in the schedule.

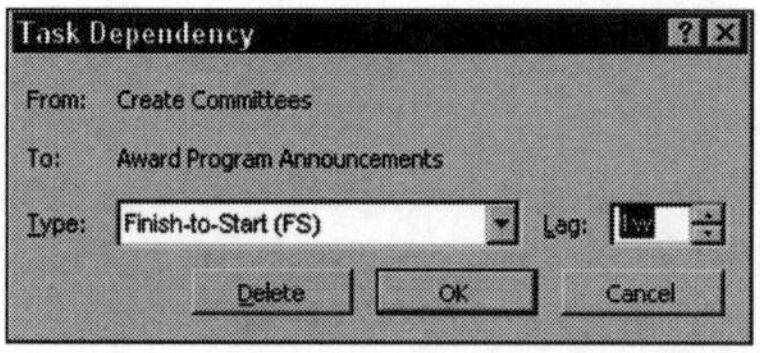

Figure 7-10:
You can
change the
task rela-
tionship as
well as the
lag time.

Chapter 8

Shedding Light on Relationships with the Network Diagram View

In This Chapter

▶ Familiarizing yourself with Network Diagram view

▶ Working with tasks and relationships in Network Diagram view

*T*he Network Diagram view is new for Project 2000; in earlier incarnations, you would find it called the PERT chart. Network Diagrams are strong on emphasizing task relationships. On the flipside, Network Diagrams don't give you a lot of visual representation of task lengths or your project's timeline. This chapter shows you how to use the Network Diagram view.

I've put together a practice file to help you while you get used to this wild-and-wacky view. The practice file has some information built into it to help you get used to the Network Diagram features. The file is called Chapter 8.mpp. See Appendix C for more information on opening and using the CD's practice files.

Getting into Network View

Network diagrams are like flowcharts, so concentrating on the implications of task links is easy in this view. To see the intricacies of task relationships, choose Network Diagram view on the view bar. The Gantt chart is replaced by the Network Diagram view, as shown in Figure 8-1.

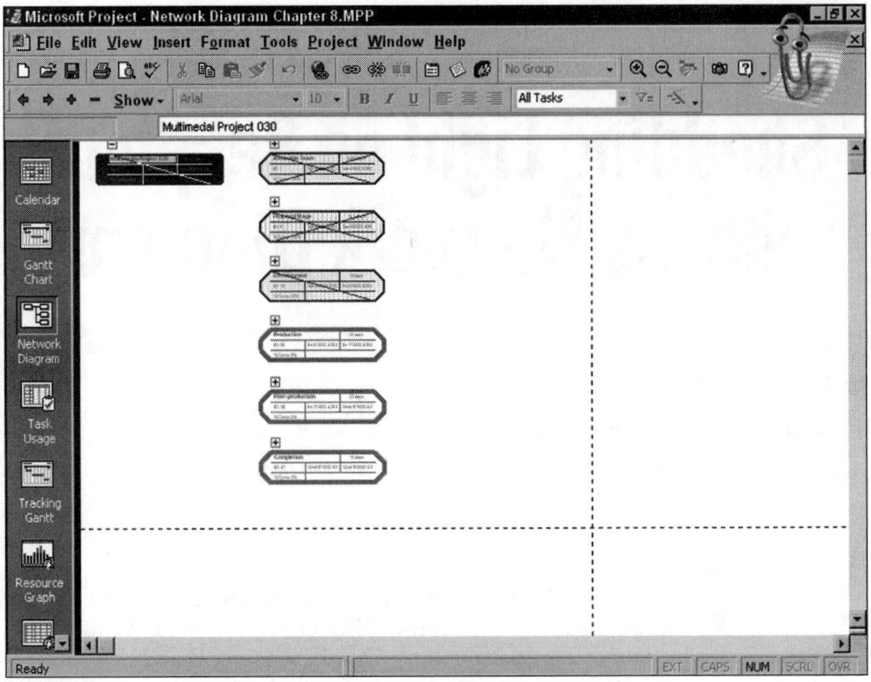

Figure 8-1:
The
Network
Diagram
view orga-
nizes tasks
relationally
without
considering
duration.

Network Diagram view is well suited for the following purposes:

✔ Reviewing project tasks in a graphical format

✔ Studying task relationships in a close-up view or a wide view

✔ Editing tasks

✔ Linking tasks

✔ Creating schedules

✔ Performing task analyses

Zooming, expanding, and peeking

Using these features enables you, the project manager, to see the whole project, portions of the project, or individual task details.

You need to know three things when you use Network Diagram view:

✔ **How to zoom:** Click the Zoom Out button on the Standard toolbar.

✔ **How to expand summary tasks:** Hold the mouse over one of the + boxes and click. Your cursor changes to an up arrow. In the example, place your cursor over the second + box in the second column and click. The tasks under that Summary task appear.

✔ **How to peek at tasks:** Hover the mouse over a task. An information box appears, giving you information about the task (see Figure 8-2). In the example, your mouse is over the third task in the second column. An exploded information box appears giving you all the information for that task. For instance, Bud is the person doing the work, and he's 25 percent finished.

Reading the Network Diagram view

In Network Diagram view, each task is contained in a box called a *node*. Predecessor tasks always precede their successors on the left side of the view. Summary tasks are always to the left of their subtasks.

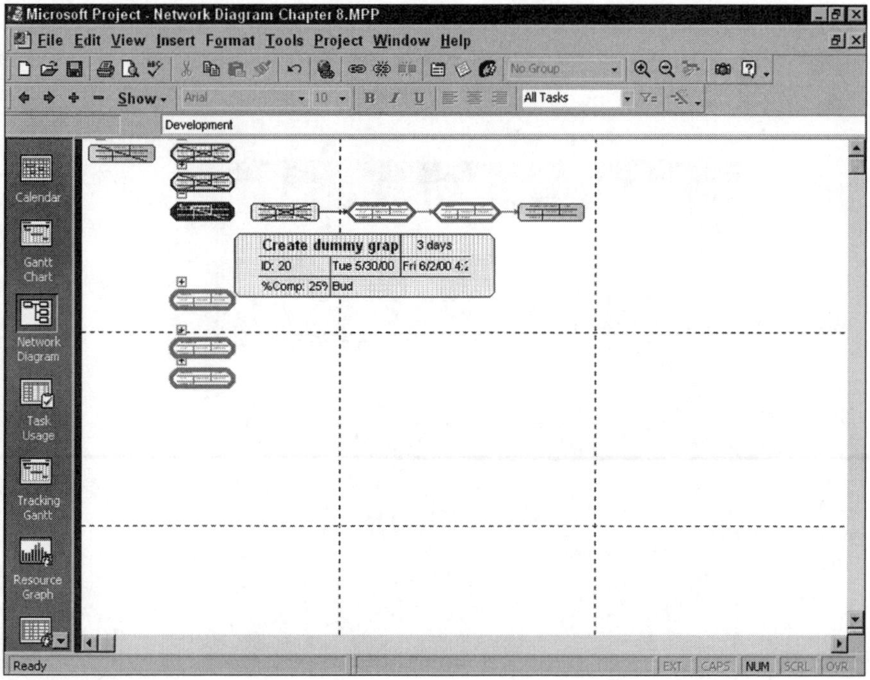

Figure 8-2:
Zooming, expanding, and peeking are effective ways to see the overall project and task details at the same time.

Clicking the Zoom In button on the standard toolbar reveals that some task boxes contain two diagonal lines, some contain a single diagonal line, and some have no diagonal line. Two diagonal lines mean the task is completed. A single diagonal line indicates a task is partially completed. No diagonal line means the task hasn't begun.

In the example, the node in the first column (the Project Summary task), has a single diagonal line. This means that the overall project isn't completed. If you place your cursor over the node, you can see that the overall project is 30 percent complete.

Understanding Network Diagram node shapes

If you're a flowchart aficionado, you know that each node shape has a particular meaning. Network Diagram nodes come in several shapes and colors, each having a specific meaning. Accessing the Box Styles dialog box is an easy way to understand the various box frames and colors. To access the Box Styles dialog box, follow these steps:

1. **Double-click anywhere in the blank area of the Network Diagram view.**

   The Box Styles dialog box appears (Figure 8-3).

2. **Click a style setting to find out how its box looks in Network Diagram view.**

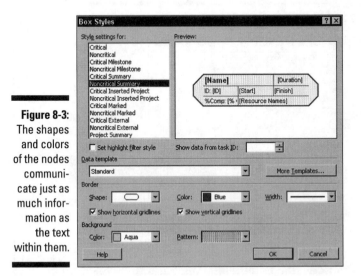

Figure 8-3:
The shapes and colors of the nodes communicate just as much information as the text within them.

The Box Styles dialog box is an editing tool, but it also illustrates the meanings of node colors and shapes. By highlighting different node borders, colors, and widths, you can see how the options are represented graphically. You can use the Box Styles dialog box to change the styles or color of any of these items.

Editing node information

Not only does the Box Styles dialog box show you node borders and interpret their meanings, the dialog box also tells you about the information contained in the nodes.

Each node box in Network Diagram has seven fields. Each field contains default task information, such as name, duration, task ID, start and finish dates, percent complete, and resource names. You can choose something else for each field.

1. **Double-click somewhere in the white space in Network Diagram view.**

   The Box Styles dialog box appears.

2. **Click the More Templates button.**

   The Data Templates dialog box appears.

3. **Click the Copy button.**

   The Data Template Definition dialog box appears (see Figure 8-4). When you click in a cell, a down-arrow button appears that allows you to select what information you want to display in that cell.

4. **Click OK, Close, and OK again to save your changes.**

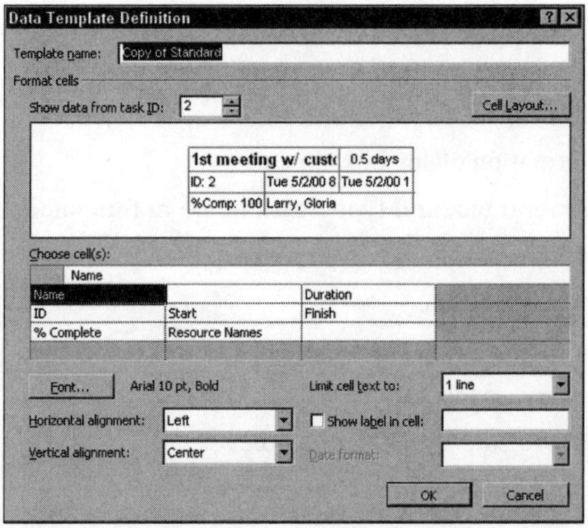

Figure 8-4:
In addition to changing box information, you can modify the box design.

Editing Tasks and Relationships

Adding a task or changing a link in the Network Diagram view is simple. And don't worry about how the changes affect the Gantt chart. Microsoft Project is keeping records for you. Any changes you make to a task or a link in the Network Diagram view appear automatically in the Gantt Chart view and are recorded in relevant tables.

Adding a task

Adding a task in Network Diagram view is quite a different process than adding one in the Gantt Chart view. Even so, it's easy.

In this chapter's sample file, suppose that you need to add a storyboard meeting for staff and freelancers. This means you need to add a storyboard task after Task 22 — Create preliminary tests, and before Task 23 — Approvals. If you want, you can zoom in once or twice to more easily read the information in the tasks. To add a new task, follow these steps:

1. **Make sure that you can read the task information. Click the Zoom In or Zoom Out button until you can.**

   In the example, click the Zoom In button on the standard toolbar and scroll until the screen looks like the one in Figure 8-5.

2. **Draw a task box next to or below the task that will be the predecessor.**

   Draw a task by clicking and dragging your cursor.

   In this chapter's example, draw a task box next to the Develop Dummy Interface task by clicking and dragging a box (see Figure 8-6).

   Another way to create a new task box next to an existing task is by selecting the existing task and then pressing the Insert key.

3. **Double-click the new task box.**

   The Task Information dialog box appears.

4. **Select the General tab, and type a task name in the Name text box.**

   In this chapter's example, type **Storyboard**.

5. **Give the task a duration.**

   In the example, give the task a 1-day duration.

6. **Click the Resources tab.**

7. **Select the first Resource Name text box.**

   Use the drop-down list to select a resource.

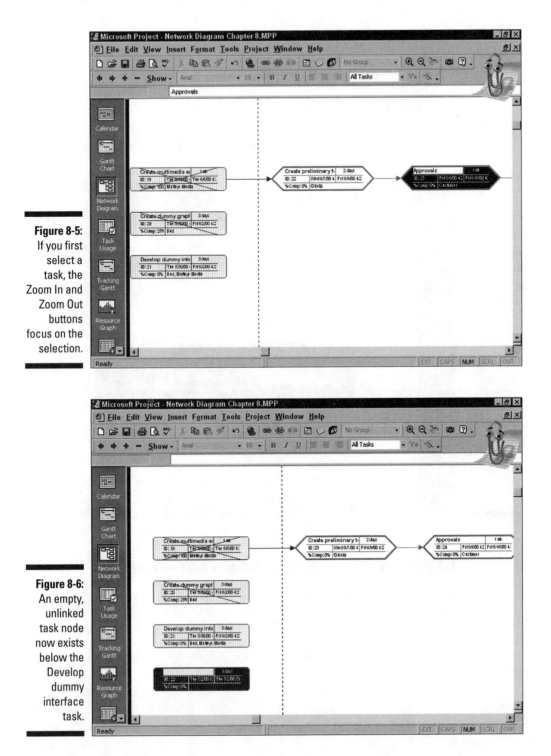

Figure 8-5: If you first select a task, the Zoom In and Zoom Out buttons focus on the selection.

Figure 8-6: An empty, unlinked task node now exists below the Develop dummy interface task.

8. **Select the second Resource Name text box and repeat Step 7 to select another resource.**

   In the example, continue adding resources until all except the Customer have been selected.

9. **Click OK.**

   The new task box contains the task information, as shown (zoomed in) in Figure 8-7. When you're done looking, you may want to zoom back out.

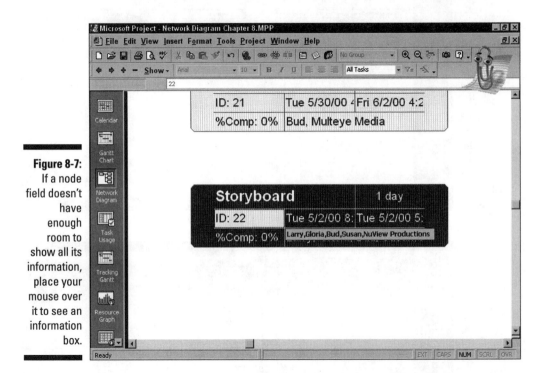

Figure 8-7:
If a node field doesn't have enough room to show all its information, place your mouse over it to see an information box.

Creating new links and removing old ones

To change an existing link or create a new link between a predecessor and a successor, click in the middle of the predecessor task and drag to its new relationship. (See Chapter 6 for more about linking.)

Use the following steps to link tasks to predecessors or successors:

1. **Click the Zoom Out or Zoom In button to show the boxes around the new tasks you want to relate.**

   Zooming makes reading task information easier.

   In the example, show the boxes around Storyboard.

2. **Place your mouse cursor on the task's new predecessor.**

   In the example, place your mouse cursor on the Create Preliminary Tests task.

3. **Hold down the left mouse button, drag to the successor, and then release the mouse button.**

   Drag from Storyboard to Approvals in the example.

4. **Place the mouse cursor on the link between two tasks and then double-click.**

   The Task Dependency dialog box appears. If necessary, use this box to change from the default Finish-to-Start relationship to another relationship type.

5. **Click OK to accept the new task-dependency information.**

   For practice, place your cursor between the Create Preliminary Tasks task and the Approvals task. Then double-click.

6. **Delete the old task dependency.**

   Microsoft Project doesn't remove your previous task relationship, so you have to remove it yourself. Do so by double-clicking the unwanted link between the two tasks, displaying the Task Dependency dialog box. Then click the Delete button to remove the old task relationship.

You can always go back to your previous setting by choosing Edit⇨Undo.

The changes you made also appear in the Gantt Chart view.

Chapter 9

Staying Ahead of Details with a Calendar

● ●

In This Chapter

▶ Creating a schedule with the calendar

▶ Putting an existing project into the calendar

▶ Cruising the calendar

▶ Customizing the calendar

● ●

*T*he beauty of the Calendar view is also its liability. On the plus side, the Calendar view enables you to see your work in a familiar manner. On the minus side, the Calendar view limits how much information you can see at a time. Ah, life! However, you can do lots of things with the Calendar view if you can live with its limitations.

The Calendar view can be helpful in two major ways. First, the Calendar view is a whiz at creating simple projects. Second, the Calendar view is a great tool for viewing, segregating, and reporting more complex projects. Accordingly, this chapter is divided into two major sections. The first focuses on how to create a simple project by using the Calendar view. The second section covers using the Calendar view for existing or more complex projects.

Creating a Simple Project in the Calendar View

The pocket or briefcase planner industry has nothing to fear about Microsoft Project's Calendar view. Planners and the Calendar view do entirely different things. They're Appaloosas and orangutans.

You can make a fully-functioning project by using the Calendar view. You can create and track a schedule of tasks and establish resources you need to complete those tasks. After you create a project in the Calendar view, you can view it in the Gantt Chart view, resource views, graphs, and in combination views. You can also make reports from projects you create in Calendar view.

Putting your project into Calendar view

Creating a project in Calendar view is fun, in a project manager sort of way. If you're building a small project, you can build it in Calendar view by clicking the Calendar button on the view bar.

 Microsoft Project uses the current date as the default project start date if you don't specify a start date. To specify a start date, choose Project⇨ Project Information. The Project Information dialog box appears. To set a new project date, change the Start Date.

Identifying tasks

Creating tasks in the Calendar view is different than creating tasks in the Gantt chart. Creating tasks in the Calendar view is a little more primitive and takes a little more work than creating tasks in the Gantt chart. The Calendar view doesn't offer you a task table and you don't get to see graphical representations like the Gantt chart view, but you just need to know a couple of basic principles and you can get the job done.

Here's how you plan a project in the Calendar view:

1. **Click the project's start date on the calendar.**

2. **Press the Insert key for each task you want to create and type it in.**

   Suppose, for example, that for your new project, you have seven tasks to enter. Press the Insert key seven times to create seven tasks. The task boxes stack on top of each other in the start date box on the calendar.

   The tasks quickly fill up the available space in the date window. A down arrow in the date's shaded area tells you that some tasks are hidden. You can access the hidden task boxes by clicking the Zoom In button or by opening the date window. Zooming magnifies the entire calendar. Opening the date window magnifies only one date. In this example, access the hidden tasks by opening the date window.

3. **Double-click the gray date bar of the date that holds the task boxes.**

   A task list appears, as shown in Figure 9-1. The check marks indicate that those tasks are visible in the window for that date in Calendar view. Unchecked tasks are visible only through the task list.

TIP

Another way to access the task list is to right-click the date bar and then select Task List from the context-sensitive menu.

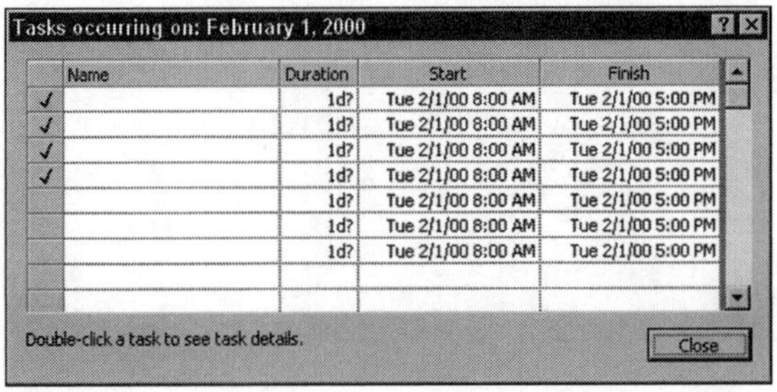

Tasks occurring on: February 1, 2000			
Name	Duration	Start	Finish
✓	1d?	Tue 2/1/00 8:00 AM	Tue 2/1/00 5:00 PM
✓	1d?	Tue 2/1/00 8:00 AM	Tue 2/1/00 5:00 PM
✓	1d?	Tue 2/1/00 8:00 AM	Tue 2/1/00 5:00 PM
✓	1d?	Tue 2/1/00 8:00 AM	Tue 2/1/00 5:00 PM
	1d?	Tue 2/1/00 8:00 AM	Tue 2/1/00 5:00 PM
	1d?	Tue 2/1/00 8:00 AM	Tue 2/1/00 5:00 PM
	1d?	Tue 2/1/00 8:00 AM	Tue 2/1/00 5:00 PM

Double-click a task to see task details.   Close

Figure 9-1:
Calendar
view's task
list.

Entering task information

After you open a task list on the screen, you can enter names in tasks. Follow these steps to enter a name in a task box:

1. **In the Name column of the task list box, double-click the first empty name box.**

   The Task Information dialog box opens. I explain more about the Task Information dialog box in Chapter 4.

2. **Type a task name in the Name box.**

   In this example, type **Develop Web Page.**

3. **Click OK.**

4. **Click Close to close the task list box.**

Using the steps above, you can practice further by entering the following tasks for the same day:

- ✓ Publish Brochure
- ✓ Contact Trade Associations
- ✓ Send Mailers
- ✓ Distribute Flyers
- ✓ Web Page Search Sign-ups
- ✓ Amend Database Forms

When you finish, your screen should look similar to Figure 9-2.

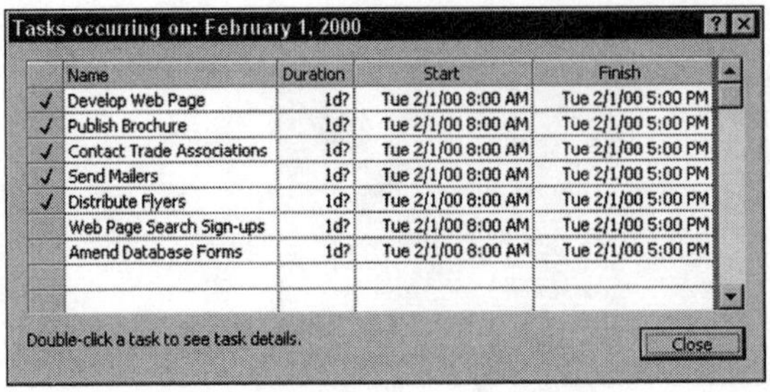

Tasks occurring on: February 1, 2000				
	Name	Duration	Start	Finish
√	Develop Web Page	1d?	Tue 2/1/00 8:00 AM	Tue 2/1/00 5:00 PM
√	Publish Brochure	1d?	Tue 2/1/00 8:00 AM	Tue 2/1/00 5:00 PM
√	Contact Trade Associations	1d?	Tue 2/1/00 8:00 AM	Tue 2/1/00 5:00 PM
√	Send Mailers	1d?	Tue 2/1/00 8:00 AM	Tue 2/1/00 5:00 PM
√	Distribute Flyers	1d?	Tue 2/1/00 8:00 AM	Tue 2/1/00 5:00 PM
	Web Page Search Sign-ups	1d?	Tue 2/1/00 8:00 AM	Tue 2/1/00 5:00 PM
	Amend Database Forms	1d?	Tue 2/1/00 8:00 AM	Tue 2/1/00 5:00 PM

Double-click a task to see task details.　　　　　　　Close

Figure 9-2:
A full day's
work!

Zooming in for a closer look at your schedule

The default Calendar view in Microsoft Project shows four successive weeks. You can change that view from four weeks to two weeks with the Zoom In button.

Click the Zoom In button on the standard toolbar once. The view changes to a two-week interval. If your start date is in one of the latter two weeks on the calendar, the tasks disappear. That's because the Zoom In command focuses on the first two weeks of the calendar. To expose your start date, use the scroll bar or press the Page Down key once. The calendar should now look like the one in Figure 9-3.

If you want, you can open the task list again to see all tasks with check marks. To open the task list, simply double-click the date bar of the date that contains the task boxes. For the sake of the next example, click the Zoom Out button to return to a four-week view.

Adding task durations in the Calendar view

Microsoft Project gives you two ways to set durations for tasks in the Calendar view. You can set task durations by using the Task Information dialog box or by dragging a task.

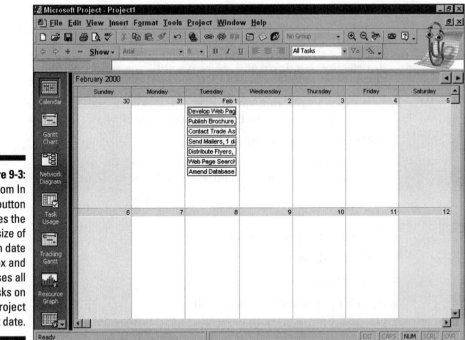

Figure 9-3:
The Zoom In
button
enlarges the
view size of
each date
box and
exposes all
the tasks on
the project
start date.

To set duration by using the Task Information dialog box, follow these steps:

1. Double-click a task.

In this example, double-click the first task, Develop Web Page. The Task Information dialog box appears.

2. Type a duration in the Duration box.

In this example, type **2w.**

3. Click OK.

You just entered a two-week duration for the Develop Web Page task using the Task Information dialog box.

If you want to enter duration by dragging a task, use these steps:

1. Move the mouse cursor to the right edge of a task.

In this example, move the mouse cursor to the right edge of the second task, Publish Brochure. The cursor changes to a vertical bar and a right arrow.

2. **Click the task and drag it downward.**

   A task information caption balloon appears, containing a duration reading.

3. **Drag the task down and sideways until you reach the duration you want.**

   In this example, drag down and back and forth until the Publish Brochure duration reading is 15d (three work weeks).

4. **Release the mouse button.**

   You successfully entered a duration by using the drag method. The second task, Publish Brochure, should now show a 15d duration.

In this chapter's example, you can add some more durations, as follows:

✔ **Contact Trade Associations:** 2 days

✔ **Send Mailers:** 2 days

✔ **Distribute Flyers:** 2 days

✔ **Web Page Search Sign-ups:** 2 days

✔ **Amend Database Forms:** 2 days

To set the above durations, follow these steps:

1. **Click the Zoom In button on the standard toolbar once.**

   The screen returns to the two-week view.

2. **If necessary, scroll or press the Page Up key to expose the starting date.**

3. **Using the dragging technique, give each of the remaining tasks a 2-day duration.**

   The resulting view looks like Figure 9-4.

Microsoft Project considers dragged durations estimates, and therefore puts a question mark beside the duration. If you want to set a precise duration for a task, use the Task Information box.

Linking tasks in Calendar view

As in the Gantt Chart view, you link tasks to create task relationships. Linking tasks in Calendar view is easy if your tasks have a Finish-to-Start relationship. To link these tasks, you simply click and drag from one task to the next (Chapter 3 covers linking tasks).

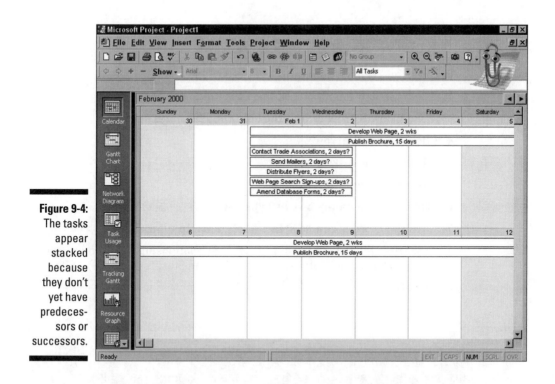

Figure 9-4:
The tasks
appear
stacked
because
they don't
yet have
predeces-
sors or
successors.

In Calendar view, as in Gantt Chart view, the default relationship type is Finish-to-Start. (See Chapter 4 for more information about kinds of task relationships.) If you want to link tasks that have a relationship other than Finish-to-Start, use the Task Information box.

Dragging to link

One of the easiest ways to link tasks is by dragging one task to another. To link two tasks that have a Finish-to-Start relationship, use these steps:

1. **Click and drag from a task to its successor.**

   An information box keeps you informed of your actions (see Figure 9-5).

2. **Release the mouse to complete the link.**

Linking within the Task Information box

If you need to use the Task Information box to link tasks with relationships other than the default, follow these steps:

1. **Double-click a task.**

   The Task Information dialog box appears.

2. **Click the Predecessors tab.**

3. **Select the first empty box in the Task Name column.**

   A small down arrow next to the entry box becomes active.

4. **Click the down arrow.**

   A list of all the tasks appears.

5. **Select a predecessor.**

6. **Select the first empty box in Type column.**

7. **Click the down arrow to select a relationship type.**

   Other than the default finish-to-start (FS) relationship, you can choose Finish-to-Finish (FF), Start-to-Finish (SF), and Start-to-Start (SS).

8. **Click OK.**

   Whew!

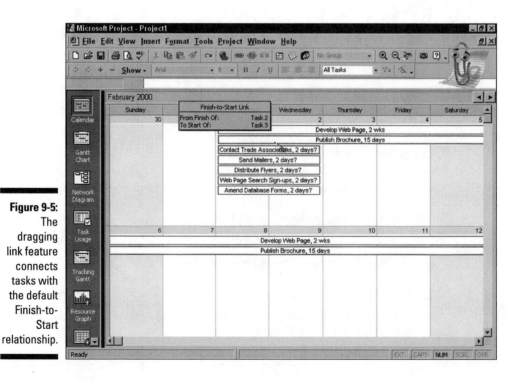

Figure 9-5:
The dragging link feature connects tasks with the default Finish-to-Start relationship.

If you want some practice building task relationships in the Calendar view, use either the dragging procedure or the Task Information box to link the following tasks and to establish their relationships.

ID	Task Name	Predecessor	Type
1	Develop Web Page		
2	Publish Brochure	1	Start-to-start
3	Contact Trade Associations	2	Finish-to-start
4	Send Mailers	3	Finish-to-start
5	Distribute Flyers	3	Finish-to-start
6	Web Page Search Sign-ups	3	Finish-to-start
7	Amend Database Forms	3	Finish-to-start

Making the information fit the calendar

After you enter task information in Calendar view, you can zoom out to change the screen to month view. Some tasks may be partially hidden in the default view, but you can optimize the screen to fit your tasks. Use the following steps to modify layout of your tasks:

1. **Choose Format⇨Layout.**

   The Layout dialog box appears.

2. **Select the Attempt to Fit as Many Tasks as Possible option.**

3. **Click OK.**

Using the Calendar View for Existing Projects

You can use the Calendar view with existing projects. Sometimes it's a convenient tool for reviewing and reporting a portion of a project's schedule. Be aware, though, that Calendar view has its strengths and weaknesses. It handles small amounts of information well, but quickly becomes unwieldy for more complicated projects.

On the CD at the back of this book, you can find Calendar 9.MPP, a file that you can use to follow along with the examples in the remainder of this section. The file opens in Gantt Chart view, as shown in Figure 9-6.

If you're working with an existing project, adding or editing tasks in the Calendar view can be messy. For example, if you add a task to the middle of a project in the Calendar view, it'll be messed up in the Gantt view. The task is linked as you indicated, but the lowest ID number is assigned to it. Who needs such problems! It's safer to add or edit the task in the Gantt view and then go back to the Calendar view to see your task nestled safe and warm where you want it.

Cruising the calendar

Notice in Figure 9-7 that the calendar opens to the project start date. Microsoft Project displays the month in the upper-left corner and sets a four-week period as the default view. Nonworking days are shaded gray.

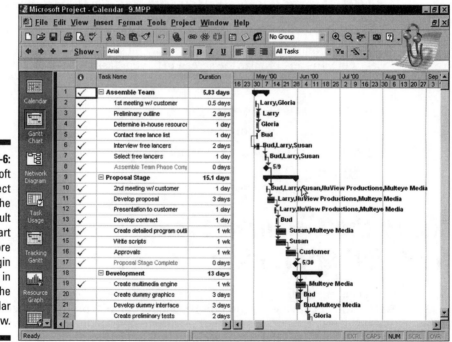

Figure 9-6: Microsoft Project opens to the default Gantt Chart view before you begin working in the Calendar view.

Try cruising around a bit. You can move around in the calendar in four ways:

- ✔ Click the up and down arrows to move from month to month.
- ✔ Click the scroll bar to slide your calendar up or down. After you click the scroll box, an information box appears, alerting you to the dates visible on the screen.
- ✔ Press Page Up and Page Down (or click the up and down arrows on the screen) to move from month to month.
- ✔ Press Alt+Home and Alt+End to jump to the start or the end of the project.

After you finish cruising, press Alt+Home to return to the beginning of the project.

Month up and down buttons ⌐

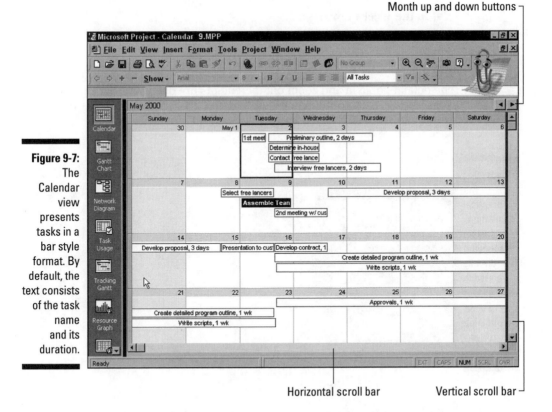

Figure 9-7: The Calendar view presents tasks in a bar style format. By default, the text consists of the task name and its duration.

Horizontal scroll bar   Vertical scroll bar ⌐

Zooming to fit a month on-screen

An entire month may not be visible on a single screen in the Calendar view. To see an entire month on your screen, you can scroll up or down, or you can click the Zoom In and Zoom Out buttons on the Standard toolbar. The best way to see an entire month is by using the Zoom dialog box. If you want to use the Zoom dialog box, follow these steps:

1. **Right-click anywhere in the white, unused portion of any date box.**

   A shortcut menu appears.

2. **Choose Zoom.**

   The Zoom dialog box appears, as shown in Figure 9-8.

3. **Select the Custom radio button.**

4. **In the Weeks box, type 5.**

5. **Click OK.**

   The Calendar view shows five weeks.

The default zoom in and zoom out increments are one, two, four, and six weeks. You can customize your view to display a particular number of weeks, or you can set a view based on specific start and finish dates.

Figure 9-8:
The practical limitations of custom zoom are directly related to the number of tasks appearing on any given day.

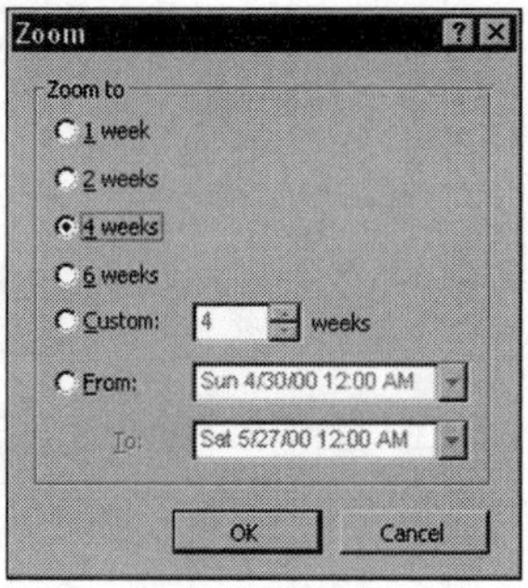

Using the layout command to see tasks

If you can see all of the weeks in your view but you can't see many of your tasks, you can use the layout command to correct the situation. But you have to decide whether you want to see all the weeks of the month or all the tasks for each day. The Layout option lets you to show fewer weeks at a time. This makes the individual day calendar boxes larger. But, of course, you can't see a month at a time.

To use the layout command to display all the tasks for each day, follow these steps:

1. **Right-click anywhere in the white, unused portion of any date box.**

   The shortcut menu appears.

2. **Choose Zoom.**

3. **Select the 4 Weeks option and then click OK.**

To make all of your tasks appear on the days to which they're assigned, follow these steps:

1. **Right-click anywhere in the white, unused portion of any date box.**

   The shortcut menu appears.

2. **Choose Layout.**

   The Layout dialog box appears, as shown in Figure 9-9.

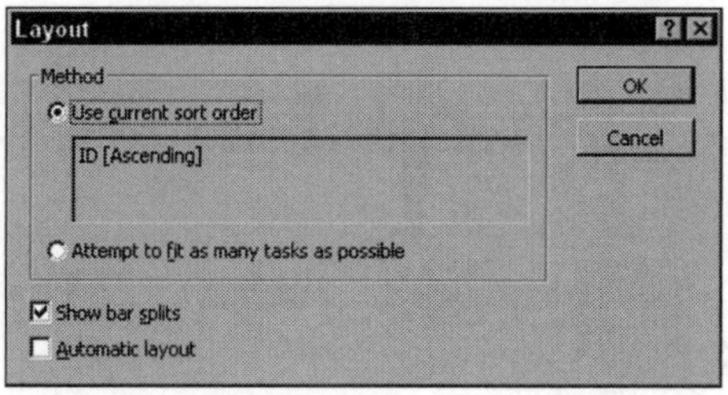

Figure 9-9:
By default, the Layout box orders tasks by their ID order.

Layout	? X
Method	
⊙ Use current sort order	OK
ID [Ascending]	Cancel
○ Attempt to fit as many tasks as possible	
☑ Show bar splits	
☐ Automatic layout	

3. **Select the Attempt to Fit as Many Tasks as Possible option and then click OK.**

   Some of the tasks now appear, as shown in Figure 9-10.

Make the week rows tall enough to show as many tasks as possible. To make week rows taller by using the automatic resizing feature, follow these steps:

1. **Place the mouse cursor over any horizontal line at the bottom of a week row.**

   The cursor turns into a horizontal line with an up and down arrow.

2. **Double-click.**

   Voilà! All the tasks fit into their date boxes.

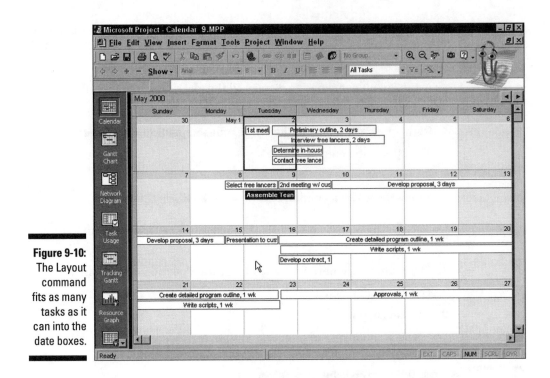

Figure 9-10:
The Layout
command
fits as many
tasks as it
can into the
date boxes.

Notice in Figure 9-11 that Microsoft Project calculated the space necessary to accommodate all the tasks and pushed the weeks down slightly so that you can see more of the tasks.

Seeing a day's tasks

Sometimes, because of a short duration, tasks are too small for their task names and information to fit in their text boxes. For example, notice in Figure 9-10 that May 2 has tasks too small to allow text identification. You can see what the tasks are and view all the other tasks on that day simultaneously by double-clicking the day's date bar.

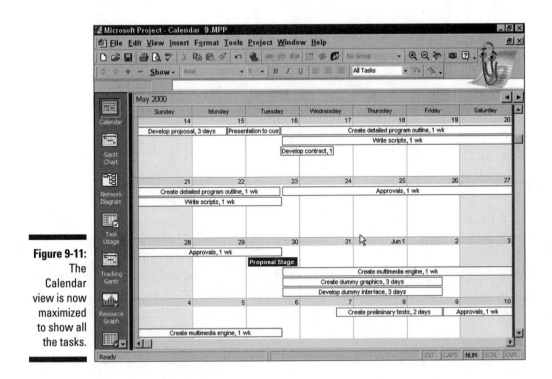

Figure 9-11:
The
Calendar
view is now
maximized
to show all
the tasks.

Chapter 10

Keeping an Eye on Resources

● ●

In This Chapter

▶ Tracking resources in the Resource Sheet view

▶ Showing resource details in different views

▶ Reviewing the allocation and cost of resources

● ●

Sometimes isolating resource information is helpful, particularly when you have a resource allocation problem in your project. Chapter 6 talks about how Microsoft Project offers views of a project (particularly task views) and why views are important.

In Microsoft Project, resource views display information from a different perspective than do task views. Two of the resource views, Resource Sheet and Resource Usage, enable you to enter and edit resource information. You use the other view, the Resource Graph view, for graphical illustration.

If you're already working on a project, this chapter will help you understand how to access views of your own work. Or you can follow along with the CD's practice file, titled Chapter 10.MPP. The practice file has some information built into it to help you get the idea of what resource views have to offer. When you open it, you'll see something like Figure 10-1. Appendix C gives you information on using the practice files on the CD.

Editing Resource Details in the Resource Sheet View

The Resource sheet, like the Task sheet, is in spreadsheet form. The Resource sheet lists resources and their related details such as initials, group designations, and maximum resource units. You can use the sheet to enter and edit resource details. To access the Resource Sheet view, click the Resource Sheet icon on the view bar. A screen similar to the one shown in Figure 10-2 appears.

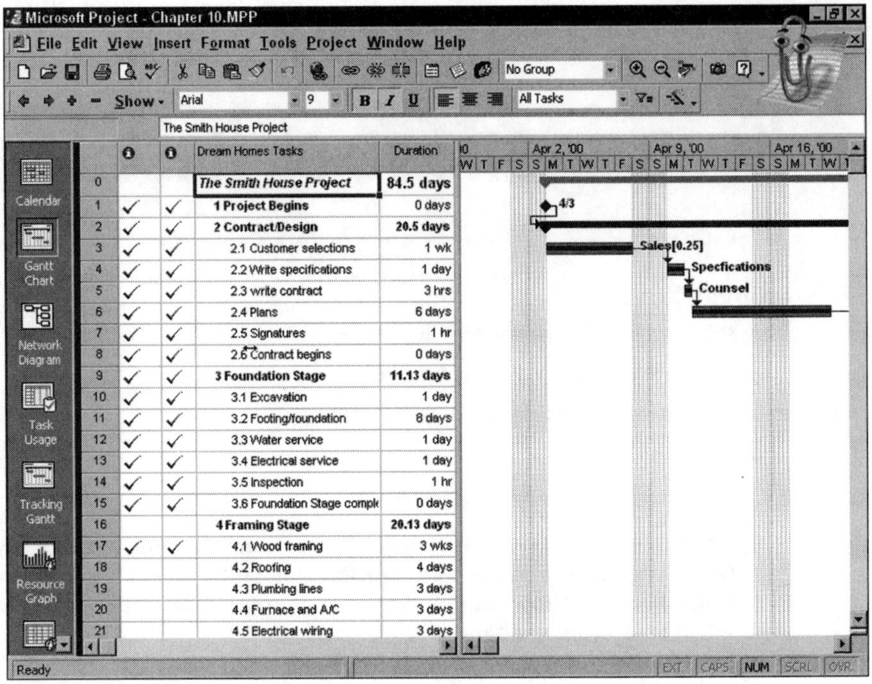

Figure 10-1: Microsoft Project opens files in the default Gantt Chart view.

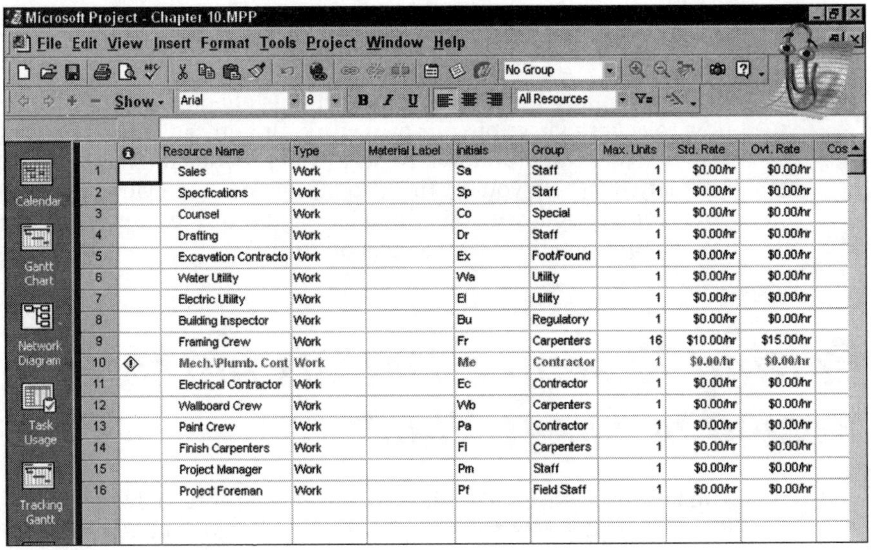

Figure 10-2: The Resource Sheet view is a handy way to review and edit individual resources and groups of resources.

Adding information to the Resource sheet is similar to entering information in spreadsheet cells. You can insert rows and columns. You can also enter information at the first available open space at the bottom of the list.

Two of the greatest features of the Resource sheet are its sorting and filtering capabilities. I discuss sorting and filtering at length in Chapter 13.

Sorting

Microsoft Project automatically assigns an identification number to each resource. By default, the Resource sheet is ordered by this ID. But the default ID numbering system simply reflects the order in which you enter resources. If there's a significance to this order, great. Often, however, the default order has no special value. You can increase the utility of the Resource Sheet view through sorting.

To put your resources into a particular order by sorting, follow these steps:

1. **Choose Project⇨Sort.**

   The Sort dialog box pops up to say "Howdy!" This dialog box enables you to sort your tasks in a myriad of ways. You can sort by Start Date, Finish Date, Priority, Cost, and ID. If you select one of these options, Microsoft Project performs the sort in descending order (first to last). If you want to sort in ascending order or if these options aren't what you're looking for, you can go on to Step 2.

2. **Click the down-arrow in the Sort By list box and select the option that suits you, as well as either the Ascending or Descending radio button.**

   For example, select the Name option and the Ascending radio button. The view now displays resource names in the order you chose (see Figure 10-3.)

   To return to the default sort, choose Project⇨Sort⇨by ID.

If you want your tasks to always appear in the order in which a particular sort puts them, select the Permanently Renumber Resources check box, as shown in Figure 10-4.

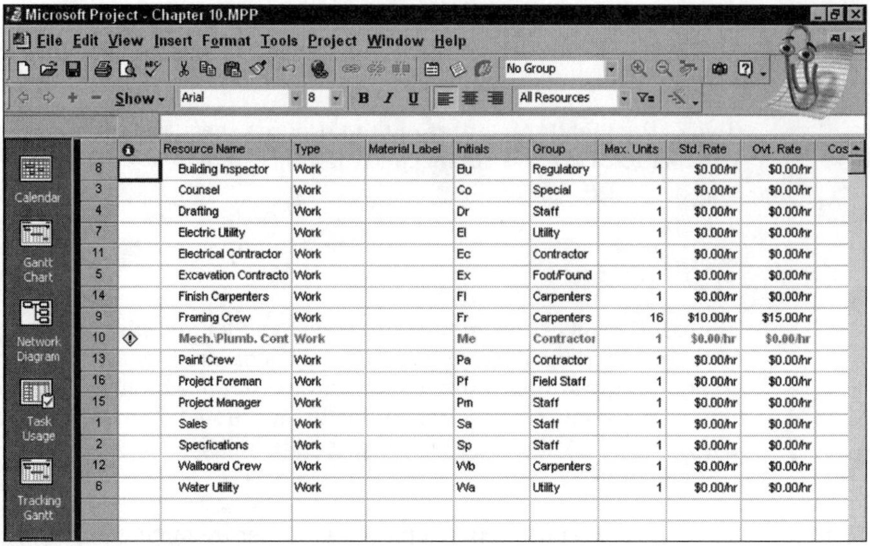

Figure 10-3: The resource ID number stays with the resource. This prevents the sort process from messing up your resource assignments to tasks.

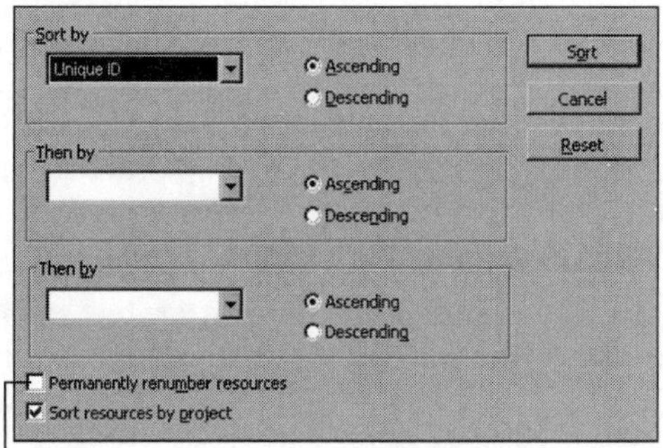

Figure 10-4: Before you perform a sort, decide whether you want to permanently renumber resources.

This check box allows you to make your sort permanent

Filtering

In addition to changing the sort order, you can change the filter of the Resource Sheet view. Filters show only what you want to see and hide the rest. When you choose a filter, you're not changing or removing anything from your project; you're only hiding unwanted information from your view. You may not realize it, but Microsoft Project is always filtering your information — not like your mother, but more like an administrative assistant. Microsoft Project isn't getting rid of anything; it's controlling the amount of information it thinks you want to see at any given time.

The default filter in the Resource Sheet view is All Resources. You see this designation in the Filter list on the formatting toolbar, as shown in Figure 10-3. Here's how to use a filter:

1. **Click the down arrow next to the Filter list on the formatting toolbar.**

2. **Select a filter.**

   In this example, select the Group option. A Group entry box appears. In the entry box, type the group name. Click OK.

In the example, the Resource Sheet view is now filtered to show only the Staff group, as shown in Figure 10-5. Play with the Resource Sheet view, sorting and filtering all you want. After you're finished and before you turn out the lights, please put the Resource Sheet view back the way you found it.

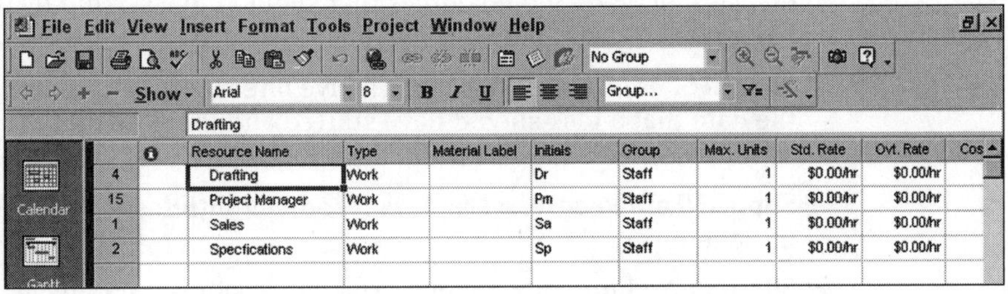

Figure 10-5:
The filtering options in the Filter list are only a fraction of the filtering options available.

The following list describes other filtering options that Microsoft Project offers:

- ✔ **All Resources:** Displays all the resources in your project

- ✔ **Confirmed Assignments:** Displays only those assignments that a resource has not declined

- ✔ **Cost Greater Than:** Displays resources costing more than an amount you specify

- ✔ **Cost Overbudget:** A calculated filter that displays resources with a scheduled cost greater than the baseline cost

- ✔ **Date Range:** An interactive filter that prompts you for two dates and then displays tasks and resources with assignments starting or finishing in the date range

- ✔ **Group:** An interactive filter that displays resources of the group you specify

- ✔ **In Progress Assignments:** Displays the assignments that have started but aren't completed

- ✔ **Linked Fields:** Displays resources linked to values from other programs

- ✔ **Overallocated Resources:** Displays resources scheduled for more work than they can accomplish in the specified time

- ✔ **Resource Range:** An interactive filter that displays resources in the ID numbers range you specify

- ✔ **Resources – Material:** Displays material resources, such as typewriters or phones

- ✔ **Resources With Attachments:** Displays resources with attached objects or notes in the Notes box

- ✔ **Resources/Assignments With Overtime:** Displays resources that are working overtime

- ✔ **Resources – Work:** Displays work resources

- ✔ **Should Start By:** An interactive filter that asks you for a date and then displays all tasks and resources that should have started by that date but haven't

- ✔ **Should Start/Finish By:** An interactive filter that asks you for two dates: the date that a task should have started and the date that the task should have finished

- ✔ **Slipped/Late Progress:** Displays resources with tasks that aren't staying on schedule

- ✔ **Slipping Assignments:** Displays resources whose tasks haven't yet been completed

- ✔ **Unconfirmed Assignments:** Displays assignments that the requested resources have declined

- ✔ **Unstarted Assignments:** Displays assignments that haven't started

- ✔ **Work Complete:** Displays resources that have completed all of their assigned tasks

- ✔ **Work Incomplete:** A calculated filter displaying resources with scheduled work less than the baseline work

- ✔ **Work Overbudget:** A calculated filter displaying resources with scheduled work greater than the baseline work

Getting Multiple Views in the Resource Usage View

From the Gantt Chart view, change to the Resource Usage view by clicking the Resource Usage icon on the view bar. The Resource Usage view displays a combination view, as shown in Figure 10-6. The Resource Usage view shows resources with their assigned tasks grouped below them. In the Resource Usage view you can enter information about a resource's task assignment. You can look for overallocated resources and resolve the problems.

The default right-hand window is a timeline that shows the date and the amount of work that individual resources perform. The Details column identifies the information as work. In fact, you can list any combination of six types of details in this column:

1. **Choose Format⇨Details.**

   The Details list appears.

2. **Select any combination of detail types.**

   Your choices are Work, Baseline Work, Cost, Actual Work, Overallocation, Remaining Availability, and Cumulative Work.

3. **If you're not satisfied with these detail options, you can choose Format⇨Detail Styles.**

   The Detail Styles dialog box appears. Select any available detail and then click Show. If you want, you can also move the detail order and customize the text and background color for each detail.

4. **Click OK to accept your changes or click Cancel to reject your changes.**

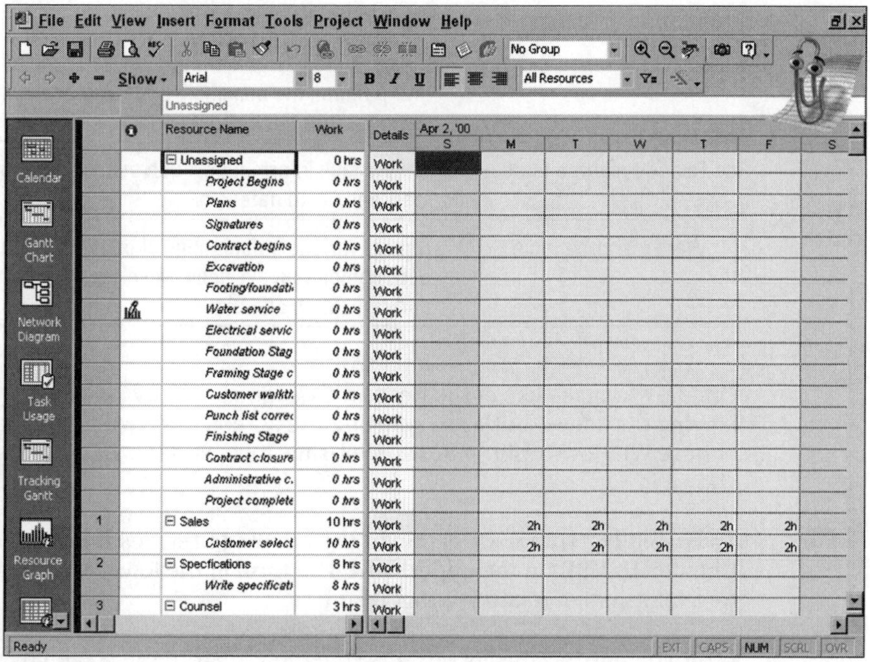

Figure 10-6:
You can scroll through information in either window with the scroll bars.

The left screen can display any of five tables. The default table is the Usage table, which associates resources with their tasks. The indicator column displays resource-relevant information. As an example, scroll within the view to Resource 10 in Chapter 10.MPP. Hover the cursor over the indicators to read Microsoft Project's messages.

To display a different table, choose View⇨Table. You can drag the vertical bar between the timeline and the table to the right until you expose all the details in the particular table. I tell you about six of the tables in Table 10-1.

Table 10-1	Microsoft Project Tables and Their Uses
Table	**What It Does**
Cost resource table	Shows information about resources, including cost, baseline cost, variance, actual cost, and amount remaining.
Entry resource table	Shows the resource's initials, group, maximum units, rate, overtime rate, cost per use, accrual method, relevant calendar, and code.
Hyperlink resource table	Creates shortcuts and associates them with a resource. Use it to jump to your computer files, files on a network, your organization's intranet, and the World Wide Web.
Summary resource table	Displays the assignment of resources, including the group name, the maximum units, the peak unit usage, the rates, the cost, and the work performed in hours.
Usage resource table	Shows task information, such as task duration and start and finish dates.
Work resource table	Shows various calculations about work, including percent completed, overtime, baseline, variance, actual, and remaining calculations.

One way to make use of the Resource Usage view is by splitting — not as in leaving the scene, but as in splitting the screen into two views. To do this, choose Window⇨Split. A Resource Usage form appears in the lower view, as shown in Figure 10-7.

To try out the split view, highlight the Framing Crew resource name (from Chapter 10.MPP) in the upper view. The form in the lower view reports the task information related to this resource.

After you finish checking out this split view, restore the screen by choosing Window⇨Remove Split. This brings back the Gantt Chart view.

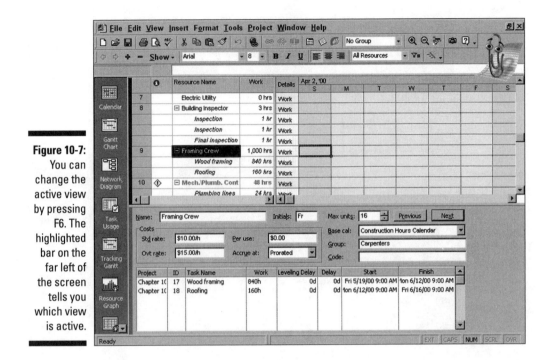

Figure 10-7:
You can
change the
active view
by pressing
F6. The
highlighted
bar on the
far left of
the screen
tells you
which view
is active.

Measuring Resource Allocation and Cost

The Resource graph shows information about the allocation or cost of resources in measurements of time. Use it for reviewing allocations for a single resource or a group of resources.

The best way to use this graph is in a split view with the Resource Usage view. To use the Resource graph, follow these steps:

1. **Choose View⇨Resource Graph, or select Resource Graph View on the view bar.**

   The Resource Graph view appears.

2. **Select Window⇨Split.**

3. **Select the lower pane, and choose Resource Usage View on the view bar.**

   The Resource Usage Chart appears in the lower split window, as shown in Figure 10-8.

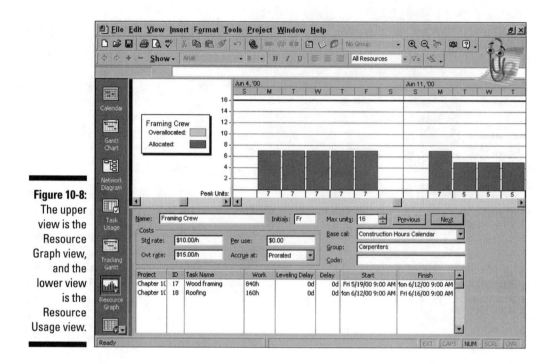

Figure 10-8:
The upper
view is the
Resource
Graph view,
and the
lower view
is the
Resource
Usage view.

You can use this split view to compare the graphical chart with work in hours. If you want, you can edit work amounts to correct overallocation or simply to spread around the fun to more people. To edit work amounts, drag the vertical bar in the Resource Usage view until you expose the Work column. Select a work cell and change the units of time. The change also appears in the Resource Graph view.

Overallocation occurs when you assign more resource time than is available for your project tasks (for example, assigning ten hours of work in an eight-hour day). I tell you more about overallocation in Chapter 13.

In the Resource graph, click the right arrow of the horizontal scroll bar in the left box until the Mech./Plumb. Contractor appears. As shown in Figure 10-9, the upper window displays any overallocated resources for the task in percentages of time, and the lower window displays indicators and actual work in hours.

Figure 10-9:
The
Resource
graph dis-
plays the
resource
(left) and a
timeline
chart (right).
The
Resource
Usage view
identifies
the
resource
and tasks
(left) and
work details
(right).

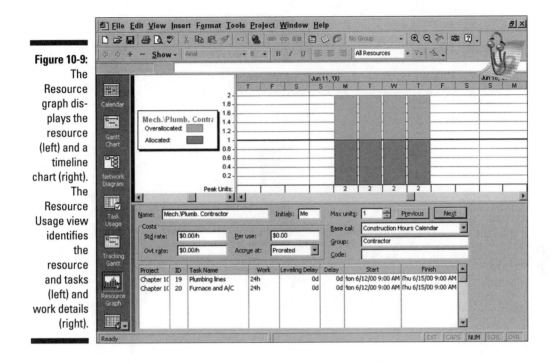

Chapter 11

Filtering and Sorting Views

● ●

● ●

So you have this beautiful, huge project. Tasks are in order and resources are assigned. Relationships are set and durations are as tight as a drum. You know how to look at the project from about every view the human brain can imagine.

Life is good — at least for an hour or so. Then you get a memo from a stakeholder requesting a listing of all resources whose tasks will occur on Tuesdays in odd weeks of all summer months. While you're still trying to figure out what an odd week is, you get a call from a contractor wanting to know whether there could be any slippage of other tasks and, if so, how they will affect her start date. Oh, and she has to know right now. And while your ear is still ringing from that one, your boss rushes in wanting a list of all tasks that cost more than $1,500, starting with the most expensive and ending with the least expensive.

Big deal! Why don't they ask for something complicated? All that you need to do is some filtering and sorting. Then you need to decide what to do during the second half of the hour.

Filtering and sorting are two of the best reasons for using software programs in project management. Quite often, you need to establish criteria for relating and finding certain details. In such situations, the least important project information may be what you needed the most just a few minutes ago.

The worth of a project-management software program is measured by its capability to solicit, associate, and interpret a group of facts from a mass of project information. With Microsoft Project, you can perform this with surprising ease and creative freedom.

A *filter* segregates information using predetermined criteria. A helpful analogy is the use of filters in photography. Choose a particular color filter, and all blue color is eliminated from a picture. In contrast, by choosing a saturation filter, all colors are screened from a picture by a predetermined percentage. As long as you use the same filter, you establish temporary group relationships that include some classes of visual information and exclude others. Using the same filter, you get the same visual relationships no matter where you point the camera.

In Microsoft Project, filters work in much the same way. For example, you can choose a filter that displays only unfinished tasks. Or, you can choose a filter that displays all tasks with a duration greater than three days.

Sorting doesn't filter information. A *sort* sets a task order based on your criteria. Unlike filtering, you don't segregate information. Instead, with a sort, you order the information in a different way. For example, you can sort the tasks in alphabetical order by task name.

In Microsoft Project, it's possible to use both filter and sort. For example, you can use a filter that lists only tasks whose costs are based on hourly rates. Then you can sort the filtered tasks by the amount per hour in ascending or descending order.

For your convenience, I include a practice file that you can use for checking out filtering and sorting. Many of the specific examples in this chapter refer to Chapter 11.mpp practice file. See Appendix C for information on opening the practice files on the CD-ROM.

Using Standard Filters

A *filter* segregates and associates project information to provide you with the specific facts you need. The underlying ingredients of a filter are test and value criteria. When you select a filter, you're saying you want to see all the tasks or resources with values that meet the conditions of a certain test. For example, the test may be that you want to see all tasks with a duration value greater than one week. Microsoft Project then searches the project databases and finds and displays all tasks with values that conform to that test criterion.

Microsoft Project provides a bunch of standard filters. These filters probably meet most of your needs. But if you're like most project managers, sooner or later, you'll need to create a new filter or two. Fortunately, creating a new filter is almost as easy as using a standard one. As you may guess, though, it's best to find out how the standard filters work before you jump into the creative mode.

Whatever view you happen to be in, you're looking at information provided through a standard filter. For example, if your file is in the Gantt Chart view, you're looking at tasks through the default All Tasks filter. Knowing which filter is active is easy. Just look at the Filter box on the formatting toolbar, as shown in Figure 11-1.

In most views, you can access standard filters and new filters by using the Filtered For command, the Filter box, the More Filters command, or the AutoFilter command. Although all four choices provide access to filters, each offers a distinct way to use those filters.

The Filtered For command

The Filtered For command changes the active task or resource view to display only the information that meets the filter criteria you choose. For example, if you want to see only completed tasks, choose Completed Tasks. You can use the Filtered For command to see both isolated and highlighted filter views.

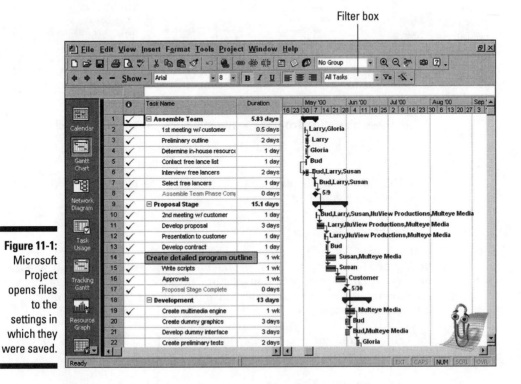

Figure 11-1: Microsoft Project opens files to the settings in which they were saved.

Isolated filter views

The default view you select from the Filtered For submenu can be referred to as an *isolated filter view,* which shows only those tasks or resources that meet the criterion of the selected filter.

To use the Filtered For command to display all completed tasks in isolated filter view, follow these steps:

1. **Choose Project⇨Filtered for: All Tasks.**

   The Filtered For submenu appears, as shown in Figure 11-2. The sub-menu lists eleven commonly used filters.

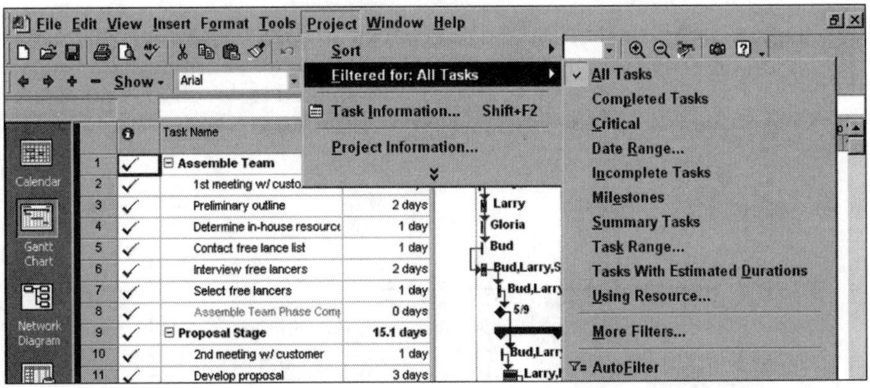

Figure 11-2:
In addition to the eleven most commonly used filters, the sub-menu can display any filter you create.

2. **Choose an option from the submenu, such as Completed Tasks.**

   Tables 11-1 and 11-2 later in this chapter explain your filtering choices in detail.

   The Gantt chart displays all tasks that meet the test of completion, as shown in Figure 11-3.

Highlighted filter view

In the Filtered For command, you can show either an isolated filter view or a highlighted filter view. A *highlighted filter view* is different from the isolated filter view in one major way: A highlighted filter view identifies the tasks or resources that meet the filter criterion and highlights them among all the other tasks or resources.

Using the Filtered For command, follow these steps to select a filter in the highlighted filter view:

1. **Hold down the Shift key.**

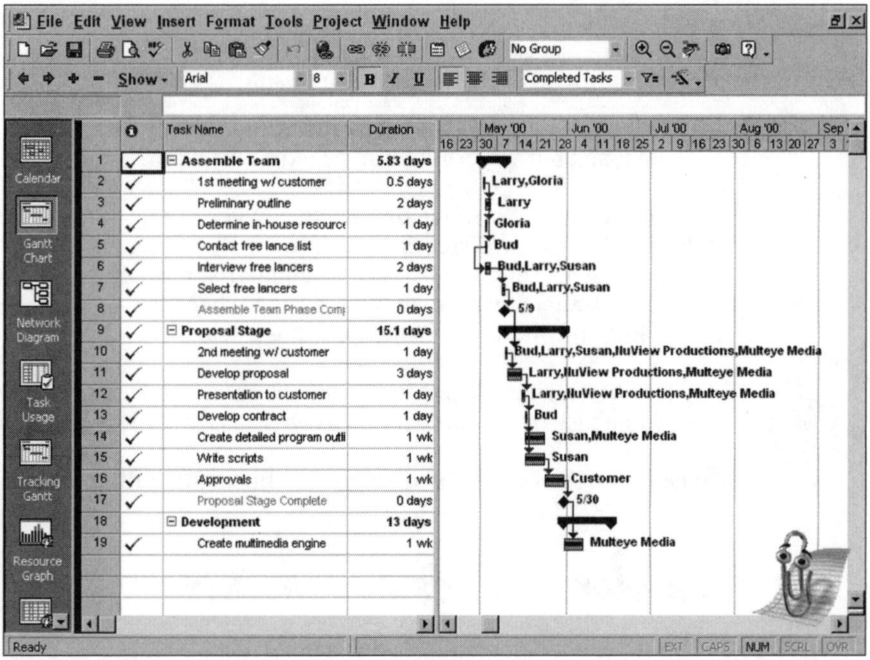

Figure 11-3:
The
Completed
Tasks filter
displays
only those
tasks that
are finished.

2. **Choose Project➪Filtered for: Completed Tasks.**

The submenu appears.

3. **Choose Incomplete Tasks.**

The Gantt chart displays all the tasks but highlights incomplete tasks.

The Filtered For command lists a submenu of commonly selected filters, including filters you create. Later in this chapter, I show you how to create a filter and list it in this submenu.

You can revert to the default filter by pressing F3.

The Filter box

The Filter box serves two purposes: It displays the current filter and provides a list of all task filters in task views or all resource filters in resource views. To use the Filter box, follow these steps:

1. **Click the down arrow next to the Filter list box on the formatting toolbar.**

2. Select a filter.

For example, selecting the Unstarted Tasks filter causes Project to show only those tasks that haven't yet begun.

Two things happen. The highlighted filter disappears and it's replaced by an isolated view of the Unstarted Tasks filter.

Each filter provides a unique perspective of your project. For example, the Unstarted Tasks view displays all tasks meeting the test of the Actual Start Date equaling NA (not applicable). By comparison, any started or completed task has an Actual Start Date not equaling NA because a date has been entered into the Microsoft Project database field.

The Filter box always displays the current filter. The Filter box also contains all available task or resource filters as well as any filters you create.

You can't use the Filter box to access the highlighted filter view.

The More Filters command

The More Filters command is a misleading name — More Than More Filters might be a better description. The More Filters command displays a dialog box that's like a command central for filters — it provides a number of options for selecting, highlighting, editing, creating, and organizing filters. To access the dialog box, follow these steps:

1. Choose Project⇨Filtered for: All Tasks.

The Filtered For submenu appears.

2. Choose More Filters.

The More Filters dialog box appears, as shown in Figure 11-4.

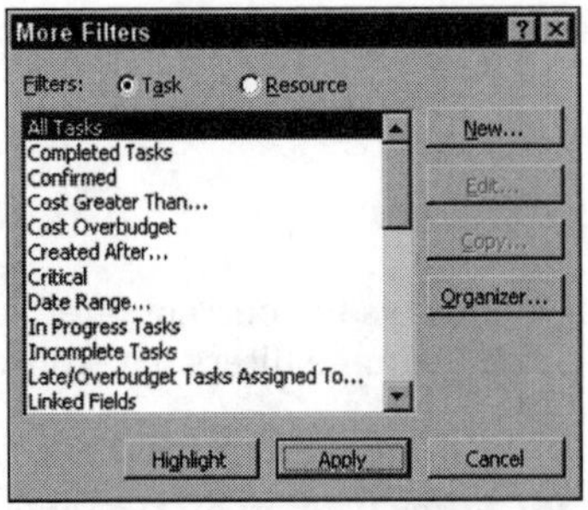

Figure 11-4:
The More
Filters
dialog box.

You can perform many functions by using the More Filters dialog box. (I describe these in Table 11-1 later in this chapter.) In addition to these creative opportunities, you can select either an isolated filter view or a highlighted filter view.

To select the isolated filter view, choose a filter and then click the Apply button. To select a highlighted filter view, use these steps:

1. **In the More Filters dialog box, select a task filter.**

2. **Click the Highlight button.**

    Press F3 to return to the All Tasks filter.

The AutoFilter command

The AutoFilter command is a nifty little feature. Using AutoFilters is a helpful way to filter task or resource information in individual columns of sheet views. That may sound technical, but it's not. To use the AutoFilter command, follow these steps:

1. **Select the AutoFilter icon on the formatting toolbar.**

    A down arrow appears in a column of the table in your Gantt Chart view.

2. **Click one of the AutoFilter down arrows for a list of available options that are relevant to information contained in that column.**

    For example, if you select the AutoFilter for the Task Name column, a list of all tasks appears for that project. By clicking one of the tasks in this list, you see a filtered view showing only that task. By clicking F3, you can return to the default All Tasks filter.

    In addition, the AutoFilter offers All and Custom, as shown in Figure 11-5. The All selection is the same as pressing F3. The Custom filter enables you to create a unique set of criteria for filtering task names.

3. **In the AutoFilter box, select one of the task names.**

    The AutoFilter displays all criteria that equal the task name you selected. The color of the column name (in this case, Task Name) changes to blue, which indicates that the information is based on the use of that column's AutoFilter.

4. **Press F3 to restore the project to the default all tasks filter.**

Where have autofilters been all my life? Could it be that they're available for all columns in a table? Yep. Well, almost. Drag the vertical bar in the Gantt chart to the far right. Notice that an AutoFilter is available for every column except the Indicator column. Every sheet view provides this feature.

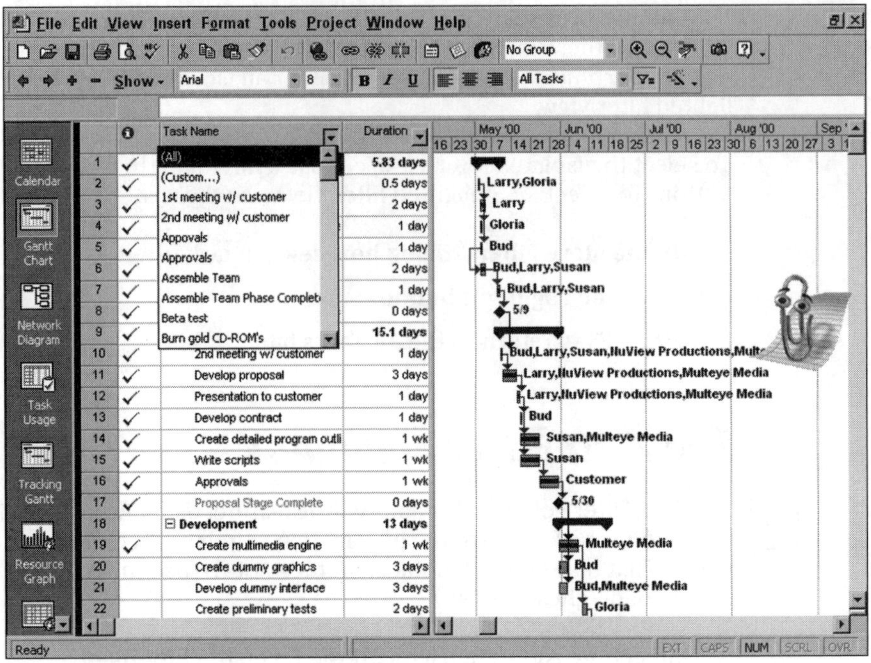

Figure 11-5:
The
AutoFilter
offers All
and Custom.

One of the most significant features of AutoFilter is the Custom command.
The Custom command is an advanced feature that anyone can use almost
immediately. To use the Custom command:

1. **Select the Finish column's AutoFilter.**

   The AutoFilter box displays all available project criteria equaling *Finish*.

2. **Select Custom.**

   The Custom AutoFilter dialog box appears, as shown in Figure 11-6.

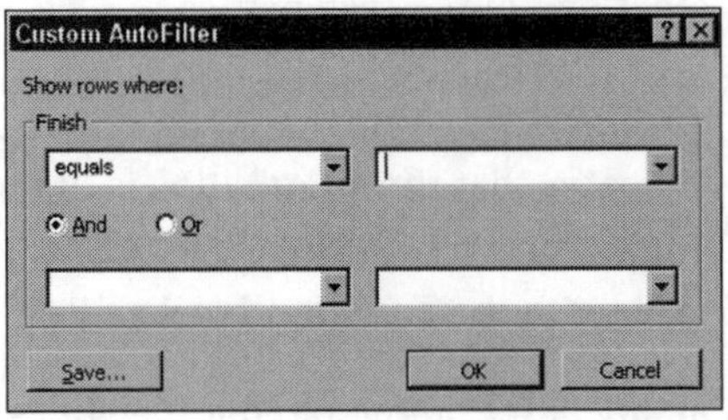

Figure 11-6:
The Custom
AutoFilter.

3. **Click the down arrow in the list box below Finish.**

    You are offered a number of comparison operators (such as does not equal).

4. **Select a comparison operator other than equals.**

5. **Click the down arrow in the text box to the right of the comparison operator.**

    The text box lists all the criteria in this project file's Finish field. By selecting one of the criteria, you are telling the AutoFilter to operate on that criteria based on the comparison operator to the left (such as does not equal). Pretty neat, huh?

6. **Click OK.**

If you want to do some more advanced AutoFiltering, use a second basis of comparison. In the Custom AutoFilter dialog box, select the And option or the Or option. Add an additional comparison and its criteria, as shown in Figure 11-7. (The left conditions are the comparison and the right conditions are the criteria unique to that project file.) By setting two comparisons, you can, for example, bookend Finish dates to show those that are after one date and before another.

Lastly, you can save your custom AutoFilter so that it becomes a permanent filter option. (Note, however, that your custom filter doesn't become your default filter for that column.) To save your custom AutoFilter as a permanent option, use the following steps:

1. **Ensure that the Custom AutoFilter is open.**

    If the information is gone, enter your double comparison again or use the one shown in Figure 11-7.

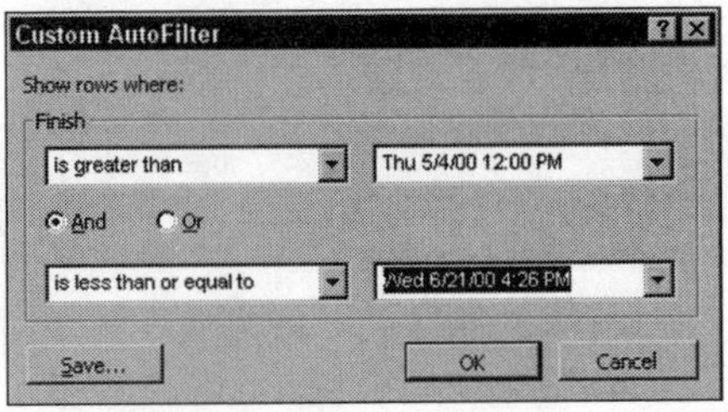

Figure 11-7:
The Custom
AutoFilter
dialog box.

2. **Click the Save button.**

    A Filter Definition dialog box appears. (See Figure 11-8.)

3. **Give your custom filter a name in the Name box.**

    Select a name that's easy to remember.

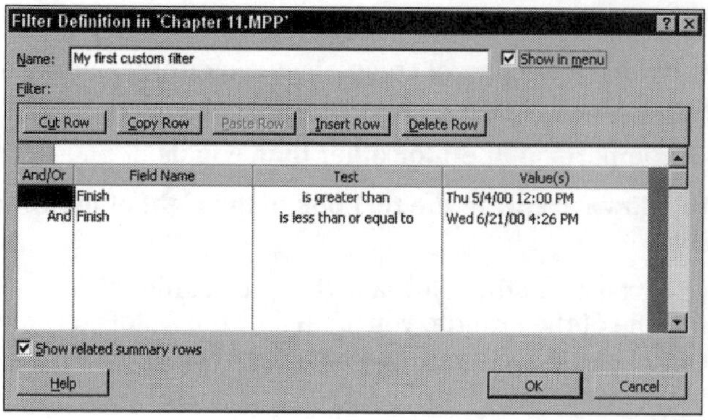

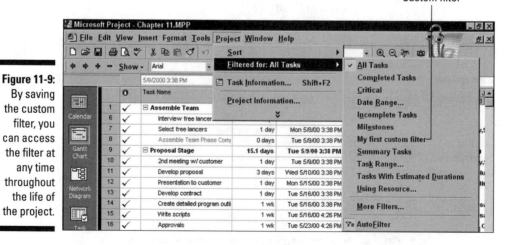

Figure 11-8:
The Filter
Definition
dialog box.

4. **Select the Show in Menu check box.**

   This will make the custom filter available in the Filter For box.

5. **If you want, make more changes to the filter.**

6. **Click OK in the Filter Definition dialog box and again in the Custom AutoFilter dialog box.**

   Two things have happened. Your view is now based on the custom criteria, and your custom filter has been added to the Filtered For menu.

7. **To see your custom filter, choose Project⇨Filtered for.**

   The Filtered For box now includes your custom filter, as shown in Figure 11-9.

Figure 11-9:
By saving
the custom
filter, you
can access
the filter at
any time
throughout
the life of
the project.

You can remove your custom filter at any time by choosing Tools⇨Organizer. The Organizer dialog box appears. Select the Filters tab. In the right column, select your custom filter and choose the Delete button.

 When you finish checking out the custom filter option, press F3 to return to the default All Filters. Choose the AutoFilter icon to turn off the AutoFilters option. The icon acts as an on/off toggle.

Customizing the highlighted display

Sometimes modifying the look of your project view is necessary or simply more enjoyable than looking at the default view. In this section, using the example, you can change the color of the highlighted filter, which has a default text color of blue. To begin customizing the highlighted display, highlight a filtered selection:

1. **Choose Project⇨Filtered for: All Tasks⇨More Filters.**

2. **Select one of the filters, such as Incomplete Tasks.**

3. **Click the Highlight button.**

As an example, for easier reading, change the text style of the highlighted filter:

1. **Choose Format⇨Text Styles.**

2. **In the Item to Change list box, select Highlighted Tasks.**

3. **Select a feature.**

   In this example, select the Underline option.

4. **In the Font Style list box, select a font style.**

   For example, select Bold Italic.

5. **In the Color list box, select a color.**

6. **Click OK.**

   The highlighted filter view displays the modified highlighted text.

Types of filters

The two major classifications of standard filters in Microsoft Project are task filters and resource filters. The task filters are accessible in all task views. The resource filters are accessible in all resource views. Tables 11-1 and 11-2 describe the task and resource filters available.

In split views, filters work for only the upper view, and they always apply to an entire project file. If you select a filter and then select a second filter, the second filter analyzes the entire file, not just the product of the first filter.

Using interactive filters

An *interactive* filter is one that asks you a question or questions and then goes hunting for the information you want. You can tell many of the interactive filters in the filter list boxes by the ellipsis marks (. . .) following the filter name, such as Should Start by. . . .

Using the Chapter 11 example, you find all tasks whose resource is Bud. Then you use the highlighted filter option to display those tasks among all the others. To do this:

1. **Press and hold down the Shift key.**

   You should continue holding down the Shift key until the last step.

2. **Choose Project⇨Filtered for⇨Using Resource.**

   The interactive question box appears.

3. **Use the down arrow to scroll to a resource name.**

   In this example, scroll to the Bud resource and select it.

4. **Click OK and then release the Shift key.**

The Using Resource filter appears in the highlighted rather than isolated option. In addition, the filter box on the formatting toolbar displays the Using Resource selection.

Table 11-1	**Types of Task Filters**
Task Filter	*What It Shows*
All Tasks	All tasks; this is the default filter
Completed Tasks	All completely finished tasks
Confirmed	Tasks agreed upon by requested resources
Cost Greater Than	Tasks that will cost more than the amount you designate; this is an interactive filter
Cost Overbudget	Tasks with a cost greater than their baseline amount

Task Filter	What It Shows
Created After	Tasks you create after the date you designate; this is an interactive filter
Critical	Critical tasks
Date Range	Tasks between two dates you specify; this is an interactive filter
In-Progress Tasks	Tasks that have started but haven't finished
Incomplete Tasks	Tasks that aren't finished (including those that haven't started)
Late/Overbudget Tasks Assigned To	Tasks assigned to resources you designate that are over the budget you set or will finish after the date you set; this is an interactive filter
Linked Fields	Tasks with text linked to other applications
Milestones	All milestones
Resource Group	Tasks associated with resources belonging to the group you specify; this is an interactive filter
Should Start By	Tasks that should have started by the date you specify, but haven't started; this is an interactive filter
Should Start/Finish By	Unfinished tasks based on a range you set in the filter; this is an interactive filter
Slipped/Late Progress	Slipped or slow tasks
Slipping Tasks	Tasks that aren't finished and are behind schedule
Summary Tasks	Tasks with subordinate tasks
Task Range	Tasks within a range of task IDs you specify; this is an interactive filter
Task with a Task Calendar Assigned	Displays tasks that have objects and a calendar assigned

(continued)

Table 11-1 *(continued)*

Task Filter	What It Shows
Tasks with Attachments	Tasks with objects or notes in the note box
Tasks with Deadlines	Displays tasks which have a deadline set
Tasks with Estimated Durations	Displays tasks with an estimated duration
Tasks with Fixed Dates	Tasks with a constraint other than As Soon As Possible and tasks that have already started
Tasks/Assignments With Overtime	Tasks where resources are working overtime
Top Level Tasks	The uppermost-level summary tasks; this filter is for projects with summary tasks within summary tasks
Unconfirmed	Tasks that have requested but unconfirmed commitment
Unstarted Tasks	Tasks that haven't started yet
Update Needed	Tasks that have experienced change and need to be sent for update or confirmation
Using Resource	Tasks that use the resource you specify; this is an interactive filter
Using Resource In Date Range	Tasks that start or finish within a timeline you determine and related to resources you designate; this is an interactive filter
Work Overbudget	Tasks with scheduled work greater than their baseline work

Table 11-2 — Types of Resource Filters

Resource Filter	What It Shows
All Resources	All resources in your project file
Confirmed Assignments	Resources that have acknowledged their assignments; this is used with workgroups

Resource Filter	What It Shows
Cost Greater Than	Resources that will cost more than what you designate; this is an interactive filter
Cost Overbudget	Resources with a scheduled cost greater than the baseline cost
Date Range	Resources with assignments within two dates you specify; this is an interactive filter
Group	Resources associated with the group you specify; this is an interactive filter
In Progress Assignments	Resources that have started assignments but haven't completed them
Linked Fields	Resources with text linked to other applications
Overallocated Resources	Overallocated resources
Resource Range	Resources within the range of ID numbers that you specify; this is an interactive filter
Resources – Material	Displays material resources, such as bricks and mortar
Resources – Work	Displays work resources, including people and equipment
Resources with Attachments	Resources with objects attached or notes in the Attachments note box
Resources/Assignments With Overtime	Resources or their assignments that are working overtime
Should Start By	Resources that should have started by a date you specify
Should Start/Finish By	Resources that should have started or finished by a date you specify; this is an interactive filter
Slipped/Late Progress	Resources associated with tasks that have slipped behind their baseline scheduled finish date or are late
Slipping Assignments	Resources with delayed assignments and incomplete tasks
Unconfirmed Assignments	Resources that have not responded with commitment to assigned tasks; this is associated with workgroups

(continued)

Table 11-2 *(continued)*

Resource Filter	What It Shows
Unstarted Assignments	Resources that have committed to assignments but have not yet begun them; this is associated with workgroups
Work Complete	Resources that have completed their tasks
Work Incomplete	Resources that have not completed their tasks
Work Overbudget	Resources with scheduled work that's greater than the baseline work

Creating Your Own Filters

So you've given Microsoft Project the benefit of the doubt. You've checked out all the task and resource filters, but none scratches the precise itch you have for details about your project. You're not a vanilla kind of project manager. You want some flavor and character in your work. No problem — create your own filter.

Follow a few rules, and Microsoft Project helps you make your project as personal as you want. You don't have to tell anybody it's easy — go ahead and impress your stakeholders!

Creating a filter by editing an existing one

The easiest way to create a new filter is by editing an existing one because most of the work has already been accomplished. Changing an existing filter slightly can make it work differently and look unique.

Using the example, you can edit an existing filter to create a new one that shows the final week before the project completion. To do this:

1. **Choose Project⇨Filtered for: All Tasks⇨More Filters.**

   The More Filters dialog box appears.

2. **Select the Task option in the Filters panel.**

3. **Select Task Range and then click the Copy button.**

   The Filter Definition dialog box appears, as shown in Figure 11-10. Copy of Task Range is a temporary name for the copy of the Task Range filter. All the changes you make will be to the copy; the original filter remains intact.

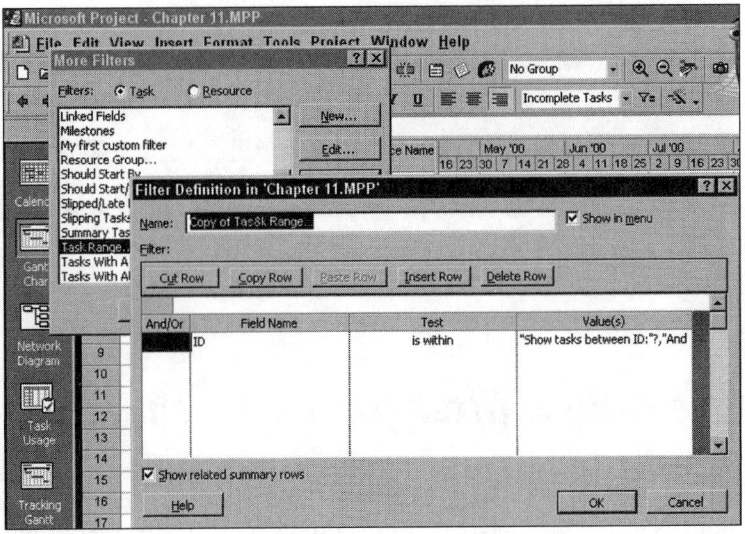

Figure 11-10:
This dialog box provides a number of options for customizing and applying filters.

4. **In the Name box, type a name.**

   In this example, type **Completion Date** (or whatever you want). The Field Name is already ID, so leave it.

5. **In the Test column, select is within.**

   A small down arrow appears next to the text box.

6. **Click the small down arrow and select a value.**

   In this example, select equals.

7. **In the Value(s) column, select "Show Tasks Between ID:"?, "And ID:"?**

8. **Drag your cursor across the text in the entry box above the column names and then press the Delete key.**

9. **In the text box above the column names, type a value.**

   In this example, type **44.** Notice that the Show in Menu check box is selected. By leaving this box checked, your new filter appears in the Filtered For submenu.

10. **Click OK.**

    Your new Completion Date filter appears in the More Filters dialog box.

11. **Click the Apply button.**

    Your new filter searches for all tasks equaling ID 45. The Completion Summary task and the Distribute milestone appear, as shown in Figure 11-11. By default, Microsoft Project displays the summary task when the filter finds one of the summary task's subtasks.

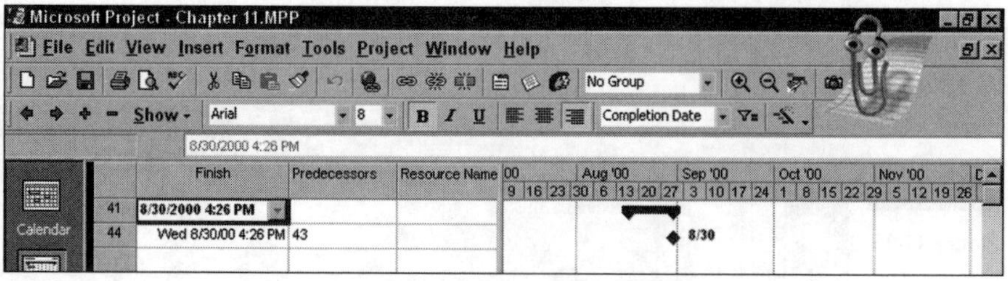

Figure 11-11:
The filter
displays the
sole task
that meets
the filter
criterion of
all task IDs
equaling 45.

Figure 11-11: The filter displays the sole task that meets the filter criterion of all task IDs equaling 45.

Creating a filter from scratch

You create a new filter in much the same way as you copy and edit one, except that you choose New Copy in the More Filters dialog box. In this section, using the Chapter 11 example, I show you how to create a filter that lists all tasks with the NuView Productions resource. To do this:

1. **Make sure that the default All Tasks filter is selected.**

   If not, press F3.

2. **Choose Project⇨Filtered for: All Tasks⇨More Filters.**

   The More Filters dialog box appears.

3. **Click the New button.**

   The Filter Definition dialog box appears.

You use the Filter Definition dialog box to set the criteria for selecting tasks or resources. After you create your filter, you're able to use it for both isolated and highlighted views. To create the Building Inspector filter:

1. **In the Name text box, type a name.**

   For example, type **NuView Schedule.** This becomes the filter's name.

2. **Select the Show in Menu check box.**

   This way, your new filter appears in the Filtered For submenu.

3. **Select the Field Name text box.**

   A down arrow appears to the right of the text edit box.

4. **Click the down arrow and scroll to select Resource Names.**

   You could simply type the field name, but this way you ensure that the name is accurate.

5. **Select the Test text box, click the down arrow, and then scroll to select Contains.**

   The Contains test displays or highlights tasks and resources that contain a value. The value is the next thing to set.

6. **Select the Value(s) text box.**

7. **Click the text edit box above the column names.**

   You know it's active when a red x and a green check mark appear to the left of the box.

8. **In the text edit box, type a value.**

   For example, type **Nu.**

9. **Click the Check Mark button to accept the text.**

   If you're following the example, your sample filter definition should look like Figure 11-12.

10. **When you're satisfied, click OK.**

    The More Filters dialog box contains your nifty new filter.

11. **Click the Highlight button.**

    All the tasks that meet the criterion of your new filter are highlighted.

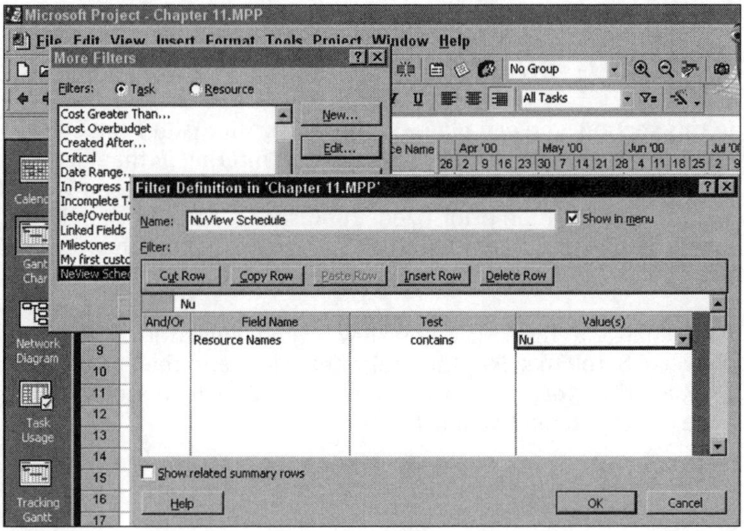

Figure 11-12:
The example looks like this if you've done everything correctly.

Sorting Your Project

Sorting tasks and resources is another way to control the display of project information. Sorting, unlike filtering, doesn't isolate or single out information. Instead, it changes the order of tasks in a descending or ascending manner based on the criteria of a particular field or fields. Is that confusing enough? Actually, it's not that bad.

By default, Microsoft assigns ascending ID numbers to tasks as you enter them into a project file. Task ID 1 is 1 simply because you entered it first. The same is true for task ID 2, 3, and so on. By using the sort option, you can use another criterion for ordering tasks.

The Sort feature works with whatever is in the active display. If you've already applied a filter to a project, the Sort feature works with the tasks or resources that resulted from the filter criteria.

Before you resort to sorting, be sure you know whether you want to maintain the original task ID relationships. The dialog box offers you the option of permanently renumbering tasks. If you choose to let the sort feature renumber tasks, it can do some strange and not-so-wonderful things to your task relationships. (In fact, allowing tasks to be renumbered may have been the inspiration for the invention of spaghetti.)

Types of sorting

In this section, you can play with the ways Microsoft Project can sort your information. Sorting is a lot different than filtering in that all the information remains visible — nothing is filtered out. You tell Microsoft Project how you want the information prioritized. Confused? It's actually kinda simple. But maybe you'd like to give it a little practice. Using the Chapter 11.MPP example, you can sort in different ways.

First, change to the Task Sheet view by choosing More Views at the end of the view bar. Scroll to select the Task Sheet view, and then click the Apply button. If necessary, expand any hash-marked columns by double-clicking the right edge of the column headings.

To use the Sort command:

1. **Choose Project⇨Sort⇨Sort By.**

   The Sort dialog box appears, as shown in Figure 11-13.

2. **In the Sort By list box, select a value.**

   In the example, select Name.

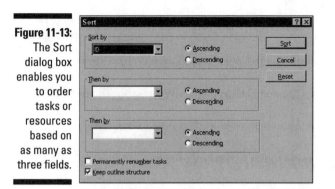

Figure 11-13:
The Sort
dialog box
enables you
to order
tasks or
resources
based on
as many as
three fields.

3. **Make sure that the Permanently Renumber Tasks check box is deselected.**

   For the example, you don't want this sort to become permanent. If you do want the sort to be permanent, however, select this check box.

4. **Click the Sort button.**

   The project is sorted to show all names in alphabetical order while maintaining summary task and subtask relationships, as shown in Figure 11-14. You can tell that the order is different by looking at the changed order of the task IDs.

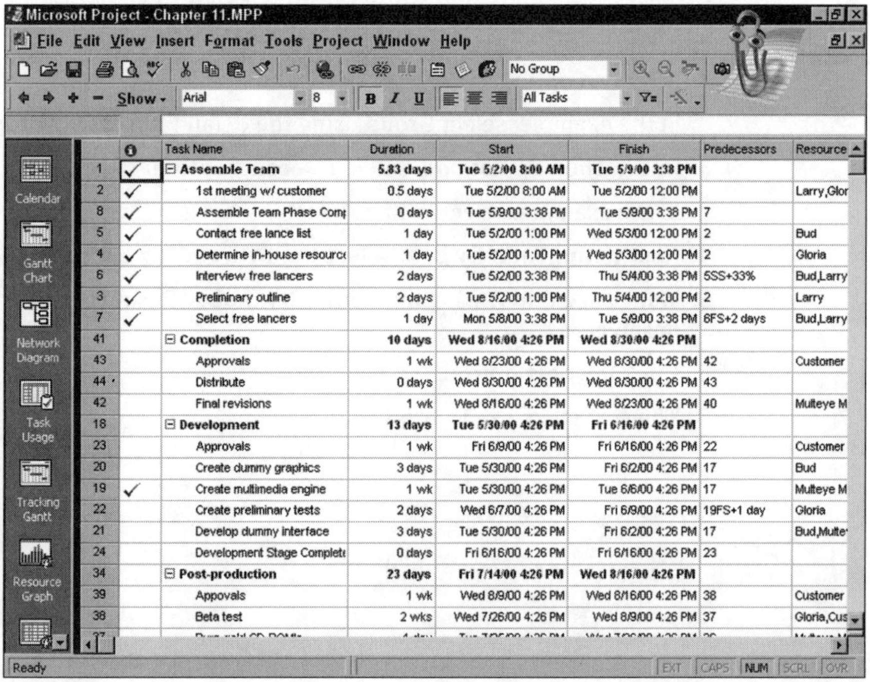

Figure 11-14:
The Sort
command
orders the
names in
ascending
order.

![Microsoft Project screenshot showing sorted task list]

		Task Name	Duration	Start	Finish	Predecessors	Resource
1	✓	⊟ **Assemble Team**	**5.83 days**	**Tue 5/2/00 8:00 AM**	**Tue 5/9/00 3:38 PM**		
2	✓	1st meeting w/ customer	0.5 days	Tue 5/2/00 8:00 AM	Tue 5/2/00 12:00 PM		Larry,Glor
8	✓	Assemble Team Phase Comp	0 days	Tue 5/9/00 3:38 PM	Tue 5/9/00 3:38 PM	7	
5	✓	Contact free lance list	1 day	Tue 5/2/00 1:00 PM	Wed 5/3/00 12:00 PM	2	Bud
4	✓	Determine in-house resource	1 day	Tue 5/2/00 1:00 PM	Wed 5/3/00 12:00 PM	2	Gloria
6	✓	Interview free lancers	2 days	Tue 5/2/00 3:38 PM	Thu 5/4/00 3:38 PM	5SS+33%	Bud,Larry
3	✓	Preliminary outline	2 days	Tue 5/2/00 1:00 PM	Thu 5/4/00 12:00 PM	2	Larry
7	✓	Select free lancers	1 day	Mon 5/8/00 3:38 PM	Tue 5/9/00 3:38 PM	6FS+2 days	Bud,Larry
41		⊟ **Completion**	**10 days**	**Wed 8/16/00 4:26 PM**	**Wed 8/30/00 4:26 PM**		
43		Approvals	1 wk	Wed 8/23/00 4:26 PM	Wed 8/30/00 4:26 PM	42	Customer
44		Distribute	0 days	Wed 8/30/00 4:26 PM	Wed 8/30/00 4:26 PM	43	
42		Final revisions	1 wk	Wed 8/16/00 4:26 PM	Wed 8/23/00 4:26 PM	40	Multeye M
18		⊟ **Development**	**13 days**	**Tue 5/30/00 4:26 PM**	**Fri 6/16/00 4:26 PM**		
23		Approvals	1 wk	Fri 6/9/00 4:26 PM	Fri 6/16/00 4:26 PM	22	Customer
20		Create dummy graphics	3 days	Tue 5/30/00 4:26 PM	Fri 6/2/00 4:26 PM	17	Bud
19	✓	Create multimedia engine	1 wk	Tue 5/30/00 4:26 PM	Tue 6/6/00 4:26 PM	17	Multeye M
22		Create preliminary tests	2 days	Wed 6/7/00 4:26 PM	Fri 6/9/00 4:26 PM	19FS+1 day	Gloria
21		Develop dummy interface	3 days	Tue 5/30/00 4:26 PM	Fri 6/2/00 4:26 PM	17	Bud,Multe
24		Development Stage Complete	0 days	Fri 6/16/00 4:26 PM	Fri 6/16/00 4:26 PM	23	
34		⊟ **Post-production**	**23 days**	**Fri 7/14/00 4:26 PM**	**Wed 8/16/00 4:26 PM**		
39		Approvals	1 wk	Wed 8/9/00 4:26 PM	Wed 8/16/00 4:26 PM	38	Customer
38		Beta test	2 wks	Wed 7/26/00 4:26 PM	Wed 8/9/00 4:26 PM	37	Gloria,Cus

You see two check boxes at the bottom of the Sort dialog box. The first is unchecked by default. The second is checked by default. With these defaults, Microsoft Project doesn't reassign ID numbers to tasks when you sort them. And all sorts will keep subtasks within their summary tasks.

After you finish reviewing the sort, press Shift+F3 to restore the default sort order.

Sorting with multiple fields

The Sort command lets you order information by multiple criteria. An example of a multiple field sort is ordering groceries by category and then by price. The first criterion is ordering by category in ascending alphabetical order, such as fruit, produce, vegetable, and so on. The second is ordering the items in each category by cost in descending order, such as bananas at 49 cents a pound, oranges at 39 cents a pound, and apples at 28 cents a pound. (You can tell how often I buy the groceries in my family!)

Using the example, sort all the resource groups alphabetically in ascending order and sort all the individual resources by their standard rates in descending order. First, you need to change to the Resource Sheet view, so select the Resource Sheet icon on the view.

To sort the resources:

1. **Choose Project⇨Sort⇨Sort By.**

2. **Select an option in the Sort By list box.**

   In the example, select Group using the default Ascending order.

3. **In the Then By list box, select a second option.**

   In the example, select Initials.

4. **Next to the Then By box, select the Descending option.**

5. **Make sure that the Permanently Renumber Resources check box is deselected.**

6. **Click the Sort button.**

   The sort looks like Figure 11-15.

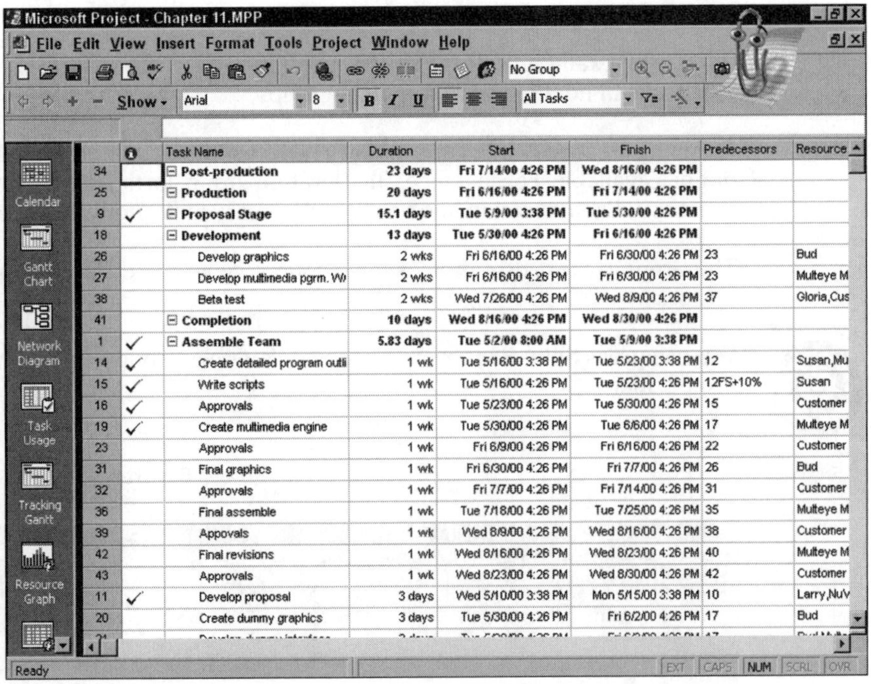

Figure 11-15:
The Sort
command
has ordered
the
resource
groups in
ascending
alphabetical
order. The
resources
within each
group are
ordered by
initials in
descending
order.

Grouping Tasks and Resources

Another way to assess your project as a whole and in parts is by using the
Grouping function. Grouping enables you to look at your tasks or resources in
groups that you define. Grouping clusters the information the way you want
it, much like sorting, but adds the function of summary information about
each group.

Grouping gives you a quick way of checking on your project's tasks by
enabling you to compare task information that shares some value with other
task information. For example, find out what tasks are critical (necessary
to be completed on time in order for the project to finish on time) and noncritical. To find critical tasks, follow these steps:

1. **Using the View bar, change to a task view.**

   In the example, change to the Task Sheet view by clicking More Views.
   Then select Task Sheet and click the Apply button.

2. **Click the down arrow in the Group By text box on the Standard toolbar (see Figure 11-16).**

3. Select a Group.

In the example, select Critical. The Task Sheet view changes to show all tasks in noncritical and critical groups.

Grouping creates a series of summary tasks with information sorted into the options available. For instance, the Duration group sorts tasks by common durations. Each duration has a unique Summary task such as Duration :0 Days.

The Group By text box choices for resource views are different than they are for tasks.

You can press Shift+F3 to return to the default No Group setting for the Project file.

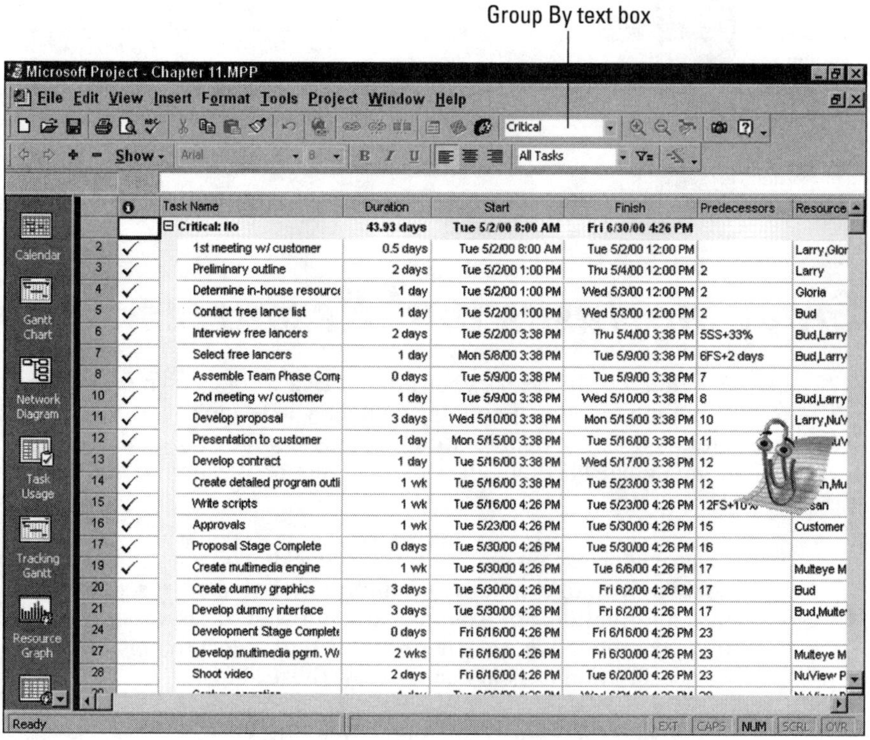

Group By text box

Figure 11-16:
The Group by function provides summary information in yellow at the top of each group.

Part IV
Refining a Project

The 5th Wave   By Rich Tennant

" RIGHT NOW I'M KEEPING A LOW PROFILE. LAST NIGHT I CRANKED IT ALL UP AND BLEW OUT THREE BLOCKS OF STREET LIGHTS."

In this part . . .

Now you focus on the endgame of the project plan, the final moments before project commencement. This involves a review of the original project scope and goals and a comparison of those early expectations with the current status. In this part, you learn to optimize your project plan, resolve cost and work overallocations, and level resource conflicts. You find out how to identify the critical path and how to crash the project's schedule.

This is where the fruit of all your efforts begins to show.

Chapter 12

Setting Budgets and Viewing Costs

● ●

In This Chapter

▶ Finding work and cost discrepancies

▶ Analyzing cost estimate problems

▶ Reducing costs

● ●

*H*ere's a wild assumption: I bet you aren't gifted at pulling money or a
rabbit out of a hat (unless your project is starting a school for magi-
cians). Even so, as a project manager, you can find money where no one else
knows it exists, and you can keep the rabbits from eating the green stuff. In
project management lingo, this magic is called *cost control.*

Suppose you've determined the tasks, created the links, set the durations,
and assigned the costs to your project. The start date of your first project
task is about to occur. In this chapter and the next, you find out how to do
the final tweaking of your project to prepare for the onset of reality. To begin,
you get rid of some unsightly bulges around the waist — excessive costs.

Setting Costs

Microsoft Project enables you to budget your project in two ways— *top-down*
estimating and *bottom-up* estimating. Top-down estimating is a quick way to
add cost information to your project. But speed sacrifices the opportunity for
accuracy that the other method of estimating costs — bottom-up estimating —
provides.

Bottom-up estimating of costs allows you to set hourly rates for resources
and to set fixed costs (such as contracts) for individual tasks. This kind of
detailed cost estimation gives you much more control throughout the project. In this chapter, I assume you want to get down into the trenches of
making a project cost-controllable, so bottom's up!

Microsoft Project defines costs as either resources with rates that you assign to a task or as fixed costs that you assign to a task. A common example of a resource rate is a cost-per-hour for laborers. An example of a fixed rate for a task is a contract fee, such as the price a writer may charge for authoring a screenplay. By using these two approaches — resource rates and fixed costs — you can estimate controllable costs for your project. You set resource rates and fixed costs by using the Resource Sheet view, which I discuss in the following section.

Using the Resource Sheet view

The Resource Sheet view provides most of the basics for estimating and controlling resource costs. If you haven't already done so, check it out by clicking the Resource Sheet View icon on the view bar.

If you're just starting your project, the first thing you need to do is to enter some resource names, such as those in Figure 12-1. After you create a resource, you can change it as much as you want. As you scroll horizontally across the sheet, notice that Microsoft Project has added a number of default values to your resource. For example, unless you change it, Project assumes that the resource is performing work as opposed to being some kind of material.

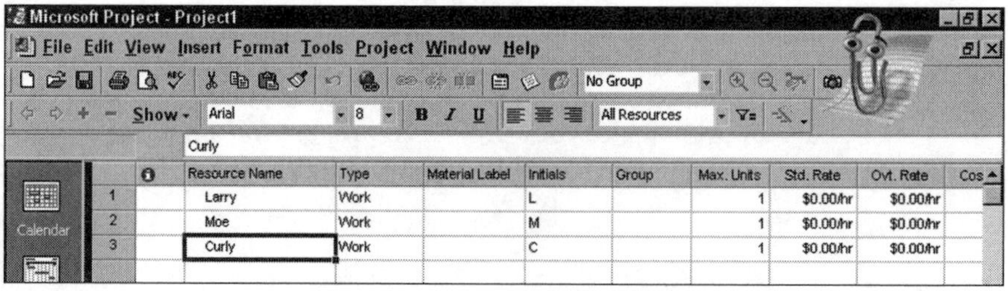

Figure 12-1:
Microsoft Project automatically assigns a number of default characteristics to a resource.

Resource types are usually either people performing work or materials being, well, materials. Microsoft Project assigns a default value of work to the resource type. You can change the resource to material easily.

Change a resource to a material by simply clicking the downward-pointing arrow in the Type column and selecting the Material option. After making such a change, the default settings change for that resource (see Figure 12-2).

Figure 12-2:
Microsoft
Project sets
other
default
values for
material
resources.

			Type	Material Label	Initials	Group	Max. Units	Std. Rate	Ovt. Rate	Cost/Use	Accrue At	Base Calen ▲
		1	Material ▼		L			$0.00		$0.00	Prorated	
Calendar		2	Work		M		1	$0.00/hr	$0.00/hr	$0.00	Prorated	Standard
		3	Work		C		1	$0.00/hr	$0.00/hr	$0.00	Prorated	Standard

Scrolling across the Resource Sheet view horizontally reveals that the sheet provides columns for standard hourly and overtime rates. You can modify when in the task assignments the costs will accrue and you can assign a standard, night shift, or 24-hour calendar.

If you know that your resource plans to change its hourly rate sometime during the project or that the resource's availability is different than the standard calendar or the other calendar choices, you can assign custom values to resources in the Resource Information dialog box. You can access the Resource Information dialog box by double-clicking a resources row in the resource sheet.

The following section explains the Resource Information dialog box in greater detail.

Customizing resource values

If you need to set custom cost values for a specific resource, a good place to perform your work is in the resource's Resource Information dialog box. To set custom values, follow these steps:

1. **Double-click in any cell within a particular resource's row in the Resource Sheet.**

   The Resource Information dialog box for that specific resource appears.

2. **Click the appropriate tab to make detail changes to the resource.**

   For instance, if you want to assign a changing hourly rate to the resource, click the Costs tab. You can set changing rates for hourly labor by entering an effective date for the change and then entering the new rates, as shown in Figure 12-3.

The Resource Information dialog box provides you the opportunity to make a number of adjustments to your resource. For example, by selecting the Working Time tab, you can set a unique work schedule for the resource. I tell you more about setting work schedules in Chapter 5. The default setting for resource costs is prorated. This means that resource costs are spread over their entire usage. You can change the cost from prorated to Start or End in the Costs tab of the dialog box. If you select Start, the resource cost is assessed at the beginning of its usage. By selecting End, the cost is not assessed until the resource has finished.

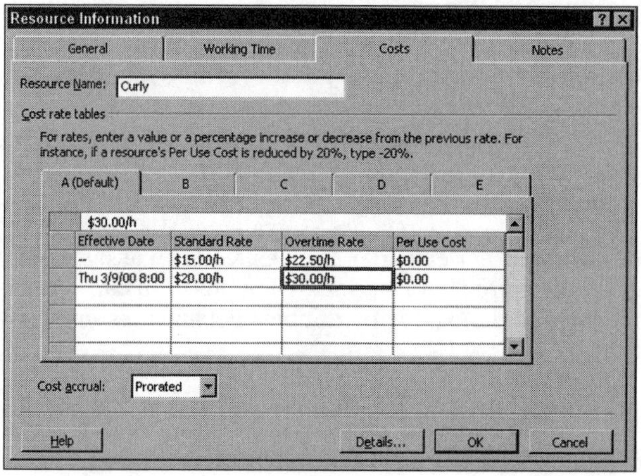

Figure 12-3:
The Resource Information dialog box enables you to customize resource values.

Controlling Costs in an Existing Project

For this chapter, I've provided a sample project file called Chapter 12.MPP in which you can make last-minute cost and work improvements to a project before its project start date. You can use this Project file for checking out Microsoft Project's cost-controlling features, or you can, of course, use your own Project file. I provide particular steps to follow on this file in this chapter, so that you can make sure that you're doing everything just the right way. When you open the sample file, you see a screen like the one shown in Figure 12-4.

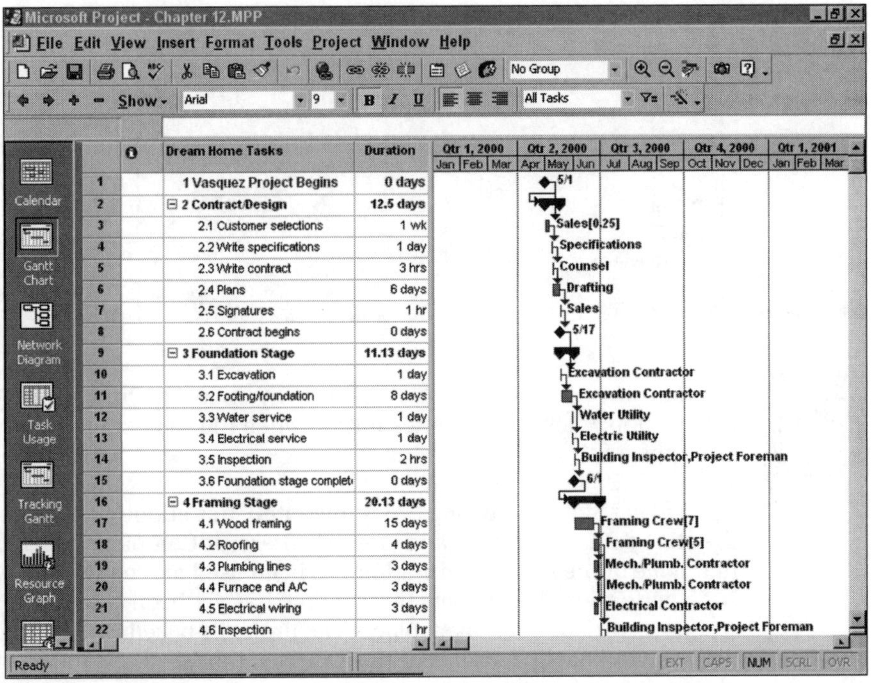

Figure 12-4:
The sample
file for
Chapter 12.

Cost and Work

You should check the pulse of your project occasionally, even before it's born. One of the quickest ways to get an overall summary view of the project is by viewing project statistics. The Project Statistics dialog box gives you an up-to-the-moment analysis of your project's relationship to the baseline estimate. To view statistics, follow these steps:

1. **Ensure that the Tracking toolbar, shown in Figure 12-5, is visible.**

   If the toolbar isn't visible, then choose <u>V</u>iew⇨<u>T</u>oolbars⇨Tracking.

2. **Click the Statistics button on the Tracking toolbar.**

   The Project Statistics dialog box appears, as shown in Figure 12-6.

Figure 12-5:
The
Tracking
toolbar.

Figure 12-6:
Check out
the Project
Statistics
dialog box
to see
statistics
about your
project.

Project Statistics for 'Chapter 12.MPP'	? ✕

	Start	Finish
Current	Mon 5/1/00 8:00 AM	Wed 8/2/00 10:00 AM
Baseline	Mon 5/1/00 8:00 AM	Thu 7/27/00 9:00 AM
Actual	NA	NA
Variance	0d	4.13d

	Duration	Work	Cost
Current	67.25d	1,908h	$59,175.00
Baseline	63.13d	1,708h	$57,175.00
Actual	0d	0h	$0.00
Remaining	67.25d	1,908h	$59,175.00

Percent complete:
Duration: 0%   Work: 0%

Close

TIP

Another way to access this dialog box is by choosing Project⇨Project Information. Click the Statistics button when the Project Information dialog box appears.

The Project Statistics dialog box shows statistics about your project, such as the start date, finish date, and cost. The Percent Complete panel indicates that none of the project's duration has been used and none of its work has been performed. This means that no time has yet been consumed and no resource work has yet taken place. The project's baseline duration was set at 63.13 days. Since the setting of the baseline, the latest estimated duration has changed to 67.25 days.

The Work and Cost columns show additional warnings. The baseline estimate of work was 1,708 hours. The estimate has escalated to 1,908 hours. The baseline cost was $57,175, and the latest estimate is $59,175. These statistics tell you that the project plan is over budget. You need to find the culprit or culprits and take $2,000 out of their piggy banks.

After you finish checking out the Project Statistics dialog box, click the Close button. Then close the Tracking toolbar by right-clicking anywhere in it and clicking Tracking on the shortcut menu. (If a toolbar is open, clicking its name on the shortcut menu toggles it closed.)

View Detailed Work and Cost Estimates

Finding the overages of work and costs is easy in the Task Usage view. This view shows tasks grouped with their assigned resources:

1. **Click the Task Usage icon on the view bar.**

   The Task Usage view appears. The default table for this view is the Usage table.

2. **Choose View➪Table: Usage➪Work.**

   The Work table appears.

3. **Scroll down to display the stages and their subtasks.**

   If you're using the Chapter 12.MPP practice file, scrolling down displays the Framing Stage and its subtasks.

4. **Drag the vertical bar separating the table and the chart to the right until the Variance column is fully exposed, as shown in Figure 12-7.**

   Doing so gives you the opportunity to compare actual work to the baseline estimate.

To simplify the work of viewing the Work view, use a filter. In the Filter list box on the formatting toolbar, select Work Overbudget. Now, two tasks and their summary tasks remain, as shown in Figure 12-8.

TIP

If you would rather highlight the overbudgeted work, choose Project➪ Filtered for➪More Filters. In the More Filters dialog box, choose Work Overbudget and then click the Highlight button.

The Wood framing task estimate has 120 hours more labor than was originally predicted. The Roofing task estimate has 80 hours more labor.

Figure 12-7:
In the Task Usage view, the Work table lists all tasks, resources, and baseline work assigned to them.

Task Name	Work	Baseline	Variance	Details		W	T	F	S	S
16 ⊟ **Framing Stage**	**1,074 hrs**	**874 hrs**	**200 hrs**	Work			10.5h	56h		
17 ⊟ Wood framing	840 hrs	720 hrs	120 hrs	Work			10.5h	56h		
Framing Crew	*840 hrs*	*720 hrs*	*120 hrs*	Work			10.5h	56h		
18 ⊟ Roofing	160 hrs	80 hrs	80 hrs	Work						
Framing Crew	*160 hrs*	*80 hrs*	*80 hrs*	Work						
19 ⊟ Plumbing lines	24 hrs	24 hrs	0 hrs	Work						
Mech./Plumb. Cor.	*24 hrs*	*24 hrs*	*0 hrs*	Work						
20 ⊟ Furnace and A/C	24 hrs	24 hrs	0 hrs	Work						
Mech./Plumb. Cor.	*24 hrs*	*24 hrs*	*0 hrs*	Work						
21 ⊟ Electrical wiring	24 hrs	24 hrs	0 hrs	Work						
Electrical Contrac	*24 hrs*	*24 hrs*	*0 hrs*	Work						
22 ⊟ Inspection	2 hrs	2 hrs	0 hrs	Work						
Building Inspector	*1 hr*	*1 hr*	*0 hrs*	Work						
Project Foreman	*1 hr*	*1 hr*	*0 hrs*	Work						
23 Framing stage complete	0 hrs	0 hrs	0 hrs	Work						
24 ⊟ **Finishing Stage**	**674 hrs**	**674 hrs**	**0 hrs**	Work						
25 ⊟ Wallboard	200 hrs	200 hrs	0 hrs	Work						
Wallboard Crew	*200 hrs*	*200 hrs*	*0 hrs*	Work						
26 ⊟ Stairway	32 hrs	32 hrs	0 hrs	Work						
Finish Carpenters	*32 hrs*	*32 hrs*	*0 hrs*	Work						
27 ⊟ Painting	320 hrs	320 hrs	0 hrs	Work						

While you're in the Work Overbudget filter, you may want to look at the Cost Table Sheet view by choosing View➪Table➪Cost. This table illustrates the variance between baseline cost and total cost. The filtered Cost table appears, as shown in Figure 12-9.

The Wood framing task is estimated to cost $1,200 more than was set as the baseline. The Roofing task is estimated to cost $800 more than its baseline.

After finding all the problems, you're ready to chase after the solutions. To prepare to fix problems, however, you should ensure that you're in the right view. Make sure that all tasks are visible (by choosing F3 for the All Tasks filter) and view your project in Gantt Chart view.

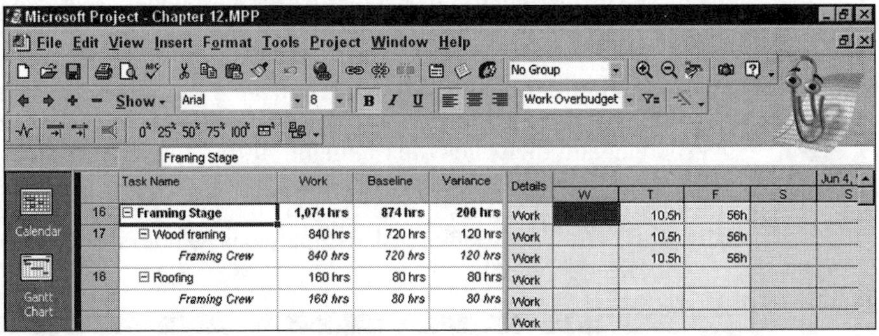

Figure 12-8:
Microsoft Project filters display a subtask with its summary task.

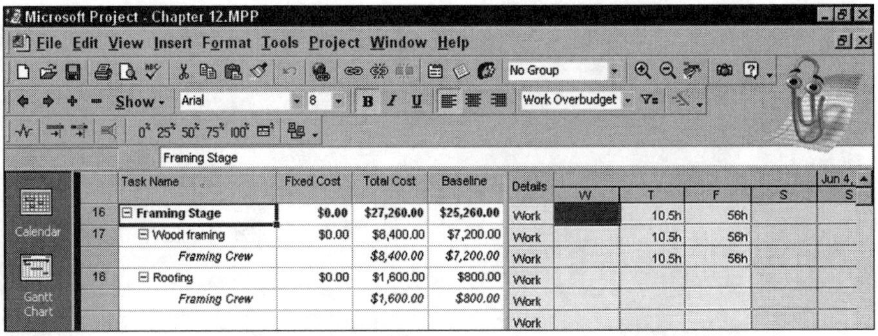

Figure 12-9:
Like the filtered Work Table Sheet view, the filtered Cost Table Sheet view shows overbudget tasks and their summary tasks.

Reducing Costs

Using Microsoft Project, you can resolve cost discrepancies any number of ways. In this section, I show you one way.

Use the Task form in a split view to make the correction:

1. **In the Gantt view, choose <u>W</u>indow➪<u>S</u>plit.**

   The Split view appears.

2. **Choose <u>V</u>iew➪Ta<u>b</u>le: Entry➪<u>C</u>ost.**

   The Cost table replaces the Entry table in the upper window.

3. **Drag the vertical separator bar to expose the Cost table so that it includes Variance.**

4. **Scroll and select the desired task.**

   In the Chapter 12.MPP example, scroll and select the Wood framing task.

5. **Click the Goto Selected Task button on the standard toolbar.**

6. **If necessary, click the Zoom Out button on the standard toolbar to show the entire task.**

   In the Chapter 12.MPP example, if necessary, click the Zoom Out button to show the entire Wood framing task's Gantt bar. The screen should look like Figure 12-10.

If the Units column in the lower window shows percentages, you can switch to decimal numbers by choosing <u>T</u>ools➪<u>O</u>ptions. Select the Schedule tab. In the Sh<u>o</u>w Assignment Units As: box, select Decimal.

To reduce a task's cost, change the makeup of resources as follows:

1. **In the lower-left pane, select the units associated with the task.**

   In the Chapter 12.MPP example, select the units associated with the Framing Crew resource.

2. **Change the units.**

   In the Chapter 12.MPP example, change the units from 7 to 4.

3. **In the Work column, replace the work hours.**

   For example, replace 840h with 480h.

4. **To add a resource, select the next free space in the Resource Name column.**

   For example, select the free space below the Framing Crew resource.

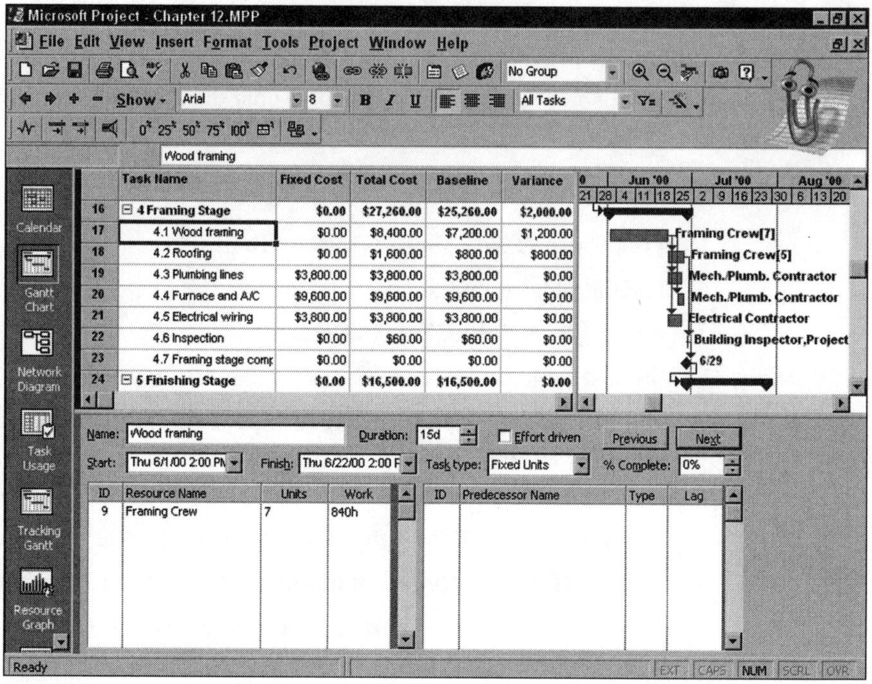

Figure 12-10:
The triple
view gives
you a read-
ing cost,
Gantt bar
placement,
and task
details.

5. **Click the down arrow and select an additional resource.**

   For example, select Day Labor.

6. **Type a unit or units for the additional resource.**

   For example, type **3** in the Units column for Day Labor.

7. **Type hours in the Work column for the additional resource.**

   For example, type **360h** in the Work column for Day Labor.

8. **Click OK.**

   If you're using the Chapter 12.MPP example, the screen should look like
   Figure 12-11.

The changes appear in the Cost table. The added resources are registered
next to the Gantt bar. (If necessary, scroll the Gantt chart horizontally to
expose the resource names.)

You can reduce costs in more ways than I mention here. For example, another
way to reduce costs is to reschedule work. By changing the work calendar,
you can avoid paying overtime. I discuss rescheduling work in Chapter 16.

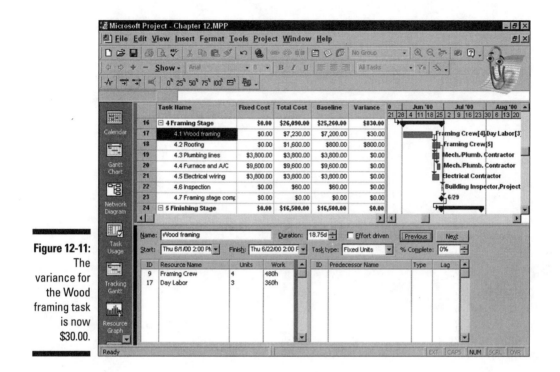

Figure 12-11:
The
variance for
the Wood
framing task
is now
$30.00.

Chapter 13

Getting Your Plan Ready for Reality

· ·

In This Chapter

▶ Correcting scheduling errors

▶ Finding overused resources

▶ Reconciling overallocations

▶ Tightening up the project timeline

· ·

*O*ne of the more fascinating stages of project management is the time just before the project start date. You have all the pieces fashioned in relative order. Some things are just as you had expected, others are slightly different, and some are out in left field.

In these predawn hours before your project meets the light of day, you have the opportunity to walk around it and look up close and from a few steps back to marvel at its strengths and to search for its potential weaknesses. And you have a final chance to make improvements that may make all the difference between success and something less.

Don't be too bothered if everything isn't trim and perfect. By the time you reach the project's start date, it's not unusual for the plan to have a little bulge around the belt. Perhaps the schedule has become longer than originally anticipated. Maybe some resources are overused and others are underused. And a bug or two in the task relationships shouldn't be a surprise.

Quite often, the most challenging task of project management is remembering and using your original goals — simply doing what you said you were going to do. Ninety-nine out of a hundred times, the best course of action is the one you spent all that time planning in the first place. In this chapter, you discover the many ways Microsoft Project can help you analyze and modify your schedule to ensure that you achieve your project's goals and objectives.

For your convenience, I've made a practice file that needs a little tweaking to prepare it for the real world called Chapter 13.MPP. You can use your own project instead of the practice file, or you can open your existing Project file and the practice file.

Determining Overallocated Resources

The term *overallocated* is very real to anyone who owns a checkbook. The term is also usually associated with things such as antacids and rapid heartbeat. In project management, overallocation is also very real and can cause some big headaches, mostly yours.

One way to determine whether any of your project's tasks are causing an overallocation is by looking in one of the resource views. For example, select the Resource Usage icon on the view bar. The Resource Usage view appears, as shown in Figure 13-1. A resource that Microsoft Project identifies as having more tasks than time to do them is marked in the information column with a yellow exclamation point indicator. This overallocation alert indicator means that a resource needs to be leveled. In Figure 13-1, Microsoft Project has marked the Drafting task for leveling.

In project management, to *level* means just what the word implies. A resource is all bunched up with task responsibilities — to the extent that the resource has more task responsibilities than hours to do them in. Microsoft Project suggests that you stretch out the tasks associated with the resource so that it can be more evenly allocated over time.

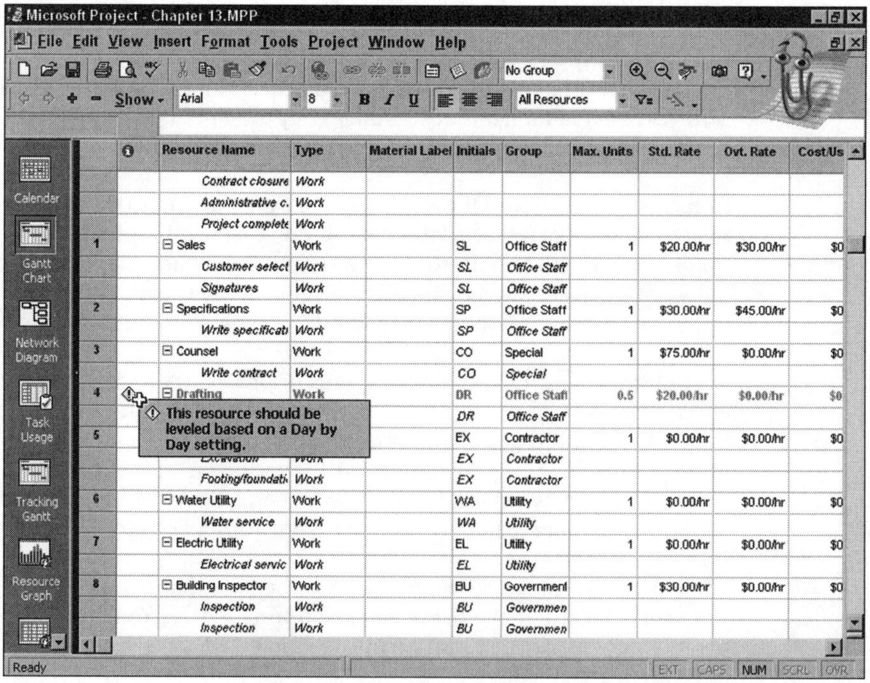

Figure 13-1: The overallocation alert often happens when you are modifying a schedule and consolidating or moving tasks.

A common example of an overallocated resource is an employee who is assigned two large jobs at the same time. Something has to give. The employee can do one of these things:

✔ Take work home evenings and weekends (working overtime or changing working time or both)

✔ Request extra assistance (additional resources)

✔ Ask to be relieved of some of the duty (task reduction)

✔ Ask for extended deadlines (resource leveling)

The above list encompasses common solutions to overallocation; of those, however, only the last, requesting an extended deadline, is leveling. When Microsoft Project suggests leveling an overallocation, it's offering this solution because it can do the leveling for you automatically. (You have to work out all the other solutions.) Leveling is often the least desirable solution to an overallocation problem. You don't want deadlines extended if, for example, your project has to be ready on a certain date.

A Resource Allocation View

You need to find out how many resources are having allocation problems and the severity of the problems. The best way to do your sleuth work is with a combination view.

Maybe the easiest and fastest way to get a bead on resource allocation problems is by using the Resource Allocation view in Microsoft Project. You can access this view by using the resource management toolbar:

1. **Right-click in the toolbar area.**

   The toolbar menu appears.

2. **Choose Resource Management from the toolbar menu.**

3. **Click the Resource Allocation View button on the far left.**

   The Resource Allocation view appears, as shown in Figure 13-2. In this view, the Resource sheet is in the upper pane and a delayed Gantt chart is in the bottom pane. The delayed Gantt chart shows only the taskbars related to the task selected in the upper pane.

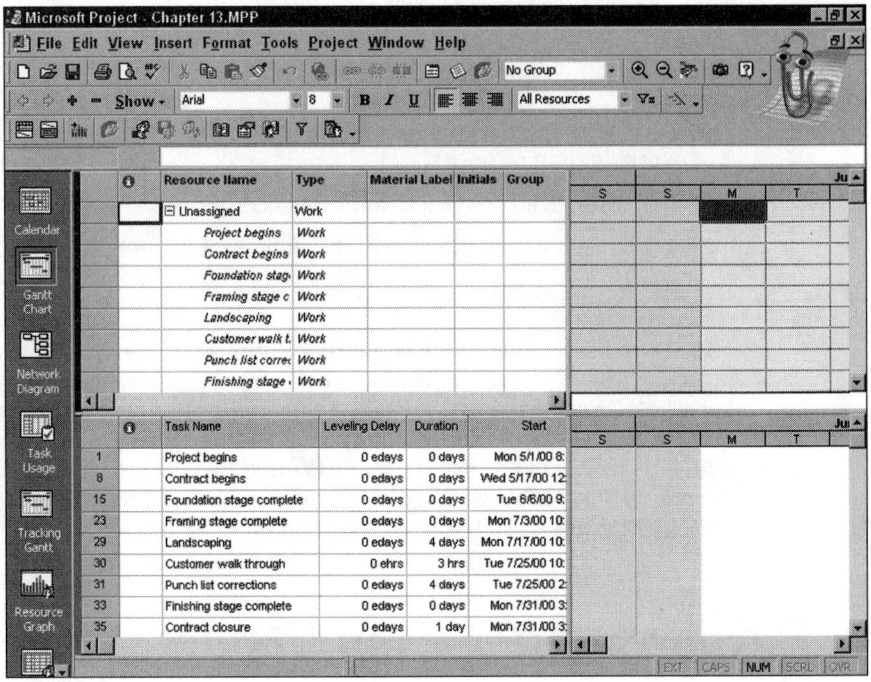

Figure 13-2:
Use the
Resource
Allocation
view to
analyze
resource
problems.

The Resource Allocation view is a pretty sharp way to analyze resource problems. Overallocated resources are designated by red text. In the practice file, drafting isn't the only resource with problems — as you scroll the upper pane, you can see that the framing crew and the mechanical/plumbing contractors have difficulties, too. Analyze the problems one at a time. To do so, follow these steps:

1. **In the upper pane, select an overallocated resource.**

   If you're using the practice example, select the Drafting resource. The delayed Gantt chart displays the task associated with the resource.

2. **Press F6 to activate the lower pane or move to the lower pane by clicking anywhere in it.**

3. **Click the Go to Selected Task button on the standard toolbar.**

   The chart and the table jump to the task dates, as shown in Figure 13-3.

The problem isn't immediately evident by looking at Figure 13-3. The draftsman is working no more than eight hours a day (and unless you're talking about a banker, this seems about right). Your next area of investigation should be to view more of the resource information. To do so, drag the vertical bar to the right until it exposes the Accrue At column, as shown in Figure 13-4.

You can now discern the problem by looking at the Max. Units column for the draftsman resource (shown on line 4). The maximum units for this resource is .5. This means the draftsman is allocated a maximum of four hours per day (assuming an eight-hour day) for each of the six days of the drafting task. The original assumption was that the draftsman would be available for eight hours per day.

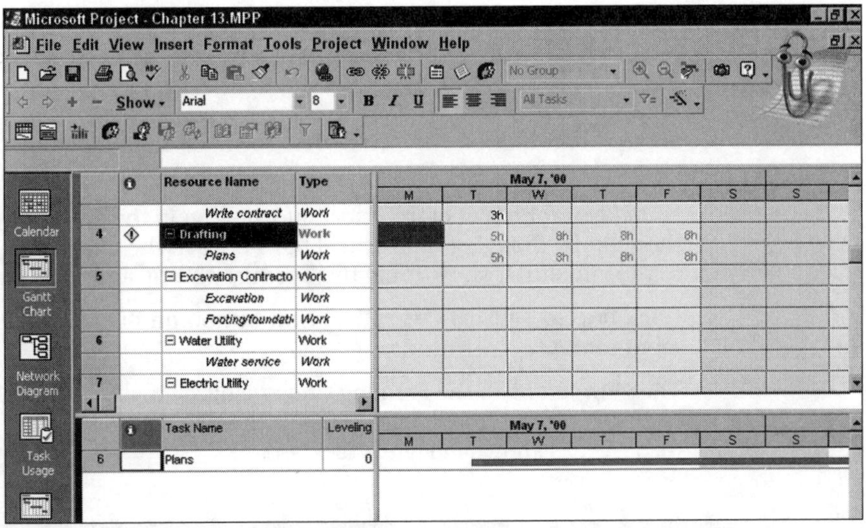

Figure 13-3:
Overalloca-
tion of
resources is
based on
the
resource's
calendar
and units.

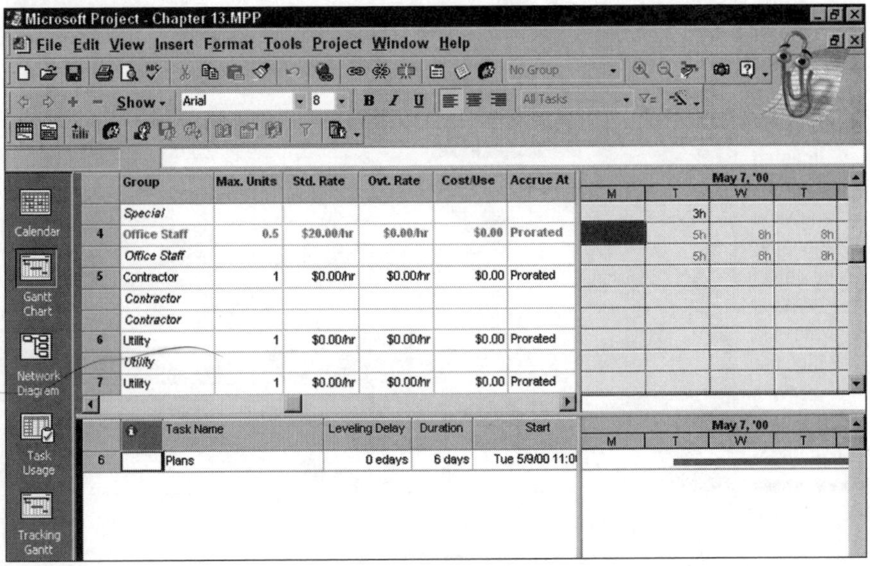

Figure 13-4:
The Max.
Units
column
reveals the
problem.

The Max. Units column shows the maximum utilization of a resource for this particular project. A value of *1* means that 100% of the resource's units can be assigned to the project. A number less than one indicates the amount of time that the resource can devote to your project. When more than one project is occurring and is tapping the same resources, you can best insure against resource overallocation by sharing a resource pool. I discuss resource pools in Chapter 14.

Sometimes overallocation requires a little digging before you can identify it. Microsoft Project helps you find overallocation wherever it may be hiding. To root out such problems, follow these steps:

1. **Set up Combination Resource view for maximum viewing of the Gantt chart.**

   You may want to get more visual information in the graphical column on the right by dragging the vertical bar between the chart and table back to the left until it shows only the Resource Name and Type columns.

2. **Click the Go To Next Overallocation button on the resource management toolbar.**

   The view jumps to the Framing Crew resource if you're using the practice project. The lower pane displays the two tasks associated with the resource, as shown in Figure 13-5.

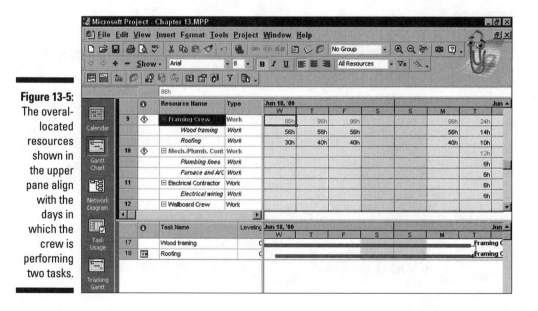

Figure 13-5:
The overallocated resources shown in the upper pane align with the days in which the crew is performing two tasks.

3. **Use the scroll bar to scroll the lower-right pane, if necessary, to expose the resource name and unit assignment for the other overallocated tasks.**

    In this example, you can scroll to expose the Wood framing and Roofing tasks. Notice that the framing crew is responsible for 7 units of the Wood framing task and 5 units of the Roofing task. A unit of 1 equals one person working for one working day. Drag the vertical bar to the right until it exposes the Max. Units column in the upper window. The maximum units for the framing crew is 10, as shown in Figure 13-6. That's the reason for this overallocation.

While you're looking at the Resource Usage details, select Mech./Plumb. Contractor. The problem with this resource is that it's currently assigned 1 maximum unit. The contractor works for a fixed fee. It doesn't matter to you how many people the contractor uses as long as the job is accomplished according to the contract. But because only 1 unit is assigned to the resource, Microsoft Project interprets that the contractor can't perform two tasks at the same time.

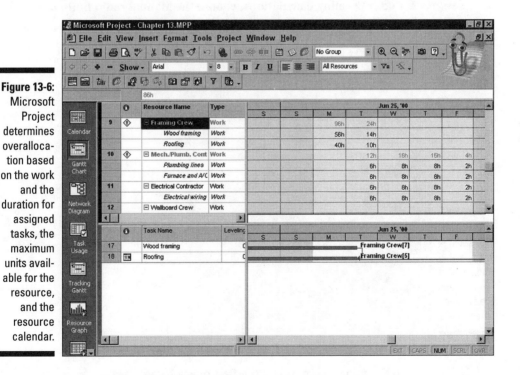

Figure 13-6:
Microsoft Project determines overallocation based on the work and the duration for assigned tasks, the maximum units available for the resource, and the resource calendar.

Correcting Resource Overallocations

You can correct resource overallocations in more than one way. In this section, using the example, you can use three solutions with the resource problems in this project. You can extend duration for the draftsman, add units for the framing crew, and delete a task for the mechanical/plumbing contractor. Each solution is the best one for the circumstances of the resource.

The best way to perform this work is manually, rather than through automatic leveling. You can perform manual leveling in the Gantt Chart view — and you don't need to have a split view either. For more information about views, check out Chapter 6.

To correct resource overallocations manually in the Gantt Chart view:

1. **Choose Tools⇨Resource Leveling.**

   The Resource Leveling dialog box appears.

2. **Under Leveling calculations, choose the Manual radio button.**

   See Figure 13-7. This selection turns off the automatic leveling option.

3. **Click OK.**

4. **Choose Window⇨Split.**

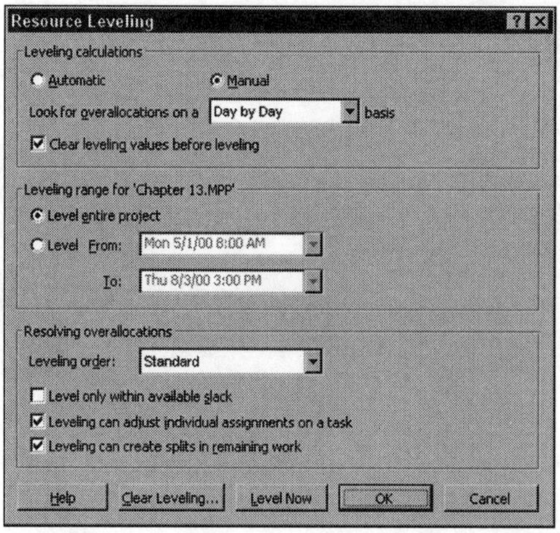

Figure 13-7:
The settings in this dialog box remain intact until you change them again.

5. **In the upper pane, select the first overallocated task.**

   In this example, select the Plans task. The Drafting resource appears in the lower pane.

6. **In the Units column, change the value to correct the overallocation.**

   In this example, change the value from 1 to **.5**. By changing a unit value from 1 to .5, you are saying that the resource is available for this project a maximum of one-half of any working day.

7. **Click OK.**

Scroll through the Gantt chart to expose the entire Plans taskbar and its resource designation. The task levels out by extending the period to 12 days. The Drafting resource limitation is maintained as 0.5 units. The solution was acceptable because adding 6 days to the task doesn't conflict with the successor date. And that's because the successor task is a fixed date later than the 12-day period.

One way to correct overallocation is to manually add resources. In this example, you correct the Framing Crew overallocation not by leveling, but by adding resources to the Framing Crew, as follows:

1. **With any task highlighted, click the Assign Resources button on the Standard toolbar.**

   The Assign Resources dialog box appears.

2. **Scroll through the list and double-click an overallocated resource. In this example, double-click the Framing Crew resource.**

   The Resource Information dialog box appears.

3. **Change the maximum units available by the number in the Units column.**

   In this example, change the value in the Units column from 10 to 12. The task cost doesn't change when you increase the available units because the assigned units remain the same.

4. **Click OK.**

   In this example, the Framing crew overallocation was caused by the same crew performing two tasks (Tasks 17 and 18) at the same time. Seven units were assigned to the Wood framing task and 5 units were assigned to the Roofing task. By increasing the maximum available resource units, you removed the overallocation.

Another way to correct overallocation is by trimming unnecessary tasks. In this chapter's example, you correct the Mechanical/Plumbing Contractor resource overallocation by removing one of two identical tasks. This schedule error comes from an earlier decision to grant both the plumbing and mechanical contracts to the same subcontractor. You aren't changing anything by removing a task because the contractor is responsible for all the crew and related resources. To remove a task, follow these steps:

1. **Highlight the unnecessary task.**

   In this example, highlight the Furnace and A/C task.

2. **Press the Delete key.**

   The resource overallocation is gone.

3. **Choose <u>W</u>indow⇨Remove <u>S</u>plit.**

   The project returns to the default Gantt Chart view.

Crashing the Critical Path

The term *crashing* has a few common uses, but none have anything to do with project management. One common meaning is to run into something, such as crashing a milk cart into a cow. Another meaning was spawned in the 1960s as a term for what you do after a night of partying — not running into a cow but falling on a couch or a floor and sleeping, usually at someone else's groovy pad.

When a project manager crashes, a higher and nobler action is happening (I hope). In project management, *crashing* is doing what's necessary to decrease the total project duration.

Understanding the critical path

So what's a critical path, you ask? Good question. A *critical path* is the series of tasks that determines the completion date of a project. Project management differentiates tasks that are on the critical path from those that aren't. The critical path of the project includes only tasks that have not been performed. For that reason, the critical path becomes smaller as the project progresses.

All the tasks in the Chapter 13.MPP project, for example, are necessary for its completion. Ignore any of them, and the customer will be quick to inform you that the project isn't complete (they have a way of noticing things like missing stairs). Even so, some Chapter 13.MPP project tasks are part of the critical path and some aren't.

To view the current Chapter 13.MPP critical path:

1. **Switch to the Gantt Chart view (if necessary) by choosing Gantt Chart on the view bar.**

   The screen should also be unsplit.

2. **Click the Zoom In or Zoom Out button on the Standard toolbar until the time scale is months over three-day segments.**

   This step makes viewing the whole project easier.

3. **Hold down the Shift key and choose Project⊏>Filtered for: All Tasks⊏>Critical.**

   The screen now displays the entire project with the critical path highlighted in underlined red text (see Figure 13-8).

An example of a noncritical task is the Stairway task. The stairway needs to be completed by the end of the project, but it can float around a little bit without affecting the start or completion of other tasks. To a lesser degree, the same is true of the Roofing task. Its start can be delayed a little bit as long as its finish date doesn't go past the finish date of the Plumbing Lines task.

An example of a critical task is the Excavation task. The start date and finish date of the house excavation directly affect the continuance and timing of successor tasks and, ultimately, the completion date of the project. In another way, the Wallboard task is critical in that its duration has a direct effect on the completion date of the project. If you can find a way of decreasing the Wallboard task's duration without increasing the cost, you would be crashing the critical path.

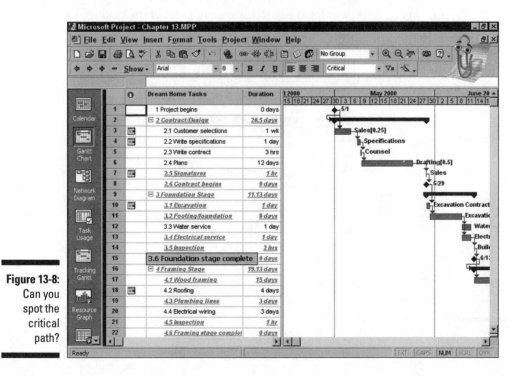

Figure 13-8: Can you spot the critical path?

Scroll the Gantt chart to expose the final task. The Project Complete milestone is August 11. That's a problem. For the sake of the example, suppose your boss would like to have the house finished by August 1. Hey, man, ya wanna crash this pad? Go ahead and work to find ways to decrease the duration of your project! And while you're at it, why not cut off some extra days in case of bad weather?

One, two, three — crash!

Crashing a schedule requires some tough analysis and some pencil sharpening. Ask yourself these three questions:

✔ Is time being used most efficiently?

✔ Can resources be changed without increasing costs?

✔ Does the project have any unnecessary Finish-to-Start relationships?

Using time efficiently

Starting with time efficiency, there's a noticeable way to crash this project's critical path. You can change the construction working calendar. In the construction trades, working six days a week without incurring overtime is common. This practice is especially true in parts of the country with harsh winters. To change the construction calendar:

1. Choose Tools⇨Change Working Time.

The Change Working Time dialog box appears, as shown in Figure 13-9.

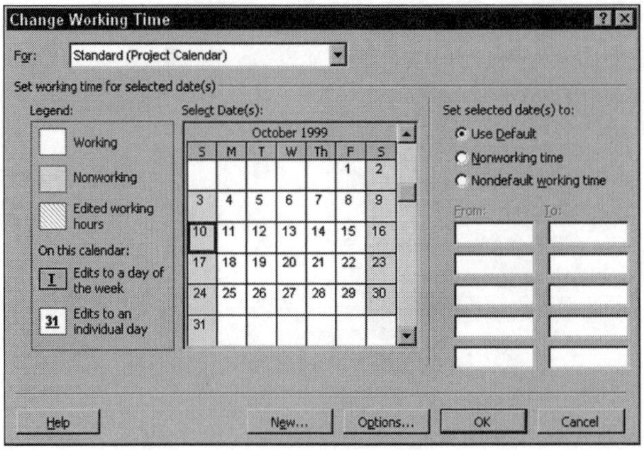

Figure 13-9:
The Change Working Time dialog box is the place to edit the default calendar and resource calendars.

2. **In the For box, select the calendar you want to change.**

   In this example, select the Construction Hours calendar.

3. **Select the heading of the day you want to change.**

   In this example, select the heading of the Saturday column.

4. **In the Set Selected Date(s) To panel, select the Nondefault Working Time option.**

   The Working Time editing area becomes active.

5. **Change the working times from the default settings to other times of your choice.**

   In this example, change the working time to the normal construction hours as set on the other days. Times should be From 7:00 AM To 11:00 AM and From 11:30 AM To 3:30 PM. The Change Working Time dialog box should now look like Figure 13-10.

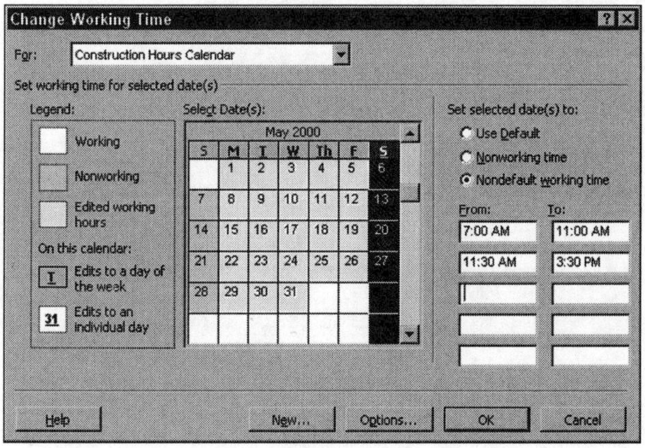

Figure 13-10:
When you change one month's setting, the settings for the entire calendar change.

6. **Click OK.**

   The Project Complete milestone changes to August 4. You're making progress.

Changing resources

Another way to crash the plan is by changing resources. Sometimes this is the simplest and most straightforward solution for the too-much-work-and-too-little-time syndrome. For example, increasing resources sometimes shortens the duration of a task without adding cost. To add resources:

1. **Select a task.**

   In this example, you can add resources to the Painting task.

2. **Click the Assign Resources button on the Standard toolbar.**

   The Assign Resources dialog box appears.

3. **Double-click the resource you want to add to.**

   In this example, double-click the Paint Crew resource.

   The Resource Information dialog box appears, as shown in Figure 13-11. Changes to this dialog box affect the amount of resource units available for a task.

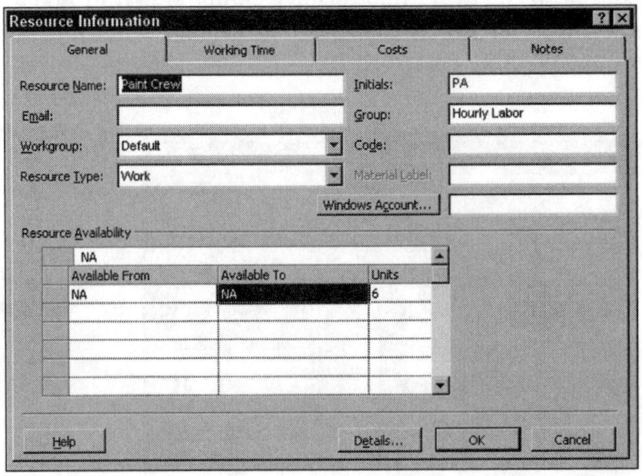

Figure 13-11:
The
Resource
Information
dialog box.

4. **Change the Units and then click OK.**

   In this example, change it to **8**.

5. **In the Resource Assignment dialog box, change the number of assigned units and then click Close.**

   In this example, change it from 4.00 to **8.00**.

   The Gantt chart changes and shows in this example that the Painting task has been reduced from two weeks to one week. In addition, the Project Complete milestone is now July 28.

Eliminating unnecessary Start-to-Finish relationships

Another thing you can do to crash the critical path is to change some task relationships. Some are unnecessarily of the Finish-to-Start variety. The Plumbing Lines task and the Electrical Wiring tasks can be made to finish with their predecessor Wood Framing task. To change task relationships:

1. **Click the Zoom In button on the Standard toolbar to weeks over days.**

   This view makes working on the Gantt chart easier.

2. **Select the task you want to change.**

   In this example, select the Plumbing lines task.

3. **Click the Go to Selected Task button on the Standard toolbar.**

4. **On the Gantt chart, double-click the arrow that touches the task.**

   In this example, double-click the arrow that touches the Plumbing Lines task. The Task Dependency dialog box appears, as shown in Figure 13-12.

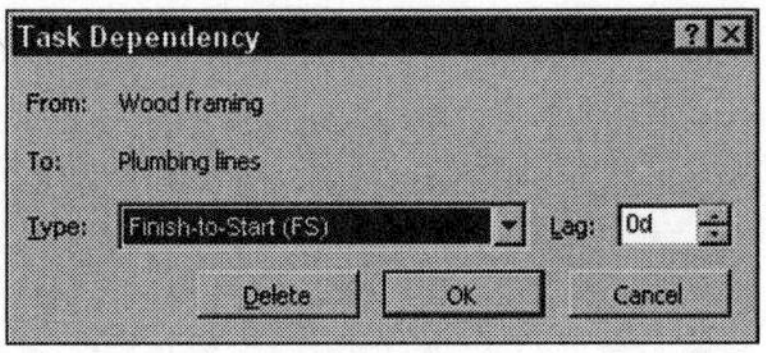

Figure 13-12:
The task dependency should be from Wood Framing to Plumbing Lines.

Task Dependency

From: Wood framing

To: Plumbing lines

Type: Finish-to-Start (FS)   Lag: 0d

Delete   OK   Cancel

5. **Change the task dependency.**

   In this example, change the task dependency to Finish-to-Finish (FF) and then click OK.

6. **Repeat Steps 2 through 5 for other tasks.**

   In this example, repeat Steps 2 through 5 for the Electrical Wiring task.

   You can also drag a task to give it the same Finish date as another task. In this example, drag the Roofing task until it has the same Finish date as the Wood Framing task (6/29/00). The Gantt chart now looks like Figure 13-13. If you make a mistake, choose Edit⇨Undo Drag.

7. **Scroll to the last task, select it, and click the Go to Selected Task button on the Standard toolbar.**

   The Project Complete milestone should say July 26. You're almost there.

Two quick changes will complete the crash. Delete the Contract closure task — it's redundant with Administrative closure. Then change Administrative closure to a one-day duration. The result should look like Figure 13-14. Your project completion date now allows for a week of rain.

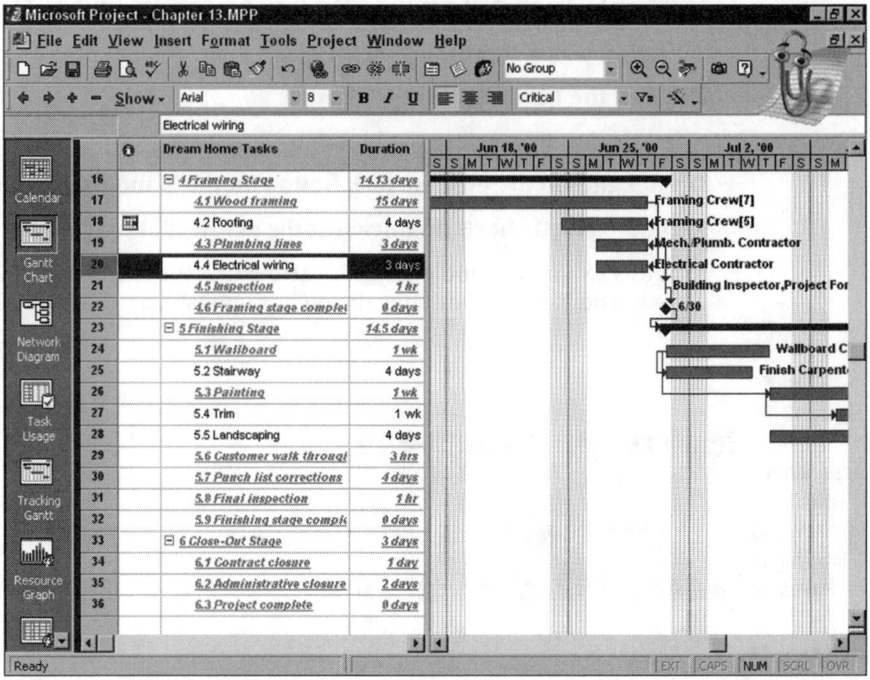

Figure 13-13:
The Gantt
chart offers
point-and-
click visual
tools for
optimizing
task
relationships.

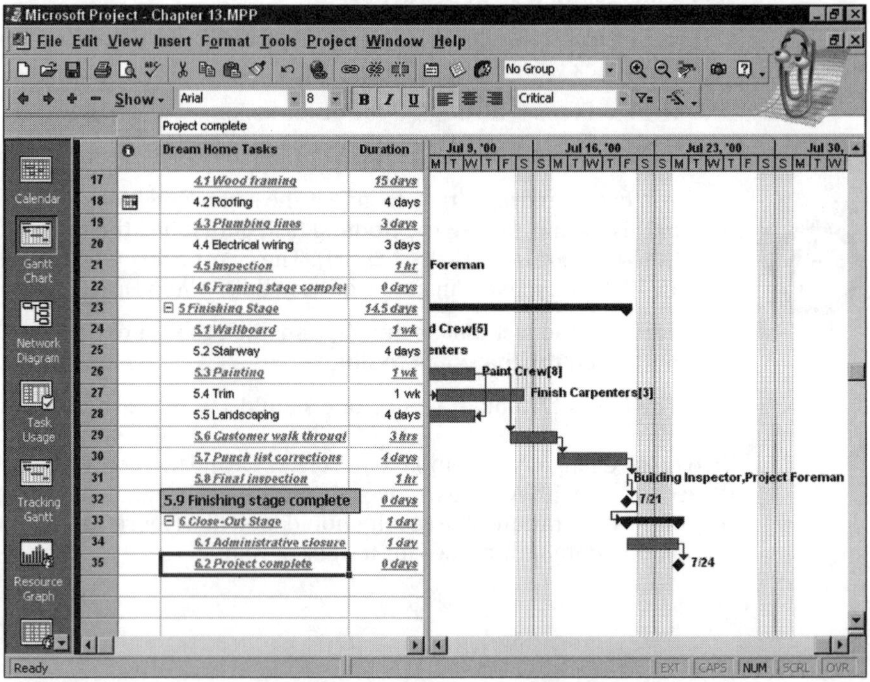

Figure 13-14:
The project
is within the
contract
time
constraints.

Last, update the baseline. To do so:

1. **Choose Tools⇨Tracking⇨Save Baseline.**

   The Save Baseline dialog box appears. Make sure the Save Baseline option is selected.

2. **Click OK.**

You've optimized your plan. Everything is as ready as it can be. Take a break and relax. Come your project's start date, you can walk into the office with a little swagger to your step. This baby's going to fly!

Chapter 14

Making Life Easier by Subdividing and Combining Projects

· ·

In This Chapter

▶ Assembling multiple projects

▶ Using windows for multiple views

▶ Creating multiple views of the same file

▶ Making a workspace

▶ Consolidating projects

▶ Appreciating the value of subprojects

▶ Sorting your project

· ·

So you're not a single-project kind of manager. You have a few balls in the air. It seems as if there are more things to do than there are resources or time to do them. And worse yet, you're not sure whether everything is okay or whether problems are lurking. Simplification sounds very attractive.

Microsoft Project can't make the world slow down, but it can reduce the chances of resource and time collisions. One way it does this is by managing multiple projects. You're about to see some simple ways to hold the reins on projects that would otherwise pull your attention and resources in conflicting directions.

You work with multiple projects in the chapter, so you can start by — you guessed it — opening a few Project files. For your convenience, I've made a small group of practice files that need a little coordinating as multiple projects. These projects are titled Sample1 Chapter 14.MPP, Sample2 Chapter 14.MPP, and Sample3 Chapter 14.MPP. Open them one after another to follow along with the examples in the chapter. For more information about opening the sample files for each chapter, please consult Appendix C.

Using Multiple Open Project Files

To display files, Microsoft Project uses standard Windows conventions, which is the best way to begin using multiple projects. Choose the Windows menu as shown in Figure 14-1. You have four window choices. Unhide appears dimmed because it's unavailable. It becomes available only after Hide is activated. Next, the menu lists Split, which is the default combination view option.

A list of the currently open project files follows these options. You can load as many project files as your computer's memory and storage allow.

Hiding and unhiding

Hiding a file is not the same as closing it. By hiding a file, you remove its name from the Window menu, even though the file remains open. Hide a window as follows:

1. Choose <u>Window</u>⇨*filename.*

Using this chapter's example, choose <u>1</u> Project1. The active window becomes Project1 in full expanded view.

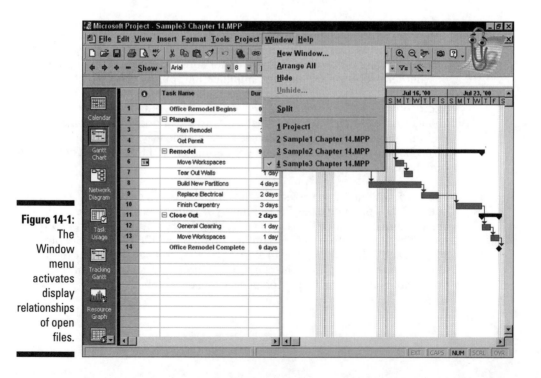

Figure 14-1: The Window menu activates display relationships of open files.

2. **Choose <u>W</u>indow⇨<u>H</u>ide.**

   Project1 disappears.

3. **To view a list of the remaining open Project files, choose <u>W</u>indow on the menu bar.**

   In the example, Project1 has disappeared from the menu and the Unhide option has become active. Projects 2 and 3 are visible in the menu — easily accessible. Exciting, huh?

If you want to always see what windows are currently hidden, follow these steps:

1. **Choose <u>W</u>indow⇨<u>U</u>nhide.**

   The Unhide dialog box appears, as shown in Figure 14-2. This is where you can practice magic and make the hidden file reappear.

2. **Click OK to bring a project out of hiding.**

   For the example, however, you don't need Project1 (after all, it's only a blank file), so just click Cancel.

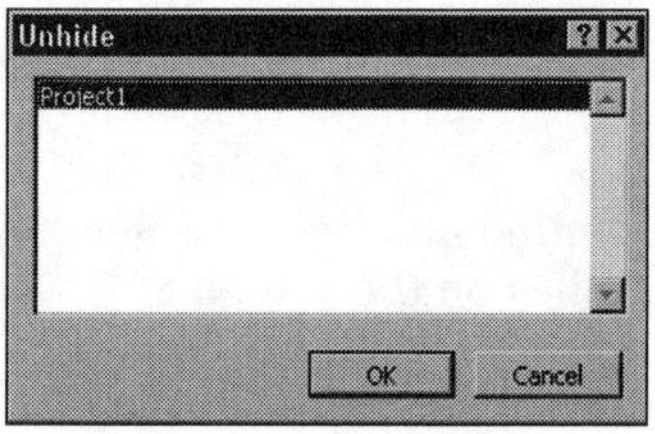

Figure 14-2:
Abracad-
abra! The
mouse is
quicker than
Project1.

Arranging all files

Sometimes, it's useful to simultaneously compare and edit information in a group of files. To do that, you need to put all the unhidden files on the screen at one time. To make the files easier to see, temporarily hide the view bar by right-clicking in the bar and selecting the View Bar option to remove the check mark.

Using the currently unhidden files:

1. **Choose <u>W</u>indow⇨<u>A</u>rrange All.**

   A three-screen display appears, similar to Figure 14-3.

2. **To activate windows, alternately click each window.**

   Each window becomes active as you click it. You can tell that it's active because the title bar changes to a vibrant color.

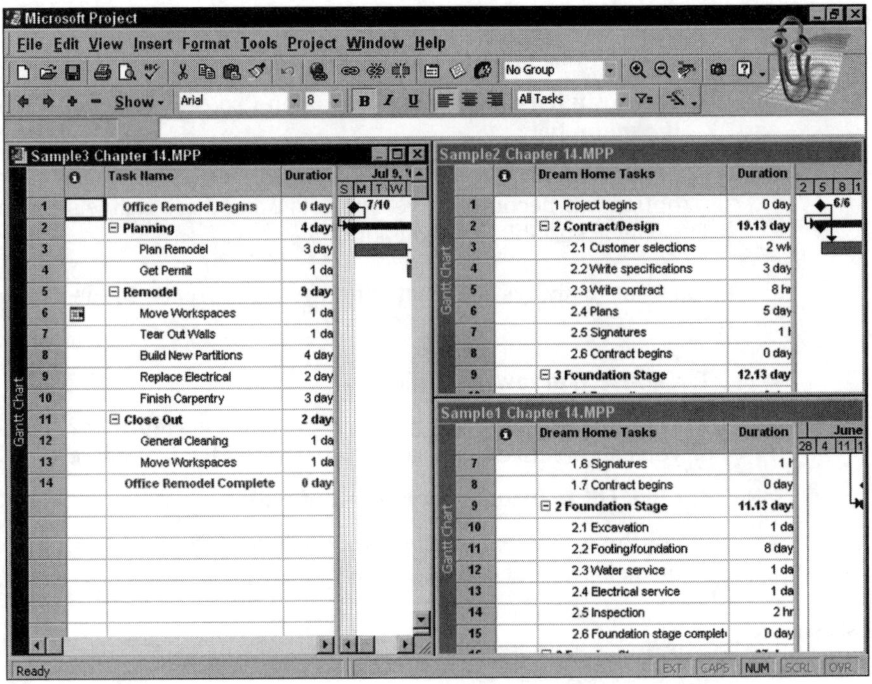

Figure 14-3:
One
example of
information
you can pull
from this
multiple
window
display is
the start
date for all
three
projects.

Although you can open a relatively unlimited number of projects, you can't display an unlimited number of project files on the screen at the same time.

To replace the Arrange All display with a single project display, use the Maximize button in the active window.

You can practice by clicking in the Sample2 Chapter 14 window to make it active and then clicking its Maximize button. The Office Remodel project is now full screen.

Instead of using the Window menu to flip through the full-screen display of unhidden project files, press Ctrl+F6. Each time you do, the screen displays the next project file (as listed in the Window menu).

Building a new window without pane, er, pain

Another nifty standard window feature is the New Window option. With the New Window option, you can create multiple views of the same project. This option acts as a shortcut to various views, and gives you the opportunity to customize combination views.

To illustrate the new window option, it would be helpful to hide two of the currently unhidden project files. Press Ctrl+F6 to display the Sample1 Chapter 14.MPP project file. Choose Window⇨Hide. Repeat to hide Sample2 Chapter 14.MPP. The Sample3 Chapter 14.MPP project file is the active display. All but one of the open Project files are hidden.

You can use the New Window option to create a combination view of the Office Remodel project. To display a combination view, use the following steps:

1. **Choose Window⇨New Window.**

   The New Window dialog box appears, as shown in Figure 14-4.

2. **Click the drop-down arrow on the View list box and select a view.**

   In this example, select Calendar. You're telling Microsoft Project that you want a new window displaying the Calendar view of the Office Remodel project. Because the Gantt Chart view of the Office Remodel project is already loaded, you have two active displays of the same project. What a country! I tell you about Gantt Chart views and Calendar views in Chapter 6.

Figure 14-4: All project files (including the hidden ones) appear in the New Window dialog box.

New Window	? X
Projects:	
Project1	
Sample1 Chapter 14.MPP	
Sample2 Chapter 14.MPP	
Sample3 Chapter 14.MPP	
View:	Gantt Chart
	OK Cancel

3. **Click OK.**

   The Calendar view of the Office Remodel project appears, as shown in Figure 14-5.

After you have two displays of the same project and because all other open project files are currently hidden, you can create that special combination view you've always wanted! Well, at least you've wanted it for the last three minutes. Simply choose Window⇨Arrange All, and the combination view appears, as shown in Figure 14-6. The highlighted bar on the far left of the screen indicates which window is active. Press Ctrl+F6 to activate the other window.

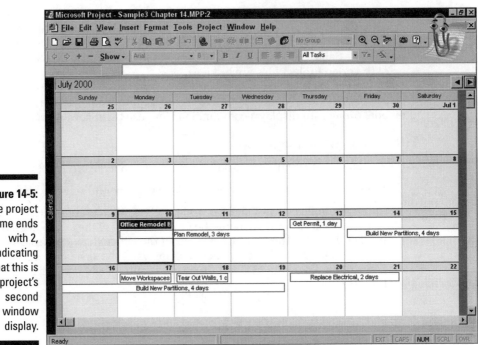

Figure 14-5:
The project
name ends
with 2,
indicating
that this is
the project's
second
window
display.

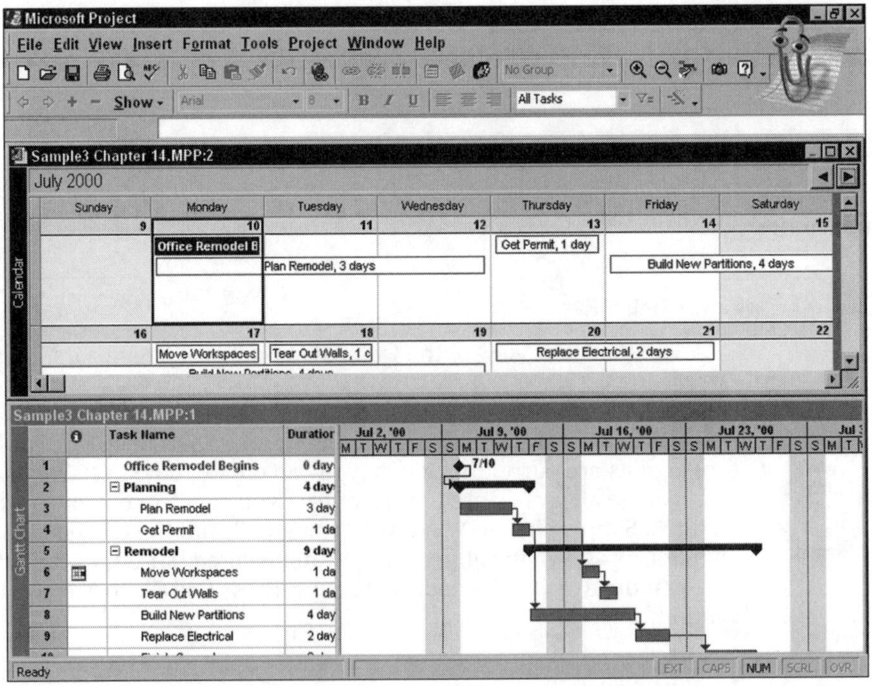

Figure 14-6:
The
combination
view uses
the standard
convention
that allows
one window
to be active
at a time.

Creating a workspace

You can create and save a file that remembers all the files you have opened. This can be helpful for picking up where you left off the day before or for guiding others to sets of information you've grouped for some ingenious purpose.

Create a workspace file of the project files you currently have open. Before you do, however, ensure that Sample1 Chapter 14.MPP and Sample2 Chapter 14.MPP are unhidden (choose Window⇨Unhide to unhide them if necessary).

Now you're ready to create the workspace:

1. **Choose File⇨Save Workspace.**

2. **Type a name in the File Name box.**

   Either use the default name, Resume, or type another one. In either case, the extension for a workspace file is mpw. See Figure 14-7.

3. **Click Save.**

   Project asks if you want to save changes.

4. **Click Yes to save changes.**

   If you're asked the same question for other project files, click Yes for them, too.

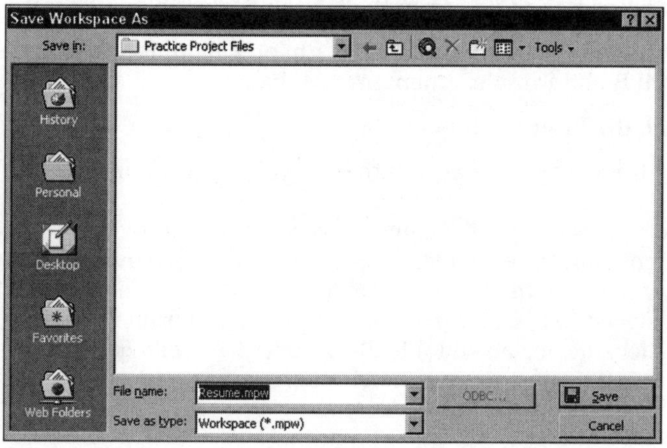

Figure 14-7:
The Workspace file is stored in the same folder as your project files unless you choose otherwise.

Save Workspace As	? X
Save in:	Practice Project Files

File name: Resume.mpw

Save as type: Workspace (*.mpw)

The MPW file contains only a call to reopen the project files; it doesn't contain the project files themselves. If you make any changes to the project files individually, those changes appear the next time you open the workspace.

Consolidating Projects

Microsoft Project offers you the opportunity to consolidate individual project files into a single window. Consolidating files makes it possible for you to manage a number of projects at once, as if they were a single project.

Consolidating a project differs from using multiple windows in one big way. In a consolidated project file, you can use all the information from all the projects as if they were a single project. For example, you can use a filter for the consolidated project that filters all the project files.

For the next example, make sure that you begin with only a new project open, so if any projects are open, close them all and then click the New button. A project, even an unsaved blank one, must be open for you to access the Microsoft Project menu options. If the view bar isn't visible (because you minimized it at an earlier point), you may want to redisplay it. To do so, right-click in the highlighted vertical bar on the left of the screen and select View Bar.

Here are the steps necessary to consolidate projects:

1. **Highlight a blank task name.**

   For this example, highlight blank Task 2.

2. **Choose Insert⇨Project.**

   The Insert Project dialog box appears.

3. **Hold down the Ctrl key and click the Project files you want to insert.**

   In this example, choose Sample1 Chapter 14.MPP, Sample2 Chapter 14.MPP, and Sample3 Chapter 14.MPP.

4. **Click the Insert button.**

   The three files are loaded into Project1, as shown in Figure 14-8.

Each file retains its specific name. Hover your cursor over the indicator icon (in the *i* column) for each file. By hovering the cursor over each indicator, you can determine the name of each inserted project. In contrast, the task name assigned to each inserted project is derived from its project title. A title is not a filename; it's an editable file property. You can edit a title, plus other file information, by choosing File⇨Properties.

Changing consolidated Project file order

After the files are loaded, you can change their order, which affects the manner in which they're displayed in the consolidated view. For example, you may want the Clark House project to follow Office Remodel. To make such a change, follow these steps:

1. **Select a consolidated Project file by clicking its ID.**

   In this example, select the Clark House project row.

2. **Click and hold down the mouse button to drag the consolidated project to a new row.**

   In this example, move the Clark House project to the row below Office Remodel. A gray T-bar appears when you are at a point where you can move the task.

3. **Release the mouse button.**

Protecting consolidated Project files

By default, Microsoft Project allows individual file edits to a consolidated file. Any edits in the consolidated file are automatically reflected in the source file or files. However, you can protect the source files by designating them as read-only. To designate an inserted project file as read-only, double-click the appropriate project indicator. Click the Advanced tab of the Inserted Project Information dialog box, as shown in Figure 14-9. Select the Read Only check box.

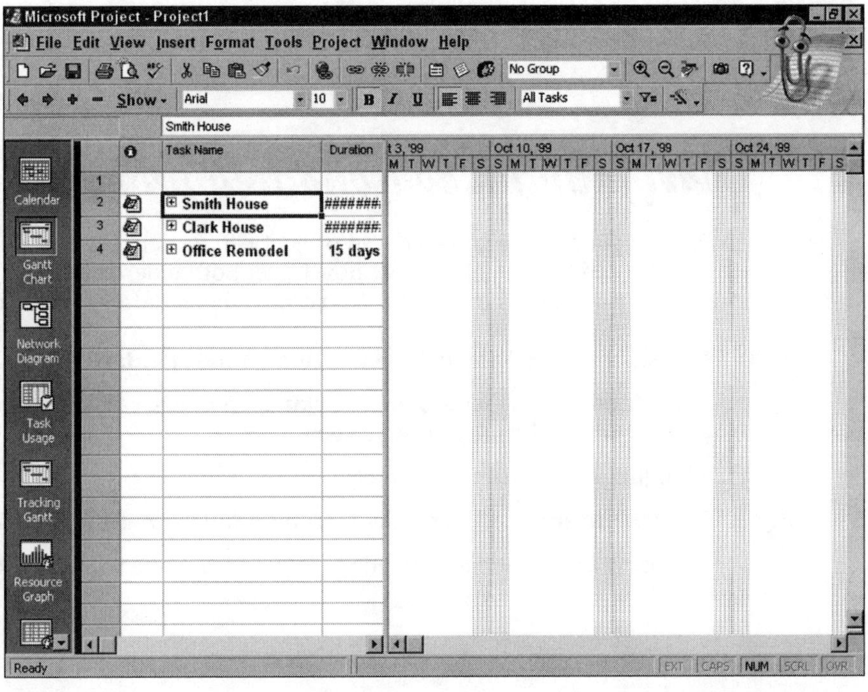

Figure 14-8:
The files are listed in the order in which you loaded them.

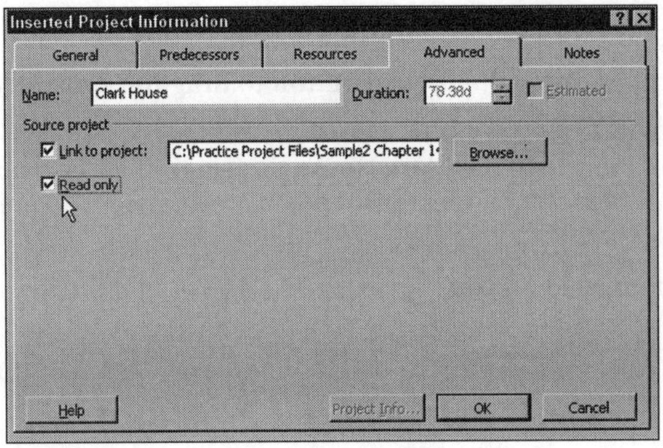

Figure 14-9:
The Inserted
Project
Information
dialog box
allows you
to associate
or dissociate
the source
project file
from the
consolidated
project file.

You can make some files read-only and others read-write. Be careful, though — you can get a big head (or was that big headache?) masterminding all this consolidation stuff.

By default, Microsoft Project attaches source files to the consolidated file. If you want to edit information in the consolidated file without affecting the source file, deselect the Link to Project check box. The Read Only check box dims because you no longer need to write-protect the linked source project. Click OK.

Navigating a consolidated project

As you can imagine, a consolidated project can be very big and bulky when fully exploded. You need to know how to get both macro and mini perspectives. Use these steps to see the big-picture consolidated view more easily:

1. **Click the Goto Selected Task button on the standard toolbar.**

2. **Click the Zoom Out tool on the standard toolbar until the full summary tasks of each of the projects appear.**

3. **Highlight the inserted projects.**

4. **Click the Show All Subtasks button on the formatting toolbar.**

The consolidated file expands to look like the one in Figure 14-10.

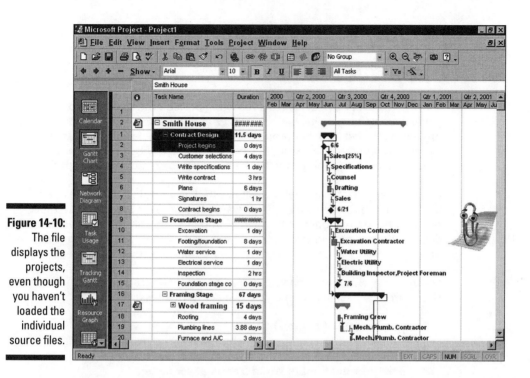

Figure 14-10:
The file displays the projects, even though you haven't loaded the individual source files.

Notice in Figure 14-10 that all the project tasks maintain their ID numbers in their respective tasks. As far as Microsoft Project is concerned, each of these three files is open and editable (unless you specified otherwise in the Consolidated Projects dialog box).

If you want to look at details of just one consolidated Project file, all you have to do is to roll up the summary task for the Project files you want to roll up, leaving the remaining Project file expanded.

Use these steps to save a consolidated project:

1. **Click the Save button on the standard toolbar.**

2. **Give your consolidated project a name.**

3. **Click the Save button.**

4. **If Microsoft Project asks whether you want to save the changes to the three projects, click Yes.**

After you're finished, please close the file but don't turn out the lights.

Simplifying Master Projects with Subprojects

If you listed every single task in a really big project, the size of the project could become unmanageable. Sometimes creating master projects with subprojects is a good idea. Subprojects are simply piece-of-the-pie projects. They are called *subprojects* because they're included as a single task in another project. You create a subproject in the same way you create any other project file.

In a master project, each subproject is listed as a single task. If you open the task, you open the subproject. This way, you can leave the details to those people who are responsible for them. Unopened, you see a start and finish date for the subproject task in the master project. Another advantage of subprojects is that you can use them in any number of projects.

For example, a number of details make up the Wood framing task in the Smith Home project. Assign a framing subproject to this task:

1. **Open Sample1 Chapter 14.MPP.**

2. **Scroll to the Wood framing task.**

3. **Click the + next to the Wood framing task name.**

   The subproject expands to reveal its subtasks, as shown in Figure 14-11.

Assigning Resources to Multiple Projects

A convenient feature of Microsoft Project is its capability of assigning resources from one project to other projects. This enables you to use the same resource pool for a number of projects. If you want, you can keep the projects linked by the shared resources, which makes you less likely to over-allocate people and equipment.

Using the Sample1 Chapter 14.MPP file, assign resources to another building project. To do this:

1. **Open the Project file for which you want to share resources.**

   In this example, open Sample2 Chapter 14.MPP.

2. **To assign resources, choose Tools⇨Resources.**

3. **Select Share Resources from the submenu.**

   The Share Resources dialog box appears, as shown in Figure 14-12.

4. **Select the Use Resources option.**

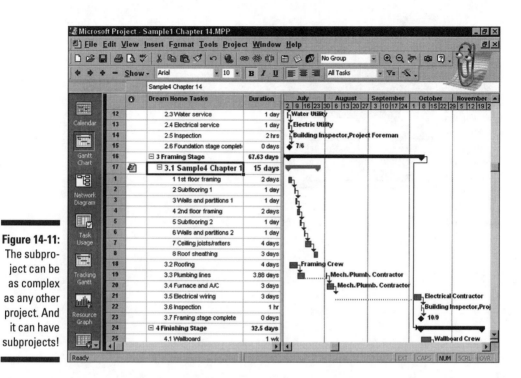

Figure 14-11:
The subproject can be as complex as any other project. And it can have subprojects!

5. In the From text box, select another Project file from the list of opened files.

In this example, select Sample1 Chapter 14.MPP.

6. Click OK.

Sample1 Chapter 14.MPP is now the source of the resource pool.

Now that Sample2 Chapter 14.MPP is a resource pool groupie of Sample1 Chapter 14.MPP, click the Assign Resources button on the standard toolbar. You'll see all your friends' sales and specifications. Project management is a friendly profession!

Establishing a shared resource relationship with another project creates a link between the projects. For example, modifying the resource pool in one project displays the modification in the other project. The advantage of sharing resources is that you can have more than one project using the same people and still avoid overallocation of resources. I talk about resource overallocation in Chapter 13.

You can make the shared project resources take precedence over the resource pool by clicking Sharer Takes Precedence at the bottom of the Share Resources dialog box (see Figure 14-12).

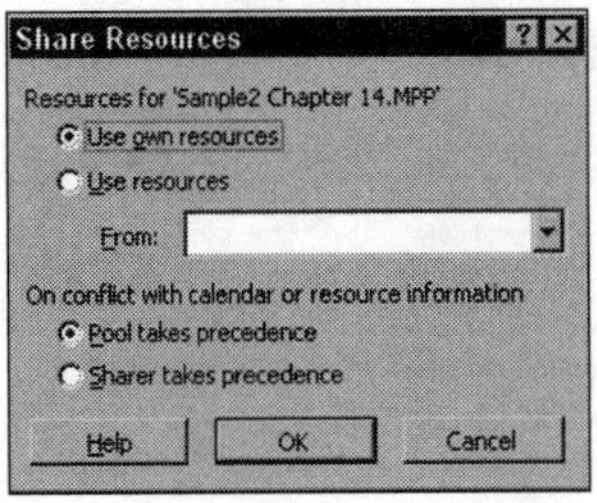

Figure 14-12:
If you change the resources of the source file, the changes affect any project file where the resources are shared.

Chapter 15

Personalizing Your Project Environment

- -

In This Chapter

▶ Customizing tables to see what you want

▶ Customizing bars to highlight Gantt chart attributes

▶ Adding recurring tasks for those weekly meetings

▶ Changing default views to fit your needs

▶ Customizing toolbars to group your favorite shortcuts

- -

*T*elling you how to make your project environment unique is a self-contradictory task — something like my teenagers having to be themselves by conforming to their peers. Ah, life! But I've never been accused of doing only sensible things, so here's an oxymoronic chapter full of standard ways to personalize your work environment.

This chapter is written partly in question-and-answer format because, well, I needed to personalize my writing environment to write a chapter about personal environments. Also, the only way this subject makes sense is by using some mini–case studies. But don't think that someone actually wrote and asked me these questions — I asked the questions so that you can consider the answers as samples of what can be accomplished.

In this chapter, you can do a bunch of stuff to make your workspace more personal. By using the same approach in other ways, you can truly make yourself at home with Microsoft Project.

I've made a Workspace file that you can use in this chapter. The Workspace file contains a couple of Project files. The name of the file is Chapter 15.MPW. For more information on opening the practice files on the CD, please refer to Appendix C.

Changing Your Default Folder

If nothing else, a project manager is a person who understands the importance of good organization. Microsoft Project is a good place to begin organizing your project management responsibilities. Here's how you start organizing your project by setting up a default folder for your Project files:

1. **Select Tools⇨Options.**

   The Options dialog box opens.

2. **Click the Save tab.**

3. **Make sure that Projects is highlighted in the File Types text box.**

4. **Select Modify in the File Locations text box area.**

   The Modify Location dialog box appears. You can use an existing folder or create a new folder for your Project files.

5. **Click the down arrow next to the Look In text box.**

   The folders of your C drive appear in the Modify Location dialog box. You can choose an existing file from here and skip to Step 8, or you can create a new folder by continuing to Step 6.

6. **Click the Create New Folder button.**

   The New Folder dialog box appears.

7. **Type the name for the folder.**

   You can choose **Project Files** if you want, or you can use choose another name or another default directory.

8. **Click OK.**

   Your new default project folder now appears in the Options dialog box.

Notice that the Save tab in the Options dialog box gives you the option of automatically saving your Project files in increments of minutes (see Figure 15-1).

If you want to tell Microsoft Project to always open your last Project file on startup, follow these steps:

1. **Choose Tools⇨Options.**

   The Options dialog box opens.

2. **Click the General tab in the Options dialog box.**

3. **Select the Open Last File on Startup check box in the General Options for Microsoft Project.**

   The Display Help on Startup check box is deactivated.

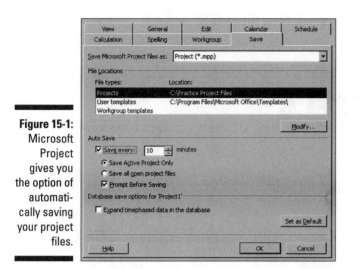

Figure 15-1:
Microsoft
Project
gives you
the option of
automati-
cally saving
your project
files.

4. **Click OK.**

   The Options dialog box closes.

Click the Open button on the Standard toolbar if you want Microsoft Project
to open your new default folder. So far, your default folder is empty. But not
for long.

Microsoft Project enables you to save all the files you currently have open as
a Workspace. That way, the next time you want to pick up where you left off,
you can open all the Project files simultaneously. You can save currently open
Project files as a Workspace by selecting File⇨Save Workspace. Microsoft
Project saves Workspace files with the extension .MPW.

Customizing the Gantt Chart Entry Table

*Question: I want the resource names next to the task names in the Gantt chart.
What do I do?*

Good idea! Why didn't I think of that? You need to do some column work to
put resources next to tasks. Use the Office Remodel Project for this example.
If the Sample1 Chapter 15.MPP file isn't on top, choose Window⇨Sample1
Chapter 15.MPP. The Office Remodel window becomes active. To customize
columns:

1. **Right-click a column in the Gantt Chart view.**

   In this example, right-click the Duration column head. A shortcut menu
   appears.

2. **Choose Insert Column from the context menu.**

   The Column Definition dialog box appears, as shown in Figure 15-2.

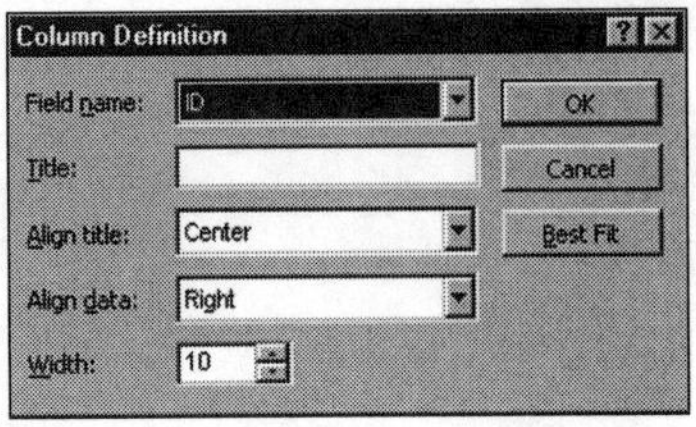

Figure 15-2:
Use the
Column
Definition
dialog box
to set
column field
conditions.

Column Definition

Field name:	ID
Title:	
Align title:	Center
Align data:	Right
Width:	10

OK
Cancel
Best Fit

3. **Select a category in the Field Name box.**

   In this example, select Resource Names.

4. **Type a Title in the Title text box.**

   In this example, type something original, such as **Reese Horses**.

5. **If you want, use the Align Title box to align the new column the same as the others.**

   The options are Left, Center, and Right. In this example, select Left.

6. **Rather than assign a character width, click the Best Fit button.**

   When you click the Best Fit button, Microsoft Project adjusts the column width to equal the widest character width of information in cells within the column.

   The column appears between the Task Name and Duration columns. You may have to scroll horizontally to bring the Duration column into view — but don't worry, it's there. New columns exist only in the Project file in which they were created.

You can change layout of existing columns. For example, you can right or center justify, or change font styles and text size. To do this, highlight a column and make changes using the Formatting toolbar.

Scheduling with the Gantt Chart

Question: I get visually confused by nonworking time. When a task duration is going across a nonworking day, I can't tell if the nonworking time applies toward the duration of a task. What can I do?

Glad you asked. One good way to remove any doubt about tasks spanning nonworking time is to put the nonworking time on top of the tasks. You can keep using the Office Remodel project for the example. To put the nonworking time on top:

1. **Double-click the open space representing nonworking time on the Gantt chart.**

   The Timescale dialog box appears, as shown in Figure 15-3.

2. **Select the In Front of Task Bars option.**

3. **Click OK.**

   The Gantt chart now hides the task or tasks crossing through nonworking times.

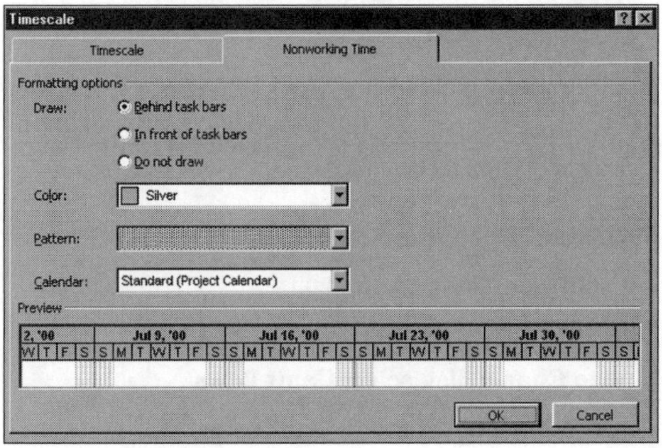

Figure 15-3:
The Timescale dialog box provides options for customizing working and nonworking time.

Question: How do I change the look of bars on the Gantt chart?

You can change the format of one bar on the Gantt chart by double-clicking it. Or, to change the format of all the bars, double-click the chart background. Either way, double-clicking displays the Bar Styles dialog box, from which you can make your format changes. For example, in the following example, you make changes to the bars in Sample2 Chapter 15.MPP. Choose Window➪Sample2 Chapter 15.MPP. The Warren Home project is now the active window.

Double-click anywhere in the working time area of the Gantt chart. The Bar Styles dialog box appears, as shown in Figure 15-4. The Bars tab has options for the Start Shape, Middle Bar, and End Shape for each task category.

Feel free to use your imagination to change the settings any way you want.

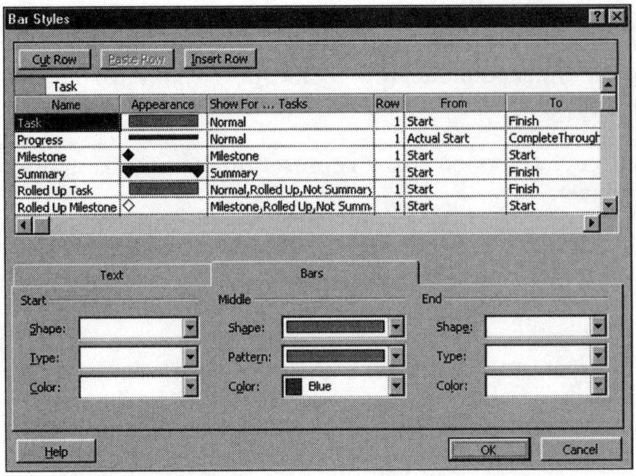

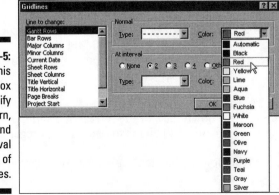

Figure 15-4:
The Bar
Styles
dialog box
shows
default
settings for
all task
categories.

Question: I get confused aligning task names with bars. What should I do?

This one's simple. All you need to do is add gridlines to the Gantt chart as follows:

1. **Right-click anywhere in the Gantt chart.**

   The Gantt shortcut dialog box appears.

2. **Choose Gridlines.**

3. **In the Line to Change list, select Gantt Rows.**

4. **Under Normal, choose a line type and color, as shown in Figure 15-5.**

   As an alternative, you can choose At Interval to add a second series of gridlines at row intervals of 2, 3, 4, or any number from 5 to 99 (using the Other option).

Figure 15-5:
Use this
dialog box
to specify
the pattern,
color, and
interval
spacing of
gridlines.

> **5. Click OK.**
>
> The Gantt chart now has gridlines.

Managing Recurring Tasks

Question: *I have to insert a bunch of weekly staff meetings into a project. How can I do this?*

Microsoft Project provides a shortcut for entering recurring tasks such as weekly staff meetings. Again, use the Warren Home project for an example:

1. Choose Insert⇨Recurring Task.

The Recurring Task Information dialog box appears, as shown in Figure 15-6.

2. Enter the task name, the duration, and the frequency of occurrence.

If you select a recurring task that falls on a nonworking day, a dialog box asks whether you want it rescheduled.

3. Click OK.

The Gantt chart now displays the weekly meetings (Figure 15-7).

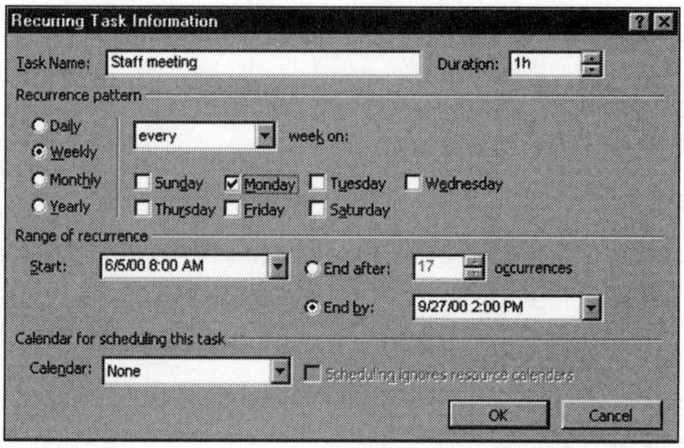

Figure 15-6:
The recurring task must be a new task; you can't edit an existing one.

Personalizing Your Workspace

Question: *Enough with this Gantt chart! How do I make something else the default view?*

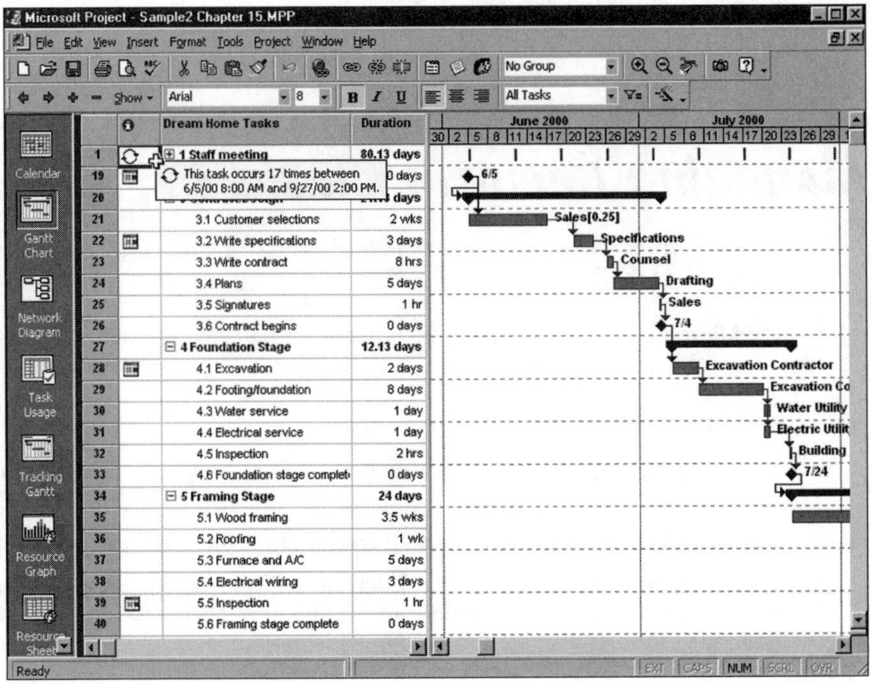

Figure 15-7:
Placing your
mouse over
the
Recurring
task
Indicator
column
reveals the
quantity of
occurrences
of the
recurring
task.

Yeah, the Gantt chart gets tiring after a while, doesn't it? You can change the default view as follows:

1. **Choose Tools⇨Options.**

   The Options dialog box appears.

2. **Click the View tab.**

3. **In the Default View list box, select another view.**

4. **Click OK.**

Customizing the Toolbar

Question: *Most of the time, I use only one button from the tracking toolbar. Can I put it into the formatting toolbar?*

As is true of all Microsoft Office family products, Microsoft Project lets you make a toolbar longer by dragging buttons onto it. To do so:

1. **Make sure that the toolbar you want to customize is visible.**

   If it isn't, right-click anywhere among the toolbars and select a toolbar from the shortcut menu.

2. **Choose View➪Toolbars➪Customize.**

   The Customize dialog box appears.

3. **Click the Commands tab.**

4. **In the Categories group, select the toolbar containing the button you want to move.**

5. **Drag the button from the Commands group to the new toolbar (Figure 15-8).**

Figure 15-8:
Drop the custom command on the active toolbar of your choice.

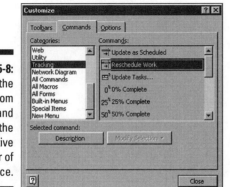

You can also place any button on any toolbar by right-clicking in the toolbar area and selecting Customize. Thanks for all the tough questions. Play hard with your project files. The work will follow.

Part V
Tracking and Reporting a Project

The 5th Wave   By Rich Tennant

"NAAAH – HE'S NOT THAT SMART. HE WON'T BACK UP HIS HARD DISK, FORGETS TO CONSISTENTLY NAME HIS FILES, AND DROOLS ALL OVER THE KEYBOARD."

In this part . . .

*I*n all the previous chapters, you've been building a vehicle that exists solely for one purpose — project management. In this part, you launch. You study how to track your project and how to make midcourse corrections. And you discover how to modify your project environment after it starts showing some pesky anomalies.

This part also shows you how to enhance and customize the look and effectiveness of your project communication. You use print preview and set margins, headers and footers, and legends. You also find out how to customize a bunch of standard reports and how to create reports from scratch.

Chapter 16

Setting a Baseline and Manually Tracking a Project

*I*n this chapter, I assume that your project is beginning or has already begun. As you're about to see, Microsoft Project is an important asset in your project-management responsibilities. It's ready and waiting to help your project plan succeed in the cold test of reality. Although you'd like the project to go without a hitch, you know that's almost impossible. Besides, if the project had no problems, it would need only a project planner — not a project manager.

A project manager has to know how the project is proceeding to be proactive as conditions change. Staying informed requires that the project manager keep a close watch on the schedule, tasks, resources, and costs. Microsoft Project enables you to analyze present circumstances in relation to the original plan so that you can make adjustments. The term for this activity is *tracking*. Microsoft Project tracks progress by comparing current circumstances to the plan you saved before your first task started. In Microsoft Project parlance, that plan is known as the *baseline*.

Tracking Your Project

Tracking has multiple meanings. One is keeping track, as in staying informed. Another is keeping on track, as in keeping the project going according to your original design.

Tracking has three major components:

- ✔ **The baseline plan:** The baseline is like a set of completed blueprints and specifications for your project, acting as your best prediction of how the project should go. You use the baseline throughout the project to maintain goals and to get things back on track.

- ✔ **Current information:** After a project begins, Microsoft Project keeps a dynamic model of the project. This model may or may not be the same as the baseline. Microsoft Project calculates upcoming start and finish dates based on the latest information. You use current information to determine how past and current schedules affect the schedule and deadlines of future tasks.

- ✔ **Actual information:** Tasks that have already started or finished are referred to as *actual*. The actual start and finish dates for tasks are designated NA until they begin and end, respectively.

By using Microsoft Project, you can perform either minimal or detailed tracking. *Minimal tracking* refers to keeping records of the start and finish dates for each task. *Detailed tracking* is not a specific action, but a range of possibilities. You can track start and finish dates as well as the percentage of task completion, duration, costs, and work. You can then use the information to maneuver your tasks through complicated situations.

You keep your project on track by systematically updating your Project file. What you update in your project file is up to you. You can:

- ✔ **Update the status of a task's completion:** You can indicate either by percentage or by dates the extent to which a task is approaching its finish.

- ✔ **Modify resources:** You can enter resource allocation changes and see the impact of those changes on the project's critical path.

- ✔ **Enter cost information:** You can keep track of your project budget and, if necessary, change costs to remain within limits.

All these updates are automatically compared to the baseline so that you can keep your finger on the pulse of the project.

After all your hard work in creating a Project file, it may seem odd to use the term *begin* for something you've been working on for such a long time. Microsoft Project interprets "begin" as the initiation of the first task. If you want, you can practice beginning a project by using a Project file I made for this chapter. In this chapter, using the Mackey Home example, you can start the project and manually track some of its progress after it begins. In doing so, you work with baseline, current, and actual information. Of course, if you prefer, go right ahead and use this chapter to work on your own Project file. The file is called Chapter 16.MPW. See Appendix C for information on finding and opening this file.

Viewing the Birth of the Baseline

You've already spent a great deal of time and effort creating the plan that establishes your baseline. When you're happy with your plan, you're ready to go ahead and set the baseline by following these steps:

1. **Click the More Views icon at the bottom of the view bar (you may need to scroll down to see it).**

   The More Views dialog box appears.

2. **Double-click the Task Sheet option in the More Views list box.**

   The screen changes to the Task Sheet view.

3. **Choose View⇨Table:.**

4. **Choose More Tables.**

   The More Tables dialog box appears.

5. **Choose Baseline in the More Tables list box.**

   Baseline, meet your project manager. Project Manager, this is your baseline table (see Figure 16-1). All your project activity and expenses are measured in comparison to the baseline you set before the project's start date.

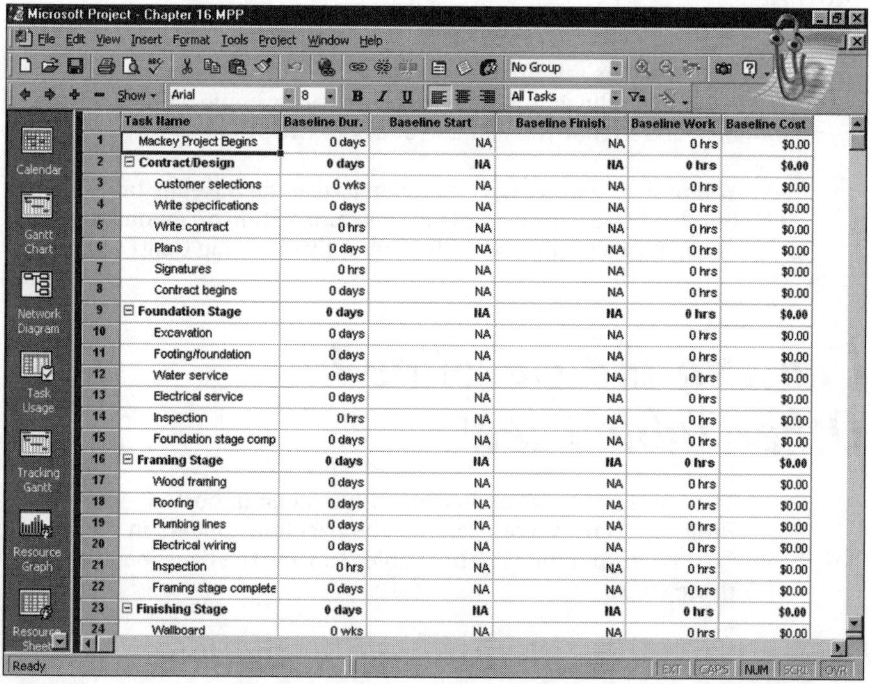

Figure 16-1: Viewing a project's various baselines.

6. Choose Tools⇨Tracking⇨Save Baseline.

The Save Baseline dialog box appears (see Figure 16-2). This little dialog box lets you save baselines and interim plans. Interim plans allow you to make mid-course corrections to your plan once the project is going. You also can choose to save a baseline for an entire project (default) or for selected tasks. In this example (which uses the Chapter 16.MPW file), stick with the Entire Project option.

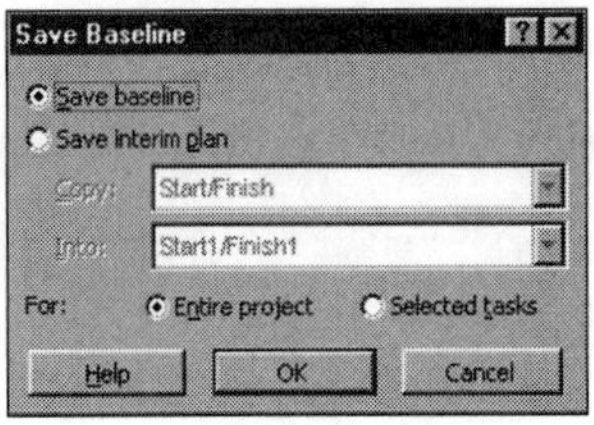

Figure 16-2:
The Save
Baseline
dialog box.

7. Click OK.

Kabam! The baseline is born before your very eyes. If you want, you can see the entire table by temporarily hiding the view bar.

You can undo the Save Baseline command any time by choosing Tools⇨ Tracking⇨Clear Baseline. This path takes you to the Clear Baseline dialog box, which allows you to clear the current baseline. The ability to clear a baseline is a terrific addition to the 2000 version of Microsoft Project.

This baseline information is set for the duration of your project unless you need to modify it for some reason. (For example, you may need to modify the baseline so that you can add a task to the project.)

You probably won't have a reason to use the Baseline table in your project, but you'll use various parts of this information on an ongoing basis. For now, change back to the Gantt Chart view by choosing Gantt Chart on the view bar.

Viewing the Baseline in Other Table Views

The baseline shows up in some of the most important analyses that Microsoft Project performs. For example, the baseline appears in the Work table, the Cost table, and the Variance table. To view the baseline in a table, follow these steps:

1. **Choose View⇔Table:⇔Baseline.**

2. **Choose Work.**

   The Work table appears.

3. **Drag the vertical bar to the right until the entire table is exposed.**

The Work table provides you with resource information about each task. The Work column is the total amount of work scheduled to be performed by all resources assigned to the task. The Variance column is a calculation of the difference between Baseline and (Current) Work. Actual is the amount of work that has been performed by all resources on the task. Remaining is the total amount of work that has yet to be performed. Percent of Work Completed (% W. Comp.) is the percentage of each task's work that has been performed.

The Cost table performs the same kind of function as the Work table except it tracks — you guessed it — cost. To see this table:

1. **Choose View⇔Table:⇔Work.**

2. **Choose Cost.**

   The Cost table appears (see Figure 16-3).

Figure 16-3:
The Cost table shows resource cost information regarding project tasks.

Task Name	Fixed Cost	Total Cost	Baseline	Variance	Actual	Remaining
1 **1 Mackey Project Begins**	$0.00	$0.00	$0.00	$0.00	$0.00	$0.00
2 **☐ 2 Contract/Design**	**$0.00**	**$1,645.00**	**$1,645.00**	**$0.00**	**$0.00**	**$1,645.00**
3 2.1 Customer selections	$0.00	$200.00	$200.00	$0.00	$0.00	$200.00
4 2.2 Write specifications	$0.00	$240.00	$240.00	$0.00	$0.00	$240.00
5 2.3 Write contract	$0.00	$225.00	$225.00	$0.00	$0.00	$225.00
6 2.4 Plans	$0.00	$960.00	$960.00	$0.00	$0.00	$960.00
7 2.5 Signatures	$0.00	$20.00	$20.00	$0.00	$0.00	$20.00
8 2.6 Contract begins	$0.00	$0.00	$0.00	$0.00	$0.00	$0.00
9 **☐ 3 Foundation Stage**	**$0.00**	**$13,770.00**	**$13,770.00**	**$0.00**	**$0.00**	**$13,770.00**
10 3.1 Excavation	$3,700.00	$3,700.00	$3,700.00	$0.00	$0.00	$3,700.00
11 3.2 Footing/foundation	$9,200.00	$9,200.00	$9,200.00	$0.00	$0.00	$9,200.00
12 3.3 Water service	$250.00	$250.00	$250.00	$0.00	$0.00	$250.00
13 3.4 Electrical service	$500.00	$500.00	$500.00	$0.00	$0.00	$500.00
14 3.5 Inspection	$60.00	$120.00	$120.00	$0.00	$0.00	$120.00
15 3.6 Foundation stage complete	$0.00	$0.00	$0.00	$0.00	$0.00	$0.00
16 **☐ 4 Framing Stage**	**$0.00**	**$17,660.00**	**$17,660.00**	**$0.00**	**$0.00**	**$17,660.00**
17 4.1 Wood framing	$0.00	$8,400.00	$8,400.00	$0.00	$0.00	$8,400.00
18 4.2 Roofing	$0.00	$1,600.00	$1,600.00	$0.00	$0.00	$1,600.00
19 4.3 Plumbing lines	$3,800.00	$3,800.00	$3,800.00	$0.00	$0.00	$3,800.00
20 4.4 Electrical wiring	$3,800.00	$3,800.00	$3,800.00	$0.00	$0.00	$3,800.00
21 4.5 Inspection	$0.00	$60.00	$60.00	$0.00	$0.00	$60.00
22 4.6 Framing stage complete	$0.00	$0.00	$0.00	$0.00	$0.00	$0.00
23 **☐ 5 Finishing Stage**	**$0.00**	**$16,500.00**	**$16,500.00**	**$0.00**	**$0.00**	**$16,500.00**

The Fixed Cost column contains the fixed cost for a task, such as contractor fees. Total Cost is the total projected cost for the task. The remaining columns are set up in the same way as those in the Work table.

The Variance table compares the difference, if any, between the project's baseline start and finish dates and the scheduled start and finish dates after the project has begun. To use the Variance table, follow these steps:

1. **Choose <u>V</u>iew⇨Ta<u>b</u>le:⇨<u>C</u>ost.**

2. **Choose ⇨<u>V</u>iew⇨Ta<u>b</u>le: Cost⇨<u>V</u>ariance.**

   After you adjust the columns to show the entire day, the Variance table appears, as shown in Figure 16-4. You may need to temporarily hide the View bar to see the entire table. The Variance table provides columns for comparing the schedule's variance from the baseline start and finish dates of project tasks.

The Variance table displays current start and finish dates. As described in the "Tracking Your Project" section, the term *current* refers to calculated information based on the latest changes or lack of changes to the project. The project is only beginning, so no variances exist between current dates and baseline dates.

Figure 16-4:
Find out which tasks aren't on track with the Variance table.

	Task Name	Start	Finish	Baseline Start	Baseline Finish	Start Var.	Finish Var.
1	1 Mackey Project Begins	6/5/00 8:00 AM	6/5/00 8:00 AM	6/5/00 8:00 AM	6/5/00 8:00 AM	0 days	0 days
2	☐ 2 Contract/Design	6/5/00 8:00 AM	7/10/00 12:00 PM	6/5/00 8:00 AM	7/10/00 12:00 PM	0 days	0 days
3	2.1 Customer selections	6/5/00 8:00 AM	6/9/00 5:00 PM	6/5/00 8:00 AM	6/9/00 5:00 PM	0 days	0 days
4	2.2 Write specifications	6/12/00 8:00 AM	6/12/00 5:00 PM	6/12/00 8:00 AM	6/12/00 5:00 PM	0 days	0 days
5	2.3 Write contract	6/13/00 8:00 AM	6/13/00 11:00 AM	6/13/00 8:00 AM	6/13/00 11:00 AM	0 days	0 days
6	2.4 Plans	6/13/00 11:00 AM	6/29/00 11:00 AM	6/13/00 11:00 AM	6/29/00 11:00 AM	0 days	0 days
7	2.5 Signatures	7/10/00 11:00 AM	7/10/00 12:00 PM	7/10/00 11:00 AM	7/10/00 12:00 PM	0 days	0 days
8	2.6 Contract begins	7/10/00 12:00 PM	7/10/00 12:00 PM	7/10/00 12:00 PM	7/10/00 12:00 PM	0 days	0 days
9	☐ 3 Foundation Stage	7/10/00 12:00 PM	7/31/00 9:00 AM	7/10/00 12:00 PM	7/31/00 9:00 AM	0 days	0 days
10	3.1 Excavation	7/10/00 12:00 PM	7/11/00 12:00 PM	7/10/00 12:00 PM	7/11/00 12:00 PM	0 days	0 days
11	3.2 Footing/foundation	7/11/00 12:00 PM	7/20/00 12:00 PM	7/11/00 12:00 PM	7/20/00 12:00 PM	0 days	0 days
12	3.3 Water service	7/20/00 12:00 PM	7/21/00 12:00 PM	7/20/00 12:00 PM	7/21/00 12:00 PM	0 days	0 days
13	3.4 Electrical service	7/20/00 12:00 PM	7/21/00 12:00 PM	7/20/00 12:00 PM	7/21/00 12:00 PM	0 days	0 days
14	3.5 Inspection	7/31/00 8:00 AM	7/31/00 9:00 AM	7/31/00 8:00 AM	7/31/00 9:00 AM	0 days	0 days
15	3.6 Foundation stage complete	7/31/00 9:00 AM	7/31/00 9:00 AM	7/31/00 9:00 AM	7/31/00 9:00 AM	0 days	0 days
16	☐ 4 Framing Stage	7/31/00 9:00 AM	8/18/00 10:00 AM	7/31/00 9:00 AM	8/18/00 10:00 AM	0 days	0 days
17	4.1 Wood framing	7/31/00 9:00 AM	8/17/00 9:00 AM	7/31/00 9:00 AM	8/17/00 9:00 AM	0 days	0 days
18	4.2 Roofing	8/14/00 7:00 AM	8/17/00 3:30 PM	8/14/00 7:00 AM	8/17/00 3:30 PM	0 days	0 days
19	4.3 Plumbing lines	8/14/00 9:00 AM	8/17/00 9:00 AM	8/14/00 9:00 AM	8/17/00 9:00 AM	0 days	0 days
20	4.4 Electrical wiring	8/14/00 9:00 AM	8/17/00 9:00 AM	8/14/00 9:00 AM	8/17/00 9:00 AM	0 days	0 days
21	4.5 Inspection	8/18/00 9:00 AM	8/18/00 10:00 AM	8/18/00 9:00 AM	8/18/00 10:00 AM	0 days	0 days
22	4.6 Framing stage complete	8/18/00 10:00 AM	8/18/00 10:00 AM	8/18/00 10:00 AM	8/18/00 10:00 AM	0 days	0 days
23	☐ 5 Finishing Stage	8/18/00 10:00 AM	9/7/00 3:00 PM	8/18/00 10:00 AM	9/7/00 3:00 PM	0 days	0 days

Tracking Your Project's Progress in Time

After your project's baseline is firmly set, you can begin tracking. Tracking is accomplished by viewing your actual information in relation to your baseline plan. The Variance table provides a good view. To access this view:

1. **Choose the Entry table by choosing View⊅Table:⊅Variance.**

2. **Choose⊅View⊅Table: Variance⊅Entry.**

   The Entry table appears.

3. **Drag the vertical bar until it's to the right of the Duration column.**

4. **If necessary, click the Zoom Out button on the Standard toolbar.**

   Zooming out makes the Gantt chart easier to use.

Suppose that the project has been progressing for a number of days. Everything was going according to plan until the construction ran into a rain day, which not only delayed construction, but also affected the availability of some resources.

You need to make some changes to the project. These changes won't affect the baseline. Instead, the baseline tells you how the changes affect the overall project.

For this example, today is July 20, 2000. You need to inform Microsoft Project of this, as follows:

1. **Choose Project⊅Project Information.**

   The Project Information dialog box appears.

2. **Type the current date in the Current Date text box or select the date in the drop-down calendar box, as shown in Figure 16-5.**

   In this example, type **7/20/00**. Don't worry, changing the current date in the Project Information dialog box doesn't affect your computer's clock.

   When entering dates, you don't need to type the current year.

3. **Click OK.**

4. **Choose Edit⊅Go To.**

   The Go To dialog box appears.

5. **Type a date in the Date box or use the drop-down calendar and click Today.**

   In this example, type **7/20/00**.

6. **Click OK.**

   The chart jumps to July 20.

Figure 16-5:
Changing
the current
date gives
you the
opportunity
to view your
project from
different
vantage
points
within the
project
timeline.

Microsoft Project informs you of the current date, July 20, by inserting a vertical dotted line on the Gantt chart.

Manually Updating the Schedule

As work on project tasks progresses, you need to enter information into your Project file. The term for this is *updating*. You can update your Project file either manually or automatically. Manual updating, which I discuss in this chapter, is a procedure in which you use tracking tools to inform the Project file of your project's progress. Automatic updating uses either an intranet or the Internet to collect information from project team members and automatically update your Project file.

Microsoft Project provides some shortcuts to aid you in your updating tasks. Some of the most common updating shortcuts are grouped together on the Tracking toolbar, which is accessible by right-clicking on any toolbar and selecting the Tracking check box.

By using the tracking tools available on the Tracking toolbar and a few others, you can make the following updates to the Chapter 16.MPW project.

Tasks 1 through 10 were completed on time and without difficulty. Task 11 is half finished and is one day behind schedule because of mud. The ground conditions aren't affecting just the Mackey project — all tasks are behind. The Electrical Service task is behind schedule and won't be performed until July 20, which affects the building inspector — the Foundation Stage inspection can't take place until electric service has been installed.

Percentage complete

Some of the friendliest tools on the Tracking toolbar are the Percentage Complete buttons. Louis Armstrong should be singing "What a Wonderful World" in the background when you use them. For example, try updating sequential tasks as 100% complete. To update a group of sequential tasks, follow these steps:

1. **Select the first task you want to update.**

   In this example, select Project Begins, ID 1.

2. **Hold down the Shift key and select the last task you wish to update.**

   In this example, select Summary Task ID 2, Contract/Design.

3. **Click the appropriate Percentage Complete button on the Tracking toolbar.**

   In this example, click the 100% Complete button. Microsoft Project updates the selected tasks. The black bar all the way through the tasks indicates completion. By selecting a summary task and choosing one of the Percentage Complete buttons, Microsoft Project interprets the percentage of completion to be true of all subtasks.

4. **To update an individual task, select the task and then click the appropriate Percentage Complete button.**

   In this example, select the Excavation task and then click the 100% Complete button on the Tracking toolbar.

Scroll through the Gantt chart to expose the first 10 or so tasks. If necessary, click the Zoom In button on the Standard toolbar. The chart should look similar to Figure 16-6. The updated taskbars on the Gantt Chart have black bars running through them. The black bars represent a percentage of completion. When you hover your cursor over a black bar, an information box appears providing tracking information. To see how the tracking information appears in tables, you can choose View⇨Table: Entry⇨Work or View⇨Table: Entry⇨Tracking.

Updating task information

You can update specific information about tasks by using the Task Information dialog box or by manipulating the Gantt chart. In either case, any changes to the task are recorded and dispersed throughout the affected fields of Microsoft Project.

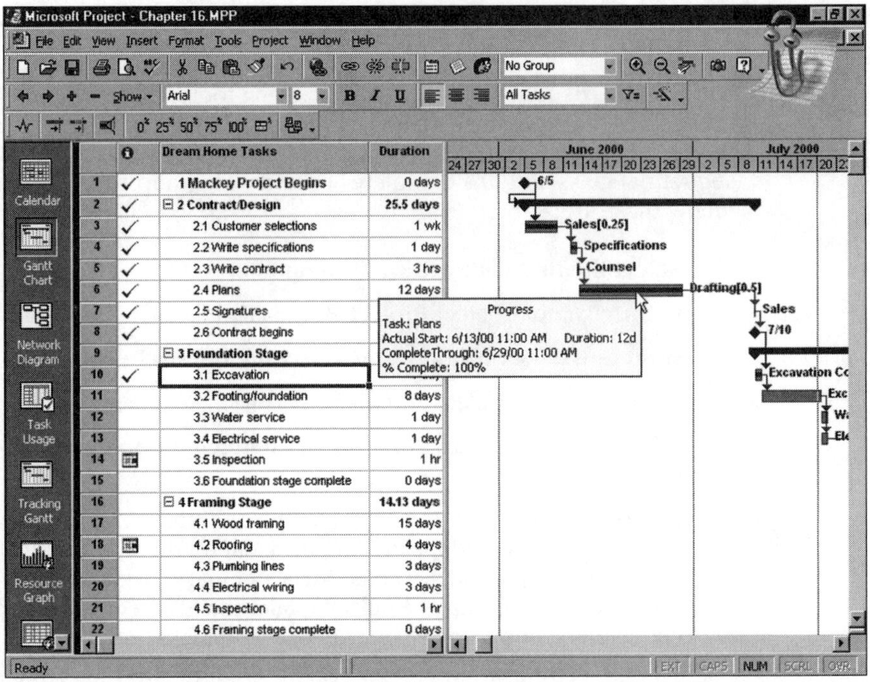

Figure 16-6:
Tasks now
have actual
dates.

Updating by using the Task Information dialog box

Using the Update Tasks button on the tracking toolbar is a convenient way to enter tracking information quickly. But using the Update Tasks button isn't the only way to update tasks. You can update tasks and perform related functions from within the Task Information dialog box by following these steps:

1. **Select a task.**

   In this example, select the Footing/Foundation task.

2. **Click Goto Selected Task on the Standard toolbar.**

   The Goto Selected Task button helps you visually keep track of the effects of your work.

3. **Double-click the task or click the Update Tasks button on the Tracking toolbar.**

   The Task Information dialog box appears. The Footing/Foundation task is 60 percent complete and one day behind schedule. You can use the Task Information dialog box to update this information.

4. **Click the General tab.**

5. **Click the Percent Complete text box to update current levels of completion.**

   In this example, type **60**.

6. **Click the Duration text box to update task duration.**

   In this example, type **9d**.

   You don't have to type *d* for days because Microsoft Project assumes that you're entering the default duration (days).

7. **Click OK.**

   The Footing/foundation task reflects your changes.

Updating Start/Finish dates and relationships using the Gantt chart

Besides using the Task Information dialog box, you can enter individual task update information easily by using the Gantt chart. In the example Project file, another task needs your attention. The Electrical Service task can't be performed until July 24, but it's currently scheduled to start on July 20. To change a task's start date by using the Gantt chart, follow these steps:

1. **Hover your cursor over the task you want to change.**

   In this example, move the cursor to the Electrical Service Gantt bar.

2. **Drag the task box to the right until the pop-up date box contains the start date of your choice and then release the mouse button.**

   In this example, drag right until the pop-up date box reads July 26.

   The Planning wizard appears. It tells you that you may be creating a task relationship problem. You can turn off this notification by selecting the Don't Tell Me About This Again option. I suggest you wait a while before you select this option: Knowing about potential problems can come in handy until you're completely comfortable with Microsoft Project.

   The Planning wizard says there's a problem because the link between tasks won't drive the start date of the later task. The wizard is saying that a task relationship exists between the two tasks (the Electrical Service task and the Footing/Foundation task). The relationship requires the later task to begin upon the completion of the previous task. By moving the first task's start date, everything is getting messed up.

3. **Choose the first option 'Move the task ('Electrical Service') to start on Wed Jul 26, '00 and remove the link'. (see Figure 16-7), which lets Microsoft Project remove the link.**

4. **Click OK.**

   The Electrical service task moves to July 26.

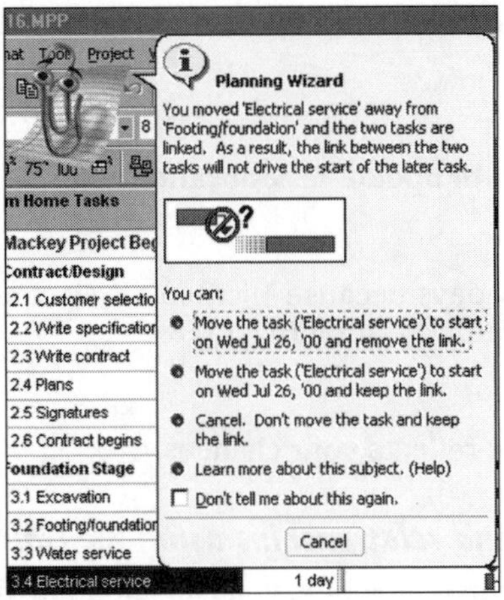

Figure 16-7:
The
Planning
wizard
appears
automatically
when you
create a
possible
task
relationship
discrepancy.

Now you need to link the Electrical Service task again. To relink a task:

1. **To reestablish a link with a predecessor, double-click the appropriate task.**

   In this example, double-click the Electrical Service task. The Task Information dialog box appears.

2. **Click the Predecessors tab.**

3. **In the text box below ID, type the predecessor task number.**

   In the example, type **11**.

4. **Select the green check mark and click OK (see Figure 16-8).**

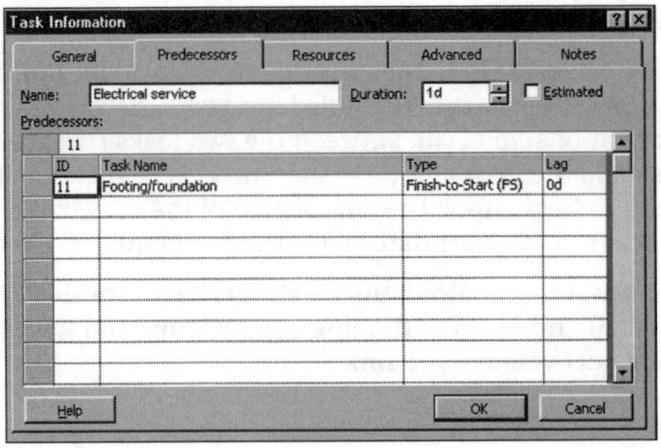

Figure 16-8:
The
Electrical
Service task
is now the
successor
of the
Footing/
foundation
task.

You can also use the Gantt chart to update detailed information about a task relationship. In this example, the Inspection task has a one-day lag from its Electrical Service predecessor. You need to remove the lag. To remove a lag:

1. **Select a task relationship you want to change by double-clicking an arrow point touching a task.**

   In this example, double-click the arrow point touching the Inspection task. The Task Dependency dialog box appears.

2. **In the Lag text box, type** 0 **to replace the 1d.**

3. **Click OK.**

Splitting tasks

One of the ways that Microsoft Project reflects reality is its capability of splitting tasks. Sometimes tasks are started and then, for some reason, put on hold for a while. You can keep track of such tasks through splitting.

Using the example Project file, suppose that the Water Service task is going to take two days with a one-day split in the middle. First, change the Water Service duration to 2d. Then, to split the task, follow these steps:

1. **Click the Split Task button on the Standard toolbar.**

   The cursor changes shape to show that it's ready to split, and then the Split Task information box appears.

2. **Place the cursor over the appropriate task on the Gantt chart.**

   In this example, place the cursor over the Water Service Gantt bar. The Split Task info box appears as shown in Figure 16-9.

3. **Click the task's Gantt bar.**

   The task splits, as shown in Figure 16-10.

   You can shorten or widen the split by clicking either part of the split task's Gantt bar and dragging it.

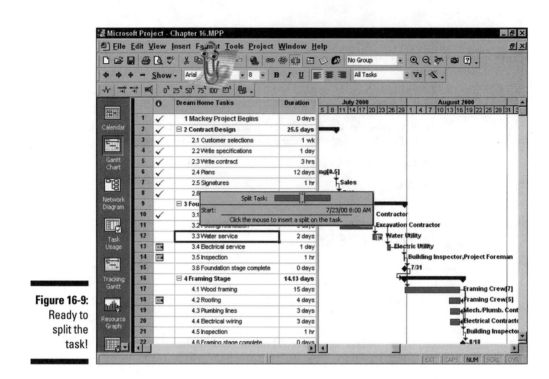

Figure 16-9:
Ready to
split the
task!

Keeping Tabs with the Tracking Gantt Table

One visually powerful view of tracking information is the Tracking Gantt table. This little hummer shows you both what you originally planned and how you're currently doing. To see what I mean, access the Tracking Gantt table:

1. **Choose Tracking Gantt on the View bar.**

2. **Select the portion of the Project file you want to view.**

   In this example, select the Footing/foundation task.

3. **Click the Goto Selected Task button on the Standard toolbar.**

4. **Using the horizontal window arrows, adjust the window to maximize your view.**

   In this example, your view looks like Figure 16-11.

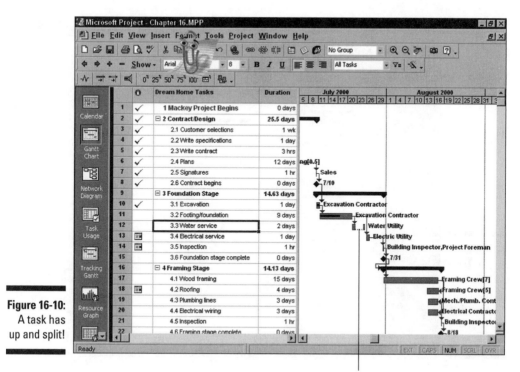

A split task

Figure 16-10:
A task has
up and split!

The Tracking Gantt view contains a lot of visual messages — mostly color changes:

- ✔ Dark gray bars are baseline tasks.
- ✔ Dark blue bars are completed tasks or portions of tasks.
- ✔ Red bars are critical path tasks.
- ✔ Light blue bars are noncritical tasks.
- ✔ Black bars are summary tasks.
- ✔ Checkered bars are percentage of completion of summary tasks.

The difference in horizontal location between the baseline bar and its partner is an indication of the schedule status. The more distance, the further the actual date is from the baseline date. The number at the end of each colored bar is the percentage of the task that's completed.

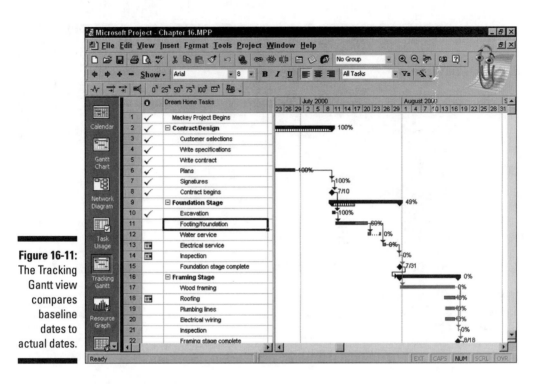

Figure 16-11:
The Tracking
Gantt view
compares
baseline
dates to
actual dates.

Tracking can be a blast as well as rewarding proof of your excellent planning. But all good athletes know that backslapping is for the end of the game, not during it. Tracking is your first defense against previously unforeseen problems. If you do it well, you'll be able to see to the horizon and — with your Microsoft Project tools — beyond.

Chapter 17

Communicating Your Views

Congratulations! Your project is a masterpiece. It's rich with resources, tight on the tasks, realistic about risks, and correct about costs. Only one challenge remains. You need to make the plan a basis of understanding among everyone involved in the project.

In many ways, a project plan is only as valuable as your ability to communicate it. Unfortunately, communicating isn't always easy. Clear and simple communication can be a moving target. The kind and quantity of information needed varies dramatically from day to day and from one group to the next. Project team members need to know schedules and resource allocations. Accountants require access to cost information. Managers must be kept abreast of work. Stakeholders want to know how things are going.

Sometimes too much information is as disastrous as too little. Other times, information is proprietary or sensitive. In some circumstances, the back of a napkin is sufficient; other circumstances require a full-blown presentation. With Microsoft Project, you can dig in, find what you're looking for, determine what and how much you'll report, customize the manner of presentation, and print the results.

I've put together a practice file that you can use to practice publishing views. If you're already working on a project, this chapter helps you understand how to publish views of your own work. You may find it helpful to open your existing Project file and the practice file. The practice file, Chapter 17.MPP, has some information built into it to help you get the idea of what Microsoft Project has to offer. See Appendix C for more information on opening practice files on the CD.

Sending the World Your Project Views

Printing a view can be as simple as clicking the Print button on the standard toolbar. The value of this approach is also its deficiency. Click the button, and the computer prints the view with a bunch of default settings. If you want, go ahead and print this little project. It eats up six pages. What you get when you use the Print button is based on a bunch of Microsoft Project defaults, most of which you can change easily by using the Print Preview button.

In many instances, the print option is exactly what the circumstances call for. But when you need a lot more control of the print function, a great alternative is just one button to the right on the standard toolbar. Print Preview's the name, and functionality's the game. (Sorry.)

Getting around in Print Preview mode

Print Preview mode has features not available by clicking the Print button. After you determine the view you want to print, you can modify the look of the view in a number of important ways. For this chapter's example, make sure that the project is in Gantt view and set to the default timescale, as shown in Figure 17-1.

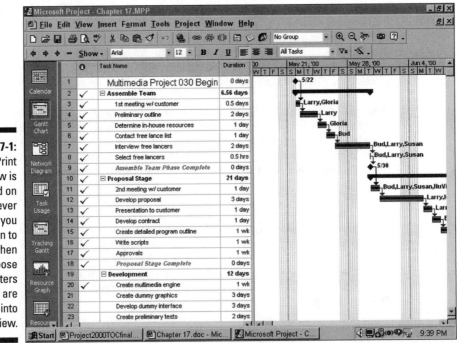

Figure 17-1:
Print Preview is based on whatever screen you happen to be in when you choose it. Any filters or sorts are carried into the view.

Click the Print Preview button on the standard toolbar. The Print Preview screen appears, as shown in Figure 17-2. The toolbar at the top has directional arrows that enable you to jump from page to page of your view. The number of pages in print preview is Microsoft Project's calculation of how many pages it takes to see whatever was in view when you chose the Print Preview command. If you zoom out before clicking the Print Preview button, fewer pages are printed. If you zoom in, more pages are printed.

The status bar at the bottom of the window displays the current page number, the page count, and a description of the layout. Multipage views are numbered and printed down and across. In this six-page example, that means that the page order will be top left, bottom left, top middle, bottom middle, top right, and bottom right.

The toolbar also has a magnifying glass and a single page button. These buttons are copycats of mouse cursor functions. As you move your cursor around the screen, the cursor turns into a magnifying glass. If you click somewhere on the screen, the information zooms to be readable and the window becomes scrollable. Click again, and it zooms back out. The same functions occur when you use the two corresponding toolbar buttons.

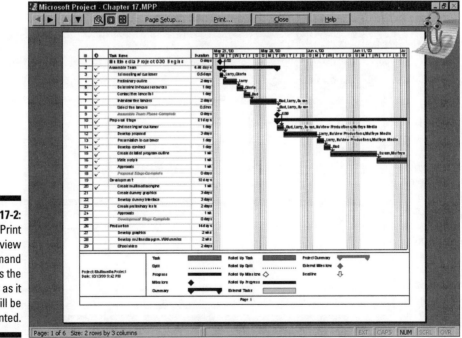

Figure 17-2: The Print Preview command displays the view as it will be printed.

Big deal, you say! Project managers are renowned for their patience, so please humor me a little longer. Click the Multiple Pages button on the tool-bar. Microsoft Project displays the whole view as it will appear in print, as shown in Figure 17-3.

You can change some or all default settings and preview your work as you make the changes. That's what the next section is all about.

Customizing Project Views with Page Setup

The Page Setup command controls certain aspects of the printed view. You can designate page orientation, margins, headers, footers, legends, and view options. In the Calendar view, you can also control units of time. Click the Page Setup button on the print preview toolbar. The Page Setup dialog box appears, as shown in Figure 17-4. The dialog box is divided into six sections, or tabs. (You can also access the Page Setup dialog box by choosing File⇨Page Setup.)

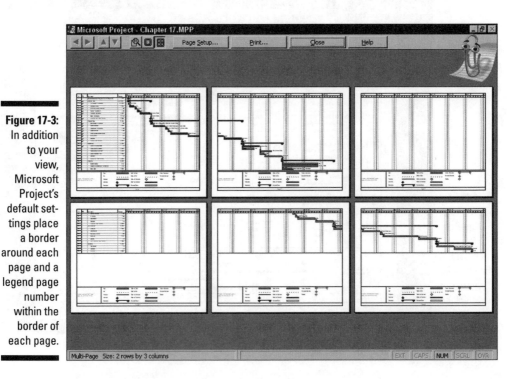

Figure 17-3:
In addition to your view, Microsoft Project's default settings place a border around each page and a legend page number within the border of each page.

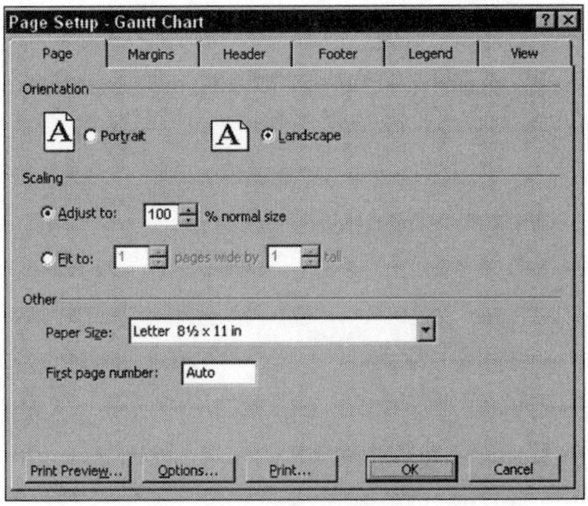

Figure 17-4:
When more than one project is active, the changes to the Page Setup dialog box apply to only the file whose view is displayed.

Setting the page layout

The Page tab offers two sets of options. The first, Orientation, permits Portrait (vertical) and Landscape (horizontal) selections. Microsoft Project's default setting is the Landscape selection. The second set of options, Scaling, enables you to size the project to a fit that best serves your printout needs.

Setting the margins

Two sets of options appear when you click the Margins tab (see Figure 17-5). In the first set of options, change the margins to see the effects of the change in the Sample box. You can further study the effect by clicking OK. The Print Preview screen adjusts to display your change. The second set of options, Borders Around, has two active selections in a Gantt view. You can turn the borders off or on around each page.

Setting headers

The Header tab offers a number of options for creating a custom header. For the next example, put the project manager's name and the current date in the header on the right margin of each page:

1. **Click the Header tab.**

2. **Select an alignment. In this example, select Right.**

3. **Select an action in the list box at the bottom of the screen.**

   In this example, select Manager Name.

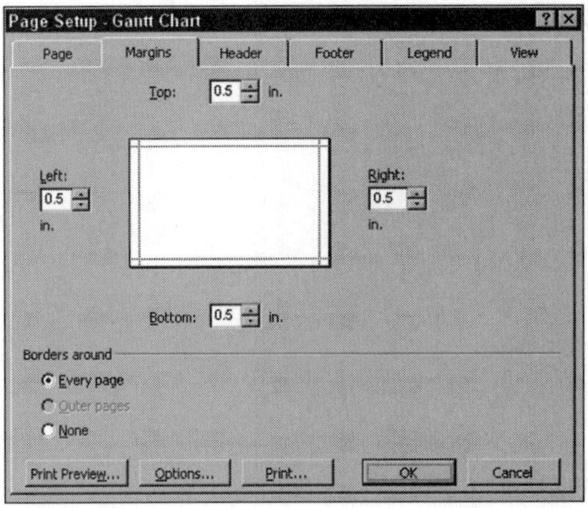

Figure 17-5:
The inactive option, Outer Pages, is available in a Network Diagram view.

4. **Click the Add button next to the list box.**

   Manager Name appears in the Selection box on the Right tab. The project manager's name appears in the Sample box.

5. **If you want, you can add another line to the header.**

   In this example, make sure that the cursor is to the right of [Manager]. This is because you're aligned right.

6. **Press Enter.**

   The cursor in the Selection box on the Right tab drops to the next line.

7. **This time, instead of using the list box, click the Insert File Name button (shown in Figure 17-6).**

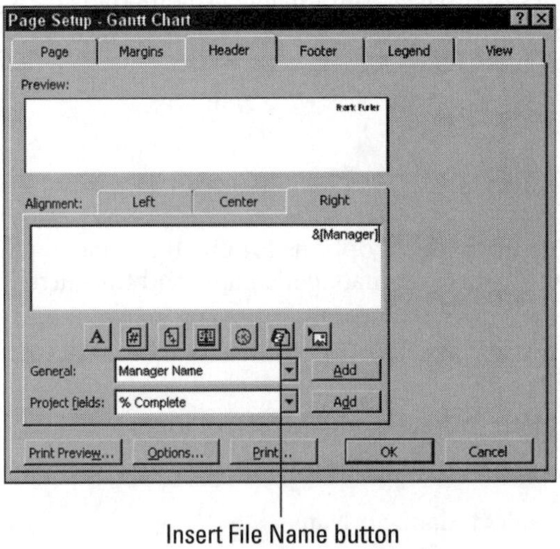

Figure 17-6:
The Header tab of the Page Setup dialog box.

Insert File Name button

The Filename code — &[File] — appears on the second line in the Selection box.

8. **Add text to the first line of code in the Selection box by positioning your cursor in front of the code and typing the text.**

   In this example, type **Manager:** (be sure to include a space after the colon). The dialog box should now look like Figure 17-7.

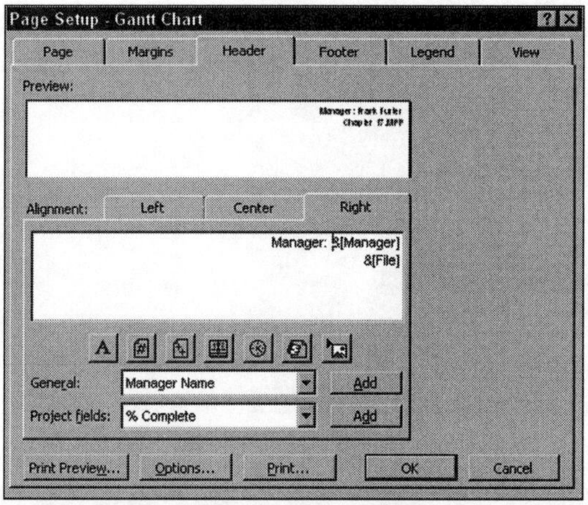

Figure 17-7:
You can customize the manager name and other goodies in fields at the bottom of the dialog box.

If you want to change the text style of your header before leaving the Header tab, follow these steps:

1. **Highlight the first line of code. Drag your cursor over the area of text you want to change.**

   In this example, I dragged over the entire manager line.

2. **Click the Text Styles button (the *A*).**

   The Text Styles dialog box appears.

3. **Select a font in the Font dialog box.**

   For this example, I selected Times New Roman.

4. **Select a style in the Font Style list box.**

   In this example, I selected Bold.

5. **Select a font size in the Font Size list box.**

   In this example, I selected 16.

6. **Change the text color by using the Color selection box.**

7. **Click OK.**

The Page Setup dialog box should now look like the one in Figure 17-8.

8. **Click OK in the Page Setup dialog box to get an overall view of your changes. Click the header once to get a close-up view, as shown in Figure 17-9.**

Figure 17-8:
The first line is bold and the header is limited to three lines.

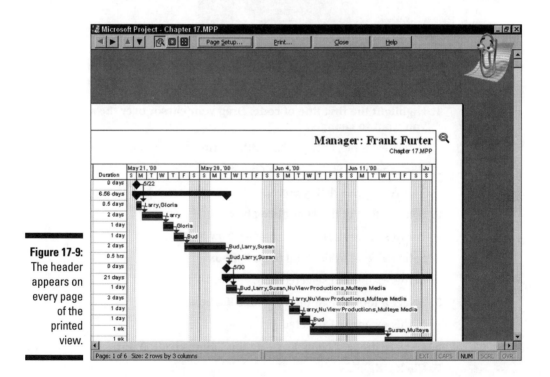

Figure 17-9:
The header appears on every page of the printed view.

Setting footers

You can click the Page Setup button to return to the Page Setup dialog box. Now click the Footer tab. The Footer tab has the same options as the Header tab. Because they're a repeat, I won't detail these options for you. But before you leave the footer, notice that Microsoft Project places a default page number in the center alignment area of the footer tab. You can remove or modify the page number if you want.

Setting the legend

The legend describes the meaning of the various bars and other symbols used in the Gantt chart or other charts. You use the Legend tab to add text to the legend area of the printed view.

Click the Legend tab in the Page Setup dialog box, and the screen shown in Figure 17-10 appears. The text options are the same in the Legend tab as they are in the Header and Footer tabs, with two additions. One additional option enables you to determine whether the legend appears on every page, on its own page, or not at all. The other option lets you determine the width in inches for the text portion of the legend.

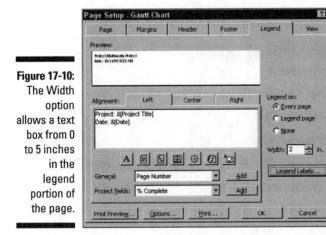

Figure 17-10:
The Width option allows a text box from 0 to 5 inches in the legend portion of the page.

Tweaking the view for printing

By default, Microsoft Project prints views pretty much in the same manner as they appear on your screen. You can change some of these defaults easily, though. To change the default settings, click the View tab and the screen shown in Figure 17-11 appears. The following list gives you some printing tips:

✔ Clicking the Print All Sheet Columns check box tells Microsoft Project to print all columns of the current sheet associated with the view.

✔ Clicking the Print First *number* Columns on All Pages check box tells Microsoft Project to print a number (left to right) of columns of the current sheet associated with the view.

✔ Clicking the Print Notes check box tells Microsoft Project to print any notes related to tasks in the view. In this example, Task 45 has a note related to it. Clicking this check box adds a note as an additional page to the end of the print job. In this example, the pages increase from six to seven.

✔ Clicking the Print Blank Pages check box toggles the selection to the Off mode. By doing this, you tell Microsoft Project to skip printing any pages that don't have tasks or task bars present. In this example, toggling off the selection reduces the print job by one page — page five (as shown in Figure 17-12).

After you finish looking at the Page Setup features, click OK.

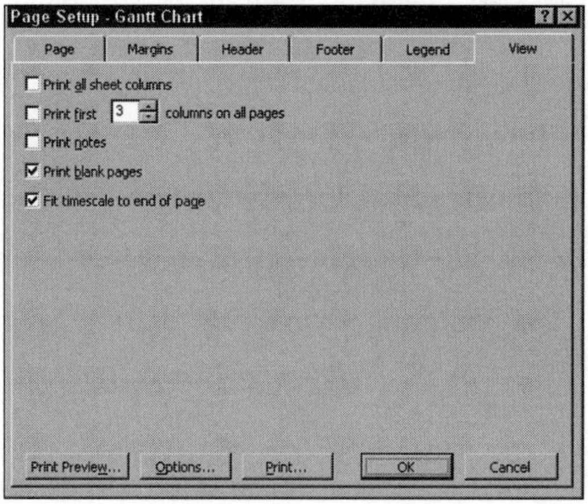

Figure 17-11:
The View tab enables you to change the Print function to be different than what appears on-screen.

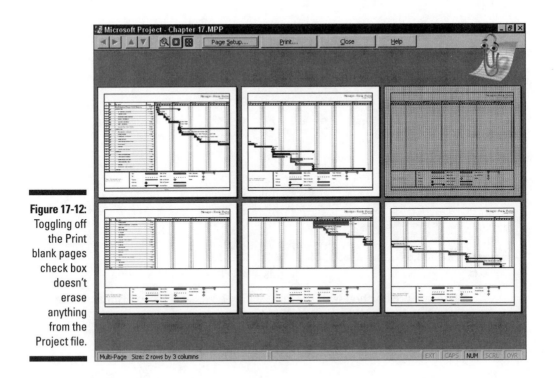

Figure 17-12:
Toggling off
the Print
blank pages
check box
doesn't
erase
anything
from the
Project file.

Printing Project Views

After you determine the page setup, you can move to the print options. Click the Print button in the print preview toolbar. The Print dialog box appears, as shown in Figure 17-13.

From the print preview toolbar, the Print dialog box offers four groups of options:

- **Print Range:** Select All to print all pages of the view. Select Pages From to print a range of pages as listed in Print Preview.
- **Printer:** Inactive in the dialog box shown in Figure 17-13. If you need to change your printer selection, close the Print Preview screen and choose File⇨Print.
- **Timescale:** Select All to print all pages of the view. Select Dates to enter different start and finish dates in the From and To boxes.
- **Copies:** Type the number of copies to be printed.

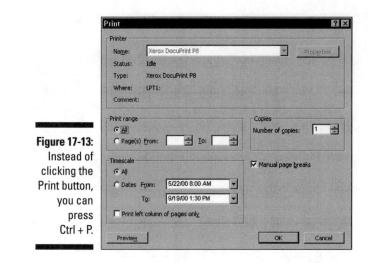

Figure 17-13:
Instead of
clicking the
Print button,
you can
press
Ctrl + P.

After you're finished with the Print dialog box, click OK to print and then
return to the Gantt Chart view.

Chapter 18

Using and Customizing Reports

● ●

In This Chapter

▶ Choosing from among 22 standard reports

▶ Customizing reports to tell the story your own way

▶ Creating reports for specific purposes

● ●

*A*s much as you've come to love the Gantt Chart and Network Diagram views, you just can't take them to all the nice places. Some people will politely ask you to leave them at the door or in the car with the windows slightly rolled down. Fear not, Microsoft Project provides you a solution for communicating information to persons of a more sensitive constitution — reports. You can take reports anywhere.

Reports summarize and present specific information in an organized manner. They're designed to focus on trends or broader aspects of your project in a manner that's used for intended stakeholders or project team members. You may get all warm and fuzzy by looking at a Tracking Gantt in combination view. Your stakeholder may get equally excited by reading a column of summary information within a report.

Microsoft Project provides five preset kinds of reports, as listed in the next section. A sixth report category, Custom, is described later in the chapter.

You're welcome to jump right in and make a report with your own project. But if you'd like, feel free to use the practice file that I've included for this chapter. The practice file, Chapter 18.MPP, has some information built into it to help you get the idea of what Microsoft Project offers for reports.

Using Standard Project Reports

Five categories of reports are ready-made in Microsoft Project and they're just waiting to be printed: Overview; Current Activities; Costs; Assignments; and Workload. Each of the categories has a list of specific reports. You can use reports as they are, or you can tweak them to meet your specific needs. To access the five kinds of reports, choose <u>V</u>iew ⇨<u>R</u>eports. The Reports dialog box appears, as shown in Figure 18-1.

Table 18-1 describes each of the reports in their categories.

Table 18-1	A Description of Reports	
Category	*Type*	*Displays*
Overview	Project Summary	The most important project information
	Top-Level Tasks	Information about top-level tasks
	Critical Tasks	Critical tasks for the project; includes summary tasks and successor tasks
	Milestones	Milestone tasks with their summary tasks
	Working Days	Working and nonworking times for resources
Current Activities	Unstarted Tasks	Tasks that haven't begun; includes predecessors and resources
	Tasks Starting Soon	Tasks that haven't started yet, given the bookend dates you specify
	Tasks in Progress	Tasks in progress and their resources' schedules
	Completed Tasks	Tasks completed in by-month breakdown
	Should Have Started	Tasks that should have Tasks started by a date you specify; includes summary tasks and successors

Category	Type	Displays
	Slipping Tasks	Tasks behind schedule; includes their summary tasks and successors
Costs	Cash Flow	Costs-per-task in one-week periods using a Crosstab report
	Budget	Budget for all tasks
	Overbudget Tasks	Overbudget tasks for the project
	Overbudget Resources	Overbudget resources for the project Resources
	Earned Value	Earned value information for all tasks
Assignments	Who Does What	Task schedules for all resources
	Who Does What When	Tasks, their resources, and work using a Crosstab report
	To-Do List	Weekly tasks for the resource you specify
	Overallocated Resources	Overallocated resources of the entire project
Workload	Task Usage	Resources assigned to tasks, including work information and totals, using a Crosstab Report
	Resource Usage	Tasks assigned to resources, including work information and totals, using a Crosstab report

A good way to envision a Crosstab report is to think of a mileage chart. In this type of chart, you find the distance between two cities by finding the box that is the intersection of the horizontal line representing one city listing and the vertical line representing the other city listing.

So how do you make a Project report work? You'll find the process is very easy. Just click a report that will fit your needs.

As an example, you can double-click Overview in the Reports dialog box. The Overview Reports dialog box appears, as shown in Figure 18-2.

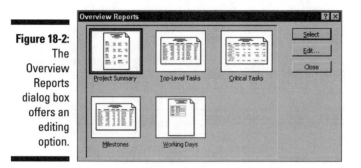

Figure 18-2:
The
Overview
Reports
dialog box
offers an
editing
option.

Double-click the Critical Tasks report. Microsoft Project opens the report in Print Preview mode, as shown in Figure 18-3. Viewing the report in Print Preview mode provides you the opportunity to customize the orientation, the margins, and the header and footer. When you're done, click the Close button on the Print Preview toolbar. You're back to the Reports dialog box.

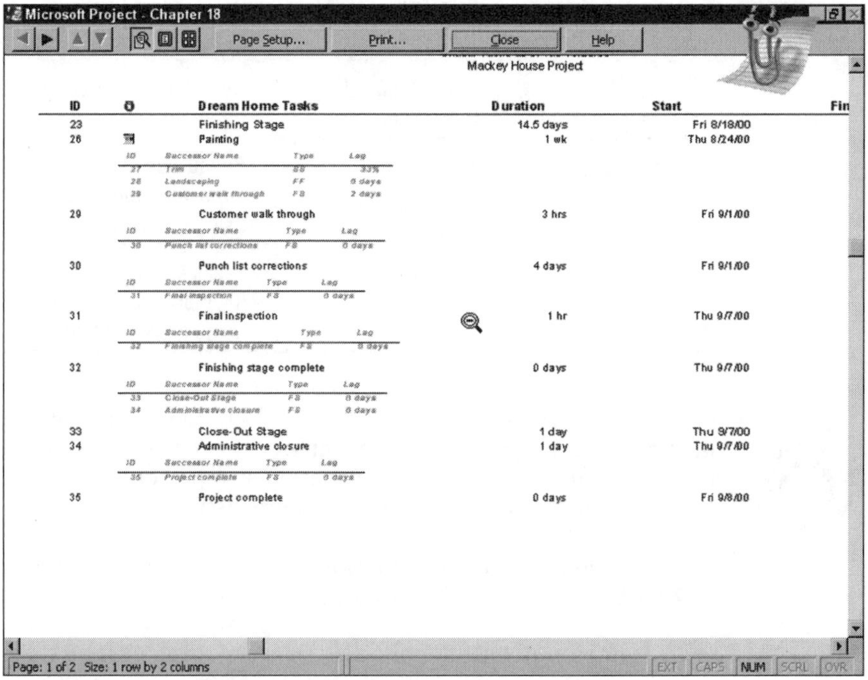

Figure 18-3:
Previewing
reports
works in
the same
manner as
previewing
charts.

Customizing a Project Report

One special selection I haven't discussed yet is the Custom reports option. By choosing this option, you're telling yourself (and soon the world) that there is no fit like a tailored one. Good isn't enough. Unless it's pleated and tucked with your own aesthetic and intellectual insight, it's just not the very best you and your public have come to expect. *My! You look mahvelous.* When you double-click the Custom category, the Custom Reports dialog box appears, as shown in Figure 18-4.

Figure 18-4:
The Custom
Reports
dialog box
offers the
options of
editing,
copying,
and creating
reports.

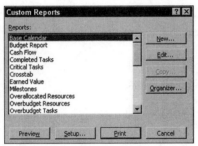

Custom means not typical. So I'm not going to tell you how you should customize your report. But, for example's sake, how about making a custom report using the Chapter 18 Project file. In this example, you customize the Critical Tasks report so that it presents information in a highlighted format instead of an isolated format. The highlighted format shows critical tasks highlighted among all the other tasks. An isolated format displays only critical tasks. To customize the Critical Tasks report in a highlighted format, follow these steps:

1. **In the Reports list, highlight the Critical Tasks report.**

2. **Click the Edit button in the Custom Reports dialog box. The Task Report dialog box appears. In the dialog box, click the Definition tab if it's not already selected (see Figure 18-5).**

   The Task Report dialog box offers highlighted (rather than isolated) reports, gray bands to separate tasks, and the opportunity to include summary tasks.

3. **Select the Highlight option and click OK.**

   You return to the Custom Reports dialog box.

4. **Click the Preview button.**

   The revised report appears in the Print Preview screen (see Figure 18-6).

5. **Scroll to see a low-resolution-quality representation of the highlighted critical tasks.**

   The highlighted critical tasks are sufficiently readable when they're printed in the report.

Experiment all you want to see how you can modify existing reports. Whatever you do, you won't change the Project file information.

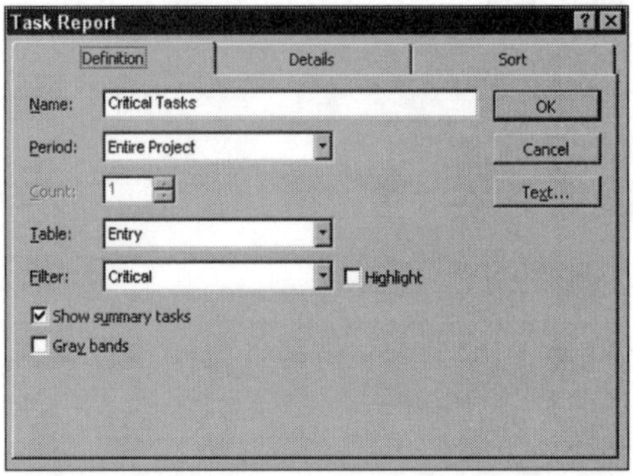

Figure 18-5:
The Task Report dialog box offers highlighted reports.

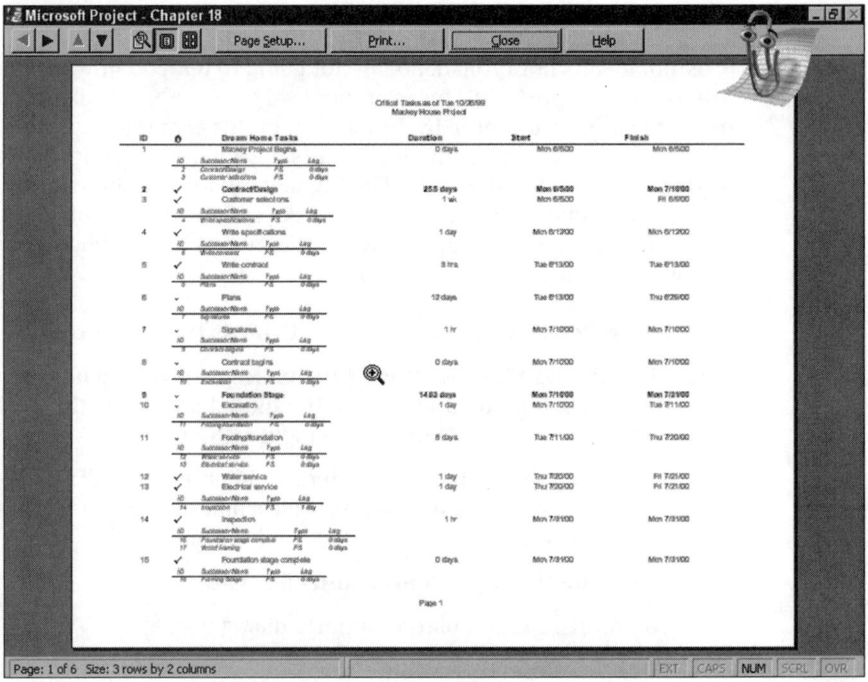

Figure 18-6:
You can skip the preview by choosing Print in the Custom Reports dialog box.

Creating a Project Report

Creating a report isn't much more difficult than using a standard report. To create a report from scratch, click the New button in the Custom Reports dialog box. The Define New Report dialog box appears. The dialog box offers you four choices:

- ✔ **Task:** Schedule, cost, information about work, and task details
- ✔ **Resource:** Schedule, cost, information about work, and resource details
- ✔ **Monthly Calendar:** Graphical representations of a calendar with tasks depicted as bars, lines, or start and finish dates
- ✔ **Crosstab:** Information about tasks and resources over a period of time

So how about using the Chapter 18 Project file to experiment with creating a report. In this next example, you create a Monthly Calendar report for the resources on the Construction Hours calendar. To do so:

1. **Double-click the Monthly Calendar option.**

   The Monthly Calendar Report Definition dialog box appears, as shown in Figure 18-7.

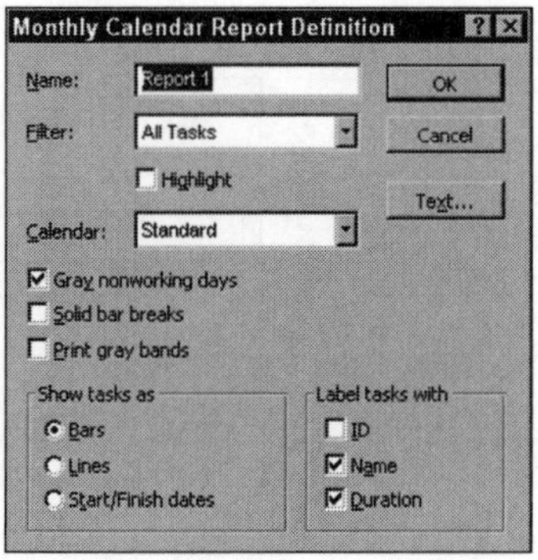

Figure 18-7:
The Task, Resource, Monthly Calendar, and Crosstab report options each have definition dialog boxes.

2. **Type a name for your report in the Name text box.**

   In this example, type **Construction Hours**.

3. **Select a filter in the Filter list box.**

   In this example select Incomplete Tasks.

4. **Select a calendar in the Calendar list box.**

   In this example, select Construction Hours Calendar.

5. **Click OK.**

   You return to the Custom Reports dialog box.

6. **Click the Preview button.**

   To make the preview somewhat interesting, click the down arrow until you come to September, 2000. The Monthly Calendar Report displays September as in Figure 18-8. The report shows all incomplete tasks assigned to resources that use the Construction Hours calendar.

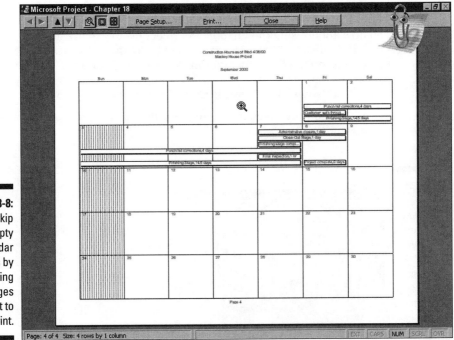

Figure 18-8:
You can skip the empty calendar pages by designating the pages you want to print.

Reports can be important to you as a project manager and to all the stake-holders of the project. They can also be powerful. An entire nation thought Mark Twain was dead because of some false reports. The key to success in reporting is properly presenting correct information at the appropriate time to the right people. Just do that. And be sure to report to us how it goes!

Chapter 19

Communicating in Workgroups with Microsoft Project Central

In This Chapter

▶ Preparing your project for workgroup communication

▶ Setting up and using Microsoft Project Central

▶ Updating your project from Microsoft Project Central

*J*ust about anyone who has developed and managed projects has experienced shrug-sigh reactions from team members and stakeholders regarding actually *using* Microsoft Project to track a working project. Sooner or later, team members eventually tell project managers that they're in the trenches trying to keep a project on time and on budget and the last thing they need is some irrelevant paper trail of status reports and task updates.

Unfortunately, in many cases, these negative reactions to a project plan are painfully true. Too quickly, today's first-rate baseline plan can turn into yesterday's inaccurate and out-of-date weather forecast. The question is, how do you keep a project file relevant? More importantly, how can your project management role ensure the success of a dynamic project?

As you find out in this chapter, the best way to manage a project successfully is with the two-way communication made possible by workgroups. And the easiest and most efficient way to maintain workgroups is with Microsoft Project Central.

Preparing to Use Microsoft Project Central

Microsoft has developed a companion product to Microsoft Project called Microsoft Project Central. Project Central keeps a project manager in the middle of all the action throughout the life of a project through the use of *workgroups*.

Microsoft Project defines a workgroup as a team of resources that a workgroup manager identifies. The workgroup shares project responsibilities during a project, and the workgroup manager and team members communicate with each other regarding task assignments, schedules, and task status.

Project Central is a Web-based management tool for workgroup communication. Using Project Central in a Web browser such as Microsoft Internet Explorer, workgroup members can accomplish the following:

✔ View tasks graphically on a Gantt chart or on a timesheet

✔ Filter and group tasks as they choose

✔ Update task status

✔ Delegate task responsibilities to other workgroup members

Setting up Project Central

Microsoft Corporation has some requirements in order for your organization to use Project Central. If you're a network guru, the requirements are pretty much of a yawner. For the rest of us though, this may sound like so much technospeak. The bottom line is that as a project manager, you need to alert the appropriate person(s) in your organization about the following information in order that you can use Project Central.

✔ You need to install Project Central on a server computer. Before you install it, ensure that Internet Server 4.0 or later and Microsoft Windows NT Server 4.0 Service Pack 4 or later are already installed.

✔ The Microsoft Project 2000 CD-ROM provides instructions for setting up Project Central. You can find the instructions in Setupsvr.htm.

✔ Microsoft has a bunch of license stuff your network guru needs to know. Basically, every workgroup member needs a Project Central license. The project manager needs the license for operating Project Central (included with the purchase of the CD-ROM).

✔ Each workgroup member also needs Internet Explorer 4.01 or later Web browser to display workgroup messages on their Web site. Or workgroup members can use the Browser Module for Project Central that comes on the Project CD-ROM.

✔ Internet or intranet access is necessary for each workgroup member.

Setting up a Workgroup

When your network guru (I call this person a *guru* because a smart project manager wants to always keep the network people happy) sets up Project

Central, he or she assigns a role of Project Central Administrator to some lucky person. Usually, network gurus maintain this role for themselves. The administrator defines subordinate workgroup roles in Project Central. Two key subordinate workgroup roles are "manager" and "team member." By default, a manager can identify himself or herself and can identify team members within Project and send this information to Project Central for workgroup communication.

Identifying a Project Central workgroup project manager

You identify yourself as the Project Central workgroup project manager in the Options dialog box within Microsoft Project. To identify the workgroup project manager, follow these steps:

1. **Open the project you want to manage, and then choose Tools⇨ Options.**

   The Options dialog box opens.

2. **Click the General tab and enter your project manager name in the User Name text box.**

   The name you enter is the project manager name by which you're known in Project Central.

3. **Click the Workgroup tab as shown in Figure 19-1.**

4. **Click the down arrow next to the Default Workgroup Messages box and select Web.**

   By doing so, you're telling Project that workgroup messages should be Web-based rather than e-mail-based.

5. **Type your Project Central server URL in the Web server text box.**

   Ask your network guru for this URL information.

6. **In Identification for Microsoft Project Central Server panel, select either the Windows User Account radio button or the Microsoft Project User Name radio button.**

   If you choose the Windows User Account option, Project Central automatically authenticates your using your Windows user account. This is the more secure of the two options, as it inherits all the password safety options from Windows 2000. If you choose the latter option, Project Central opens a logon page requiring you to identify yourself and to enter your Project Central password. This password is blank until you change it.

7. **Click the Create Account button.**

   When you press this button, Project automatically sets up your project manager personal account in Project Central.

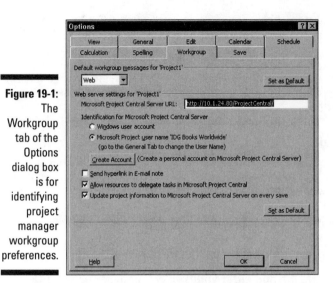

Figure 19-1:
The
Workgroup
tab of the
Options
dialog box
is for
identifying
project
manager
workgroup
preferences.

The Workgroup tab of the Options dialog box also gives you a couple of other controls related to Project Central. By selecting the Allow Resources to Delegate Tasks in Project Central Server radio button, you can enable team members to assign task responsibilities to other team members. You also can have Project automatically update your project information to Project Central every time you save the file.

Assigning team members

Assigning team members to Project Central is a little different than identifying yourself as the project manager. After you develop your project and assign resources to tasks, you can at any time populate Project Central with your team members and inform your team of their respective tasks. To assign team members, do the following:

1. **Right click in the Project toolbar area and select Workgroup from the toolbar menu.**

   The Workgroup toolbar appears below your already-selected toolbars (Figure 19-2).

2. **Click the TeamAssign button.**

   The Workgroup Mail dialog box appears, asking you if you want to Team Assign all tasks or one that you have highlighted. The default choice is to assign all the tasks.

3. **Click OK to send the team assignments to Project Central.**

   When the send is complete, an information box appears, telling you that the assignment procedure was successful.

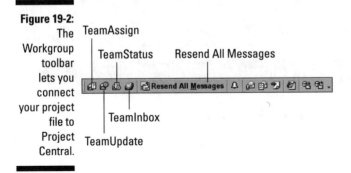

Figure 19-2:
The Workgroup toolbar lets you connect your project file to Project Central.

In addition to the TeamAssign function, you can also use four other buttons on the Workgroup toolbar:

- ✓ **TeamUpdate:** Notifies team members about changes in task information or changes in task assignments.

- ✓ **TeamStatus:** Reqests updated information from team members regarding their task assignments.

- ✓ **TeamInbox:** Connects you to your home page in Project Central where can check for information submittals from team members.

- ✓ **Resend All Messages:** Does just what it says. By pressing this button, you resend any previously sent messages.

Using Project Central

After assigning a team, you're ready to begin workgroup communication using Project Central. Click the TeamInbox button in the Workgroup toolbar to launch your Web browser and to go to your Project Central URL. If your settings on the Workgroup tab of the Options dialog box (Tools➪Options) is set to log in using the Microsoft Project username, your first page of Project Central will be a login page (Figure 19-3). The drop-down list includes your name and the names of each of your team members plus the administrator, other managers, and their team members.

The first time you log on, Project Central assigns you *blank* as your password. As a result, you shouldn't enter anything in the Password text box. When you enter Project Central, a dialog box appears, asking if you want to change your password from *blank* to a unique password. If you choose to do so, Project Central leads you through a short password-creation procedure.

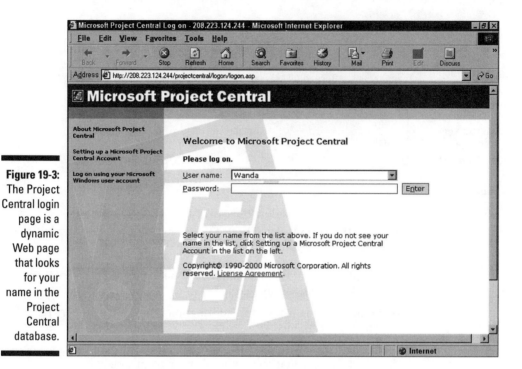

Figure 19-3:
The Project
Central login
page is a
dynamic
Web page
that looks
for your
name in the
Project
Central
database.

Your Project Central home page

When you enter into Project Central, you're greeted by your personal home page (Figure 19-4). The page is well written and pretty much self-explanatory. The left side of the page is a list of hyperlinks available from the home page. On other pages, your selections will be specific to area you are working within. The top of the home page is a menu bar that's identical to the list on the left, but is visible on every page of Project Central.

Within the body of the home page are paragraphed choices that pertain to your relationship to the workgroup.

Outlook option

The topmost option is a nifty little number that enables you to view Project Central from within Microsoft Outlook. If you click the Display button, Outlook adds a Project Central icon to your shortcut bar.

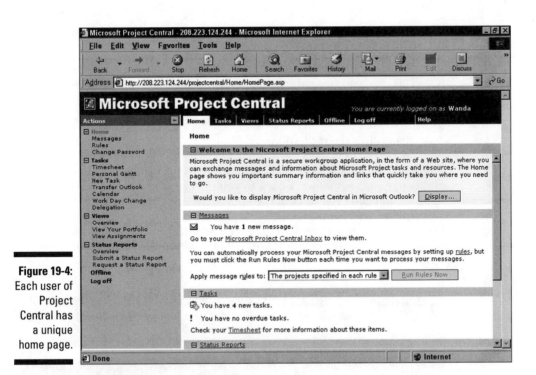

Figure 19-4:
Each user of Project Central has a unique home page.

Messages

The Messages portion tells you whether you have any news from the project manager (if you're a team member) or from the team members (if you're a project manager). Clicking the Messages hyperlink takes you to your personal Project Central Inbox. There, you can open any messages such as a TeamAssign message. If, as a project manager, you're also a team member, you'll get TeamAssign messages just like any other member of the workgroup.

Assigning yourself to a task helps you understand how Project Central processes information to and from team members.

One of the powerful features of Project Central is that it gives team members the option to accept or decline a task assignment. If a team member cannot perform a task, he or she can change the accept cell from *yes* to *no*. If team members want to make a comment about a task assignment, they can enter text of any length in the comments cell of the appropriate task before they reply to the project manager.

Tasks

Clicking the Tasks tab on the Project Central home page takes you to your unique tasks page in Project Central (Figure 19-5). The tasks page has oodles of options. Some of the most notable are:

✔ View your tasks in various filters. For example, you can choose to view only those tasks that have not yet begun.

✔ Show your Outlook tasks in the same view with your workgroup tasks. This can help you ensure that you're not inadvertently doubling up on some of your time.

✔ Change the timescale period to any time range that you choose.

✔ Change to a Gantt Chart view.

Perhaps the most important function within the Tasks tab is a team member's ability to report actual work back to you the project manager. The team member can enter the work in the appropriate task date cell(s). When the work information is up-to-date, the team member can simply click the Send Update button, and a timesheet report is sent to you the project manager. When you receive these task reports, you can click the Update button to update the project with the new information.

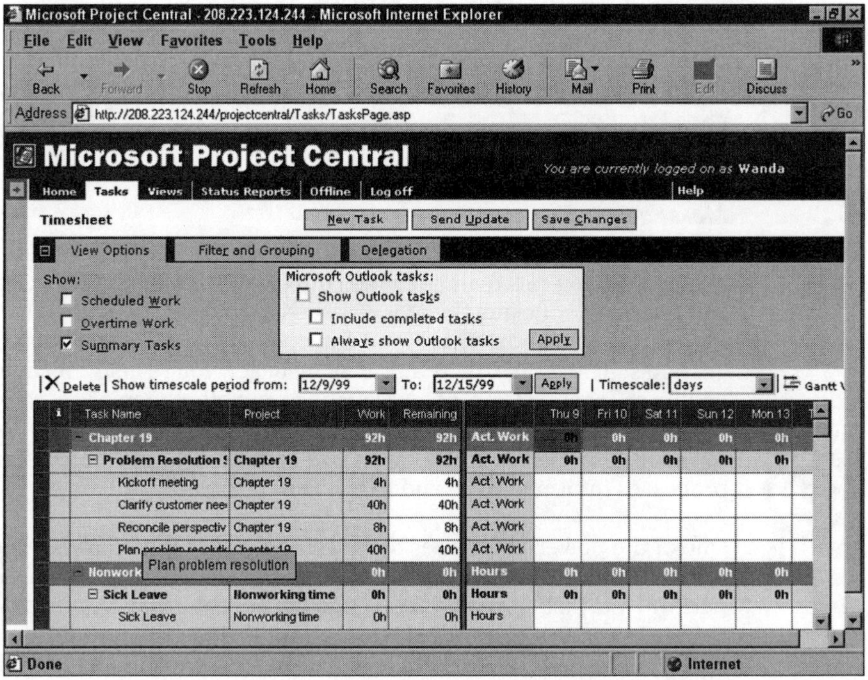

Figure 19-5:
The Tasks tab is where team members record work.

Status Reports

Another powerful workgroup tool provided to your unique project manager's Project Central home page is the Status Report function. Clicking the Status Reports tab takes you to a page that walks you step-by-step through a process of defining a detailed status report that you can request of your team members. When your team members respond with their status reports, you can then assemble the information in such a way that best fits the needs of your stakeholders.

Working with workgroup updates

As team members perform work on their tasks, they can use Project Central to send you task updates. Task updates come to you, the project manager, in Project Central as a message, as shown in Figure 19-6.

In task update messages, team members inform you of work that has been performed for specific tasks. Click the Update button to automatically update the Project file. The file reflects the completed work on the task.

Figure 19-6:
An update message is a message back from a team member regarding task performance.

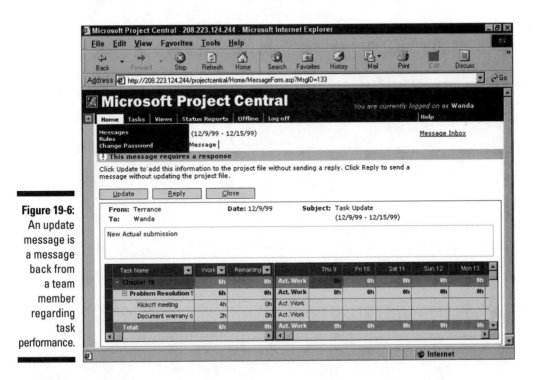

Part VI
The Part of Tens

The 5th Wave   By Rich Tennant

WHY DOGS DON'T USE LAPTOPS

THERE HE GOES AGAIN.
I'LL BET IF I LEANED
AGAINST A TREE, I
COULD DO IT.

In this part . . .

The two chapters in this part serve as an introduction to the many toolbars in Microsoft Project 2000 and an introduction to the world of project management. This part suggests ways that you can increase the efficiency of your project as well as your stature as a project manager. I hope you have a big garage for storing all these tools. And here's betting that you're pleasantly surprised about all the services dedicated to making your project a success.

Chapter 20

Ten Terrific Toolbars

In This Chapter

▶ Finding toolbars to suit your needs

▶ Customizing: Using toolbars as shortcuts

*T*oolbars are a handy way to access commands. But, just like any other accumulation of tools, toolbars can make your job easier or they can clutter up your workspace. In fact, one of the quickest ways to spot pros is their skill in knowing what's necessary for the job. The tools they want are at hand. Other tools remain stored until needed.

Microsoft Project offers 11 toolbars. Two of those, the standard and formatting toolbars, are discussed throughout this book. They're like the tape measure and the pencil — always there and available. This chapter briefly describes the other nine toolbars, each with its own group of goodies. And this chapter describes how you can design another toolbar — your own.

Open any of the toolbars by right-clicking in the toolbar area and selecting from the toolbar shortcut menu. The toolbars that are currently in view have check marks next to their names.

- ✔ Custom Forms Toolbar
- ✔ Drawing Toolbar
- ✔ Resource Management Toolbar
- ✔ Tracking Toolbar
- ✔ Visual Basic Toolbar
- ✔ Web Toolbar
- ✔ Workgroups Toolbar
- ✔ Network Diagram Toolbar

Custom Forms Toolbar

The Custom Forms toolbar takes you where normal forms seldom tread. A *form* is a type of view that gives you detailed information about a resource or a task. A typical example of a form is what you see in the Gantt Chart view when you choose Window⇨Split. In the split view, the bottom window is the Task form.

The Custom Forms toolbar, shown in Figure 20-1, provides shortcuts to performing work you would otherwise do with a standard form. For example, you can select a task or a resource in your project file and then select a custom form tool to modify that task or resource information. Buttons on the Custom Forms toolbar are described in Table 20-1.

Figure 20-1:
The Custom
Forms
toolbar.

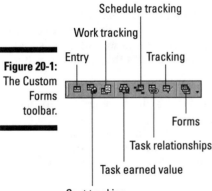

Table 20-1	Buttons on the Custom Forms Toolbar
Button	*What It Does*
Entry	Displays information you find in the Entry table
Cost Tracking	Displays a cost tracking form
Work Tracking	Displays a work tracking form
Task Earned Value	Displays an earned value form
Schedule Tracking	Displays a schedule tracking form
Task Relationships	Displays a form for reviewing or entering task relationships
Tracking	Displays a tracking form
Forms	Displays eight task and four resource forms

Drawing Toolbar

The Drawing toolbar, shown in Figure 20-2, provides tools that you can use to spiff up your Gantt chart and make it more informative. For example, you can draw a box, add text to the box, color the box, and draw an arrow from the box to a task. You can also attach the box to a task or to a specific place on the project timeline. See Table 20-2 for an explanation of buttons on the Drawing toolbar.

Figure 20-2:
The Drawing toolbar.

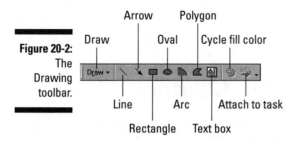

Table 20-2	Buttons on the Drawing Toolbar
Button	*What It Does*
Draw	Provides a menu of layering options after you select a drawing.
Line	Creates a line as you left-click and drag.
Arrow	Creates an arrowed line as you left-click and drag.
Rectangle	Creates a rectangle as you left-click and drag.
Oval	Creates an oval as you left-click and drag.
Arc	Creates an arc as you left-click and drag. Continue to hold down the left mouse button to move the arc in any direction. After you release the button, the concave area of the arc fills with white.
Polygon	Creates a polygon as you left-click, release, move to another spot, left-click, and so on. Complete the polygon by clicking over the original point. Adjust the polygon shaping by clicking one of the handles that surround the polygon after you select it.
Text Box	Creates a text box as you left-click and drag. Then type your text.

(continued)

Table 20-2 *(continued)*

Button	What It Does
Cycle Fill Color	After you select a drawn object, this cycles through 16 colors and a transparent option.
Attach to Task	Somewhat hampered by a misleading name, this provides a number of editing functions for a drawn object, such as changing the object's size in precise increments, attaching the object to a date or a task, and selecting a custom line color, line size, and pattern.

Resource Management Toolbar

Resource views and management are discussed in detail in Chapters 5, 8, 10, and 13. Table 20-3 gives a brief description of each of the shortcuts on the Resource Management toolbar, shown in Figure 20-3.

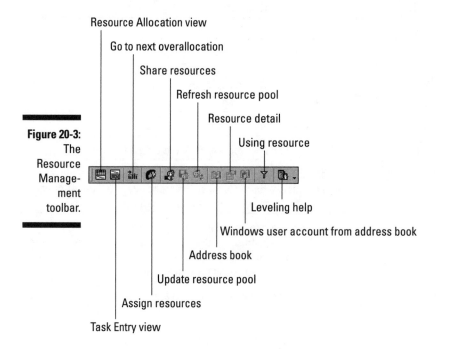

Resource Allocation view

Go to next overallocation

Share resources

Refresh resource pool

Resource detail

Using resource

Figure 20-3:
The Resource Management toolbar.

Leveling help

Windows user account from address book

Address book

Update resource pool

Assign resources

Task Entry view

Table 20-3	Buttons on the Resource Management Toolbar
Button	*What It Does*
Resource Allocation View	Displays the Resource Allocation view, which is a split view that contains the Resource Usage view in the top pane and the Leveling Gantt view in the bottom pane.
Task Entry View	Displays the Task Entry view, which is a split view that contains the Gantt Chart view in the upper pane and the Task Form view in the lower pane.
Go to Next Overallocation	A handy shortcut for finding tasks with overallocated resources.
Assign Resources	Opens the Resource Assignment dialog box identical to the Assign Resources shortcut on the standard toolbar).
Share Resources	Opens the Share Resources dialog box, which you can use to assign resources from one project to another.
Update Resource Pool	Provides the means to share your resource pool changes and availability with other managers.
Refresh Resource Pool	Updates your resource pool with changes made to the shared pool by other managers.
Address Book	On a network, displays your e-mail system's address book if the system is MAPI-compliant. (Talk to your network administrator about this.)
Resource Details	Shows a resource's business information and e-mail address.
Windows User Account From Address Book	Enters NT user account information from Network address book, if your network uses Windows NT 4 or later.
Using Resource	An interactive filter that asks you what resource you want to use as the filter. After you select the resource, the filter displays all associated tasks.
Leveling Help	A shortcut to a Help procedure that walks you through the process of leveling resources.

Tracking Toolbar

The Tracking toolbar, shown in Figure 20-4, is discussed in detail in Chapter 16. Table 20-4 describes each Tracking toolbar shortcut.

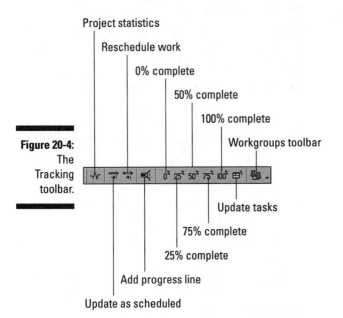

Figure 20-4:
The
Tracking
toolbar.

Table 20-4	Tracking Toolbar Buttons
Button	*What It Does*
Project Statistics	Displays the Project Statistics dialog box, which you use to get a thumbnail description of a project's status.
Update as Scheduled	Updates the schedule of selected tasks occurring before the current date.
Reschedule Work	After you have entered a status date, reschedules selected unfinished tasks to begin or continue on the status date. Tasks that have already begun become split tasks.
Add Progress Line	Changes the cursor into a progress line tool and opens a dialog box that designates that date on which the cursor rests. After you click, a progress line is added to the Gantt chart. Peaks to the left of vertical indicate tasks behind schedule. Peaks to the right of vertical indicate tasks ahead of schedule.

Button	What It Does
0% Complete	Marks selected tasks as not begun.
25% Complete	Marks selected tasks as 25% complete.
50% Complete	Marks selected tasks as 50% complete.
75% Complete	Marks selected tasks as 75% complete.
100% Complete	Marks selected tasks as complete.
Update Tasks	Opens the Update Tasks dialog box for the task you have selected. Use it to register percent complete, actual or remaining duration, and actual start and finish dates.
Workgroups Toolbar	Toggles the Workgroups toolbar open or closed.

Visual Basic Toolbar

The Visual Basic toolbar, shown in Figure 20-5, has four tools that run, record, and edit macros, and a fifth that you use to set levels of security against viruses.

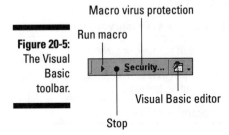

Figure 20-5:
The Visual
Basic
toolbar.

Macro virus protection

Run macro

Security...

Visual Basic editor

Stop

Web Toolbar

Tools on your Web toolbar activate your Web browser to navigate on the World Wide Web or on your intranet. The Web toolbar is valuable if you have task information saved as Web pages on the Internet or on an intranet. The Web toolbar is shown in Figure 20-6. See Table 20-5 for a description of buttons on the Web toolbar.

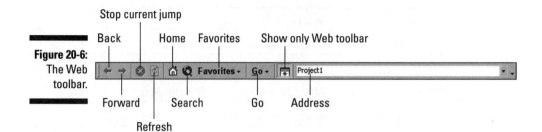

Figure 20-6:
The Web
toolbar.

Stop current jump

Back   Home   Favorites   Show only Web toolbar

Forward   Search   Go   Address

Refresh

Table 20-5	Web Toolbar Buttons
Button	*What It Does*
Back	Moves you back one site among sites you've visited during the current session
Forward	Moves you forward one site among sites you've visited during the current session
Stop Current Jump	Stops your current hyperlink jump
Refresh Current Page	Refreshes the current page
Start Page	Opens your browser's default home page or as you set it in the browser's options
Search the Web	Opens your browser's search page
Favorites	Displays your list of favorite sites from your browser
Go	Displays a shortcut menu of browser functions
Show Only Web Toolbar	Hides (or unhides) all other visible toolbars except the standard and formatting toolbars
Address	Shows your most recently visited sites

Workgroups Toolbar

You can use Microsoft Project as a communications tool among team workgroup members. As project manager, you can communicate with team members by using e-mail, an intranet, or the World Wide Web.

If you're planning to communicate with team members via e-mail, all team members must use a 32-bit, MAPI-compliant e-mail system. For Web-based communications, workgroup members need a Web browser, a Web server, network access, a network identifier, and an Internet connection and address. See your network administrator for more information.

Table 20-6 provides a brief description of each tool on the Workgroups toolbar, shown in Figure 20-7.

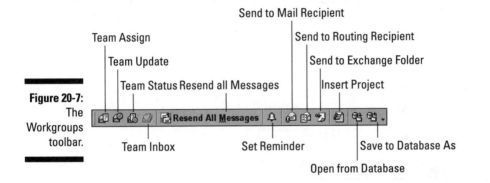

Figure 20-7:
The
Workgroups
toolbar.

Table 20-6	Buttons on the Workgroups Toolbar
Button	*What It Does*
Team Assign	Tells a team member that you want to assign him or her to a task or tasks
Team Update	Informs a team member about changes in his or her assignments
Team Status	Asks a team member for the current status of task responsibilities
Team Inbox	Opens the Team Inbox, a message center in Microsoft Project for the project manager to view Web-based messages from team members
Resend All Messages	Does just what it says: Clicking this button resends all previous messages to the workgroup
Set Reminder	Sets reminders in Microsoft Office Outlook for selected tasks
Send to Mail Recipient	Sends e-mail to project team members
Send to Routing Recipient	Adds or modifies the mail route slip
Send to Exchange Folder	Sends a copy of the project file to a Microsoft Exchange-based folder
Insert Project	Inserts another project file into your displayed file
Open from Database	Opens a project file that was saved to a database
Save to Database As	Saves a project file to a database file

Network Diagram Toolbar

The Network Diagram toolbar is quite different from the other toolbars. This little hummer is a floating toolbar that provides shortcuts to some Network Diagram evaluation tools. Table 20-7 describes each tool on the Network Diagram floating toolbar, shown in Figure 20-8.

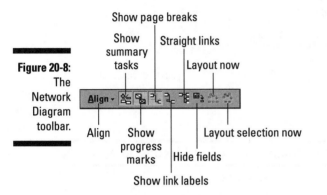

Figure 20-8:
The
Network
Diagram
toolbar.

Show page breaks
Show summary tasks
Straight links
Layout now
Align
Show progress marks
Hide fields
Show link labels
Layout selection now

Table 20-7	Network Diagram Toolbar Buttons
Button	**What It Does**
Align	Sets the alignment options for the boxes in the Network Diagram view.
Show Summary Tasks	This is a toggle button that expands to show all tasks and contracts to show only summary tasks.
Show Progress Marks	This is a toggle button that shows or hides task completion indicators (an X for complete and and \ for in progress).
Show Page Breaks	This is a toggle button that either shows or hides how nodes will appear on pages when printed.
Show Link Labels	This is a toggle button that either shows or hides task relationships (Finish-to-Start, Finish-to-Finish, Start-to-Start, and Start-to-Finish).
Straight Links	This is a toggle button that changes links styles from rectilinear (right angles) to straight lines.

Button	What It Does
Hide Fields	This is a toggle button that hides field information and only shows nodes as sequential numbers in task order.
Layout Now	Applies the selections in the Layout dialog box to the active view.
Layout Selection Now	Applies the selections in the layout to the selected boxes only.

Customizing a Toolbar

Because you're well on your way to becoming a project management pro, you can also customize any toolbar by adding tools from other toolbars. To do so, just press and hold the Alt key, move the cursor over the tool you need, press and hold your left mouse button, and drag the tool to the appropriate toolbar.

Chapter 21

Ten Innovative Ways to Spruce Up Your Project

● ●

In This Chapter

▶ Breaking the mold

▶ Seeing the world of project management in different ways

● ●

*T*he ten resources in this chapter can help you discover new and better ways to accomplish your project-management tasks. When your responsibilities outweigh your skills and resources, you can feel overwhelmed. But you're not alone! A plethora of resources (human and otherwise) is available to help you with your job.

The Project Management Institute

The recent extraordinary growth of project management and the number of practitioners is due, in part, to the Project Management Institute (PMI). This nonprofit professional association provides a wealth of written materials and training opportunities. Within this organization, you can associate with fellow project managers and tap into a network of expertise in your community, industry, and special area of interest. Considering what you get by belonging, membership is cheap (about $115 per year).

You can contact PMI at Project Management Institute, 130 South State Road, Upper Darby, PA 19082. The telephone number is 610-734-3330. The fax number is 610-734-3266. Its Web site is at www.pmi.org.

Two of the most important resources available through PMI are the Project Management Body of Knowledge and the Project Management Professional certification, both of which I describe in this chapter.

Project Management Body of Knowledge

The basics of project management are universal. Over the years, professionals have synthesized project-management principles and practices into a standard known as the Project Management Body of Knowledge. The 180-plus-page document is available on the *Microsoft Project 2000 For Dummies* CD-ROM. This document is one of the best freebies you'll ever find.

Master of Project Management Degree

Project management degree programs are available at colleges and universities around the country. One that I recommend is ITT Technical Institute's Master of Project Management (MPM) degree. The ITT objectives in the MPM program are to help students prepare for participation in project management activities upon graduation; provide high quality graduate instruction to help students prepare for advancement and professional development in their chosen career; and foster critical thinking, communication, and teamwork. Designed for working adults, the 21-month, 56 credit-hour MPM program emphasizes the practical issues of project management in a team-oriented format.

You can contact Dr. Shuster at ITT Technical Institute, 9511 Angola Court, Indianapolis, IN 46268. The telephone number is 800-937-4488. The Institute's Web site is at www.itttech.edu.

PMP Certification

Sooner or later, Project Management Professional (PMP) certification is a goal of all professional project managers. This may or may not be for you, but it's worth your investigation and consideration. Like other professions, such as law and accounting, project management is based on a recognized set of standards. The purpose of PMP certification is to provide recognition of your abilities as a project manager. The certification is based on a combination of testing and proven experience and service in the field of project management. Refer to the section, "Project Management Institute" to find out contact information.

Group Involvement

For a stimulating and challenging experience, you can't beat one-on-one contact with people who share common interests. You can accomplish this through involvement in a local PMI chapter or by joining an online shared-interest group.

Project managers throughout the world regularly attend monthly PMI chapter meetings. These self-governing chapters are great for exchanging ideas and information. Check your telephone directory for a local project management society, or contact PMI at 610-734-3330 or at www.pmi.org.

You can buddy up online by joining a regional chapter of MPUG (Microsoft Project Users Group). This organization provides a forum for users of Microsoft Project to share their ideas and experiences.

Members are informed of regional and national meetings, they get quarterly newsletters, a membership directory, beta Microsoft software, and a project manager's secret decoder ring. Well, actually, the ring is my idea. Interested? Just go to www.mpug.org.

Project Management Newsgroups

If you like working with newsgroups, Microsoft has one for users of Microsoft Project. Ask questions, tell whoppers, and exchange information with other newsgroup members. If you're industrious and a little lucky, you may even run across users in your own field of endeavor. Access the newsgroup by going to http://support.microsoft.com/support/news in your web browser. Click Microsoft Office Family of Products. Then click Project For Windows. After you sign up, your initial download will be a few hundred e-mails. But don't worry, the messages don't take up much space. Besides, you're among friends.

The Microsoft Project Report

Extra, extra, read all about it! Microsoft Project Report is a bi-monthly e-mail newsletter. In each report you'll find news and information helpful to users of Microsoft Project. The Report delivers to your door general project management news, information about Microsoft seminars in your area, access to sample templates, and big and small Project case studies from all over the world. For your free subscription, go to www.microsoft.com/office/project/projnews.htm.

Books and Periodicals

I don't mean to keep touting PMI, but the Institute has a great online bookstore offering what it claims is the world's largest up-to-date source of project management books.

You can look for a specific book among its 1,000-plus titles or browse to find sources of information. And, if you're a member of PMI, you can buy at a discount.

Web Search

If you have a few hours, do a Web search of project management. A large number of individuals and organizations offer services in project management. As is typical of such searches, a lot of your search will be marginal in value. However, some good sites are out there, too, such as `www.projectmanagement.com/main.htm`.

Microsoft Project Help

One of the least costly and most helpful study resources is the one you've been using — Microsoft Project. Microsoft Project's Help function is surprisingly helpful (ahem) in its organization and depth. One especially useful connection it offers is technical support.

At the time this book was written, Microsoft still offered limited free technical support. In the United States, no-charge support from Microsoft support engineers is available with a toll call between 5 a.m. and 9 p.m. Pacific Standard Time, Monday through Friday (except holidays) and on Saturdays from 9 a.m. to 3 p.m. To find out if you are eligible for this no-charge support, go to `www.Microsoft.com/support` and follow the classification listings that relate to you.

Part VII

Appendixes

In this part . . .

*E*ver wonder where your appendix goes after the doctor removes it? Right here in the Appendix part along with the Glossary, information on importing and exporting data, and an appendix dedicated to the all-important CD-ROM.

Appendix A

Glossary

Accrual method: When the cost of a resource occurs. This may be at the start of a task, prorated during the task, or at the end of the task.

Actual: The facets of a task that have begun, including dates, cost, and work accomplished.

Base calendar: The primary calendar for a project.

Baseline: Also called the baseline plan or simply the plan. The final copy of all project aspects before the project start date. The baseline is used as a point of reference after the project begins.

Calendar: A list of the working time periods and nonworking time periods in a project.

Collapsed outline: The outline of tasks where all or part of the subtasks are hidden under summary tasks.

Combination view: A screen showing two views. The bottom view shows details of a highlighted feature in the upper view.

Consolidation: A combining of projects.

Constraint: A condition that limits the start or the finish of a task.

Critical path: A sequence of tasks that must finish on or ahead of schedule for a project to be completed on time.

Critical path method (CPM): A procedure for setting the start and finish dates of tasks to ensure an on-time completion of a project.

Date line: A dashed line running vertically in the Gantt chart to indicate the computer's system date or a current date set in Project⇨Project Information.

Demoting: To set a task as a subtask in a task outline structure.

Duration: The units of time of a task or group of tasks. Duration units are minutes, hours, days, and weeks.

Expanded outline: An outline view in which all subtasks are visible.

Field: A data entry point in a table.

Filter: A condition or group of conditions that acts as the basis for an information search in a project.

Fixed cost: A cost, such as a contract agreement, that remains the same independent of the duration or the number of resources used.

Fixed duration: A type of scheduling that sets a fixed length for a scheduling task. Numbers of resources have no effect on fixed duration tasks.

Gantt chart: A graphic depiction of a project. The length of Gantt bars in a Gantt chart represents duration. Lines between tasks represent task relationships.

Interactive filter: A filter that asks the user for information as the basis of a search of matching information in a project.

Lag time: A set length of time that's established between a task and its predecessor as the basis for the task to start.

Legend: Reference information on a chart explaining the relevance of graphic representations.

Leveling: A procedure of lengthening task durations to decrease demands on a resource or a group of resources.

Linked tasks: Tasks connected in some kind of relationship.

Master project: A project containing one or more subprojects.

Milestone: A task that indicates a beginning, a completion, or a significant event in a project. Milestones have a duration of 0d.

Network Diagram chart: A flow chart depicting relationships among tasks. Tasks appear as boxes, or nodes. Task relationships are illustrated by connecting lines.

Node: The box in a Network Diagram chart containing properties of a task.

Outline: A structured format in the Gantt Chart view containing higher-level summary tasks and lower-level subtasks.

Overallocation: The overassignment of tasks to a resource in a particular time period.

Predecessor: A task that precedes another task.

Promote: In an outlined project, to move a subtask to a higher level. Promoting is performed by decreasing the indent (sometimes called *outdenting*).

Recurring task: A task that repeats at regular intervals throughout all or a portion of a project.

Report: A compilation of project information that you print.

Resource: A person or equipment that performs work.

Resource calendar: A designation of working and nonworking days and hours for a specific resource or group of resources.

Resource-driven task: A task whose duration is directly affected by the number of resources assigned to it.

Resource pool: A list of resources compiled so that they are available to all tasks.

Resource view: A view that shows resources instead of tasks.

Schedule: The current status of a plan.

Slippage: How much a task is behind its baseline start date, finish date, or both.

Subproject: A project file shown as a single task in another project file.

Subtask: A task indented under a summary task.

Successor: A task that follows another task.

Summary task: A task that comprises a summary of the duration, cost, and work of a group of subtasks.

Task: One of the planned activities of a project.

Task view: A view of a project based on task information.

Template: A Microsoft Project file format that enables you to use an existing schedule as the basis for making a new schedule.

Timescale: Units of time used to depict a project schedule. The timescale has levels of measurement — the major timescale and the minor timescale.

Variance: The difference between baseline data and current data.

View: Any one of a large number of possible presentations of project information.

Work Breakdown Structure (WBS): A hierarchical structure used to organize tasks for reporting schedules and tracking costs. With Microsoft Project, you can use the outline feature, use task IDs, or assign a WBS code to each task in the task detail form.

Workspace: A group of project files that can be opened at one time. Workspace files are created by choosing File⇨Save Workspace.

Appendix B

Working with Data from Other Applications

Microsoft Project accommodates the addition of text, spreadsheet information, graphic objects, sound, movies, and animation. By using applications resident in Windows 2000 (or using more elaborate applications, such as Adobe Photoshop or Premiere), you can customize your Project file to present product update discussions, customer interviews, project photos, or just about anything else you want. Microsoft Project can also send data to and receive data from databases.

Using the Clipboard

Using the clipboard to import objects may seem archaic at first, but it's actually slick. Microsoft Project uses the Windows copy-and-paste features to place data from other applications into a project.

Pasting text

You can create a list of items in a word processor and, through pasting, change the list to tasks in Microsoft Project. The value of this is somewhat questionable, but it's good to know if you've already created lists in another application, such as in a proposal.

To perform this function, open a word processor such as Microsoft Word. Create a list of items or use an existing list. Select the list and copy it to the word processor's clipboard. In Microsoft Project, select an empty task name cell, and then click the Paste button on the standard toolbar. The items in the list appear as tasks.

Pasting graphics or multimedia

You can also paste a graphic, a sound, or another kind of object. When you paste it, the object or a representation of the object appears in the Gantt chart. After it appears, you can drag the object to an appropriate spot.

Using the Paste Special command

You can take advantage of object linking and embedding (OLE) with the Paste Special command. After you've created and copied something to the clipboard — for example, text from your word processor — you can paste the clipboard contents into a project in two ways. You can designate that you want to be able to activate the text by using the word processor, or you can paste a picture of the text into your document.

To place text in the Gantt chart, for example, open a word processor such as Microsoft Word. Create text or use an existing text file. Select the text and copy it to the word processor's clipboard. In Microsoft Project, choose Edit⇨Paste Special. The Paste Special dialog box appears, providing choices for displaying the contents of the clipboard. As you select each choice, a Result message appears below the highlighted item. The Result description explains the way that selection would affect the clipboard object.

The object of the clipboard can be text, spreadsheet information, graphics, or multimedia objects. If you want, rather than display the object in the Gantt chart, you can select the Display as Icon check box. An icon appears that represents the originating application. When you place the icon in the Gantt chart, you can double-click the icon to display the object.

Inserting Objects

You can place objects in the Gantt chart not only with the clipboard but also by inserting them. To do this, choose Insert⇨Object. The Object dialog box appears. The Create New option lets you select an application from a list and open it. After you have created the object, you return to Microsoft Project. The object is embedded in the Gantt chart. The Create from File option enables you to embed or link an existing object file. In either case, Create New or Create from File, you can display an application icon rather than the object itself.

Using Project with Databases

You can open database information into Microsoft Project or save a project file to a database format. To open a database file:

1. **Click the Open button on the standard toolbar.**

   The File Open dialog box appears.

2. **In the Files of Type list, select Microsoft Access Databases.**

3. **Double-click the file you want to open.**

4. **To import all the data in your project, select the Entire Project option and then select the name of the project you want to open in the Name of the Project in the Database to Import box.**

5. **Click Open.**

To save a Microsoft Project file in a database file format:

1. **Choose File➪Save As.**

2. **In the Save as Type box, select Microsoft Access Databases.**

3. **In the File Name box, type a name for the exported file.**

4. **Click Save.**

   The Export Format dialog box appears.

5. **To save all the data in your project, select the Entire Project option, and then type a name for the project in the Name to Give the Project in the Database box.**

   You can export particular fields to a database by clicking the Selective Data option and then selecting the import/export map to use for exporting.

6. **Click Save.**

   The file is saved in the Microsoft Access Database format.

Appendix C

About the CD

H ere's a sample of the programs and practice files that you find on the *Microsoft Project 2000 For Dummies* CD-ROM:

- ✔ **Internet Explorer 5.0:** A browser for anywhere you want to go on the Internet

- ✔ **Paint Shop Pro 6.0:** 30 image formats, enhanced painting tools, and built-in special effects filters

- ✔ **Practice Microsoft Project files:** Files created especially for this book to help you get a quick start with Microsoft Project 2000

System Requirements

Make sure that your computer meets the minimum system requirements listed below. If your computer doesn't match up to most of these requirements, you may have problems using the contents of the CD.

- ✔ A PC with a 486 or faster processor.

- ✔ Microsoft Windows 95 or later.

- ✔ At least 32MB of total RAM installed on your computer. For best performance, we recommend that Windows 95-equipped PCs have at least 64MB of RAM installed.

- ✔ At least 50MB of hard drive space available to install all the software from this CD. (You need less space if you don't install every program.)

- ✔ A CD-ROM drive — double-speed (2x) or faster.

- ✔ A monitor capable of displaying at least 256 colors or grayscale.

- ✔ A modem with a speed of at least 14,400 bps.

If you need more information on the basics, check out *PCs For Dummies,* 6th Edition, by Dan Gookin; or *Windows 98 For Dummies* or *Windows 95 For Dummies,* 2nd Edition, by Andy Rathbone (all published by IDG Books Worldwide, Inc.).

Using the CD with Microsoft Windows

To install the items from the CD to your hard drive, follow these steps:

1. **Insert the CD into your computer's CD-ROM drive.**

2. **Choose Start⇨Run.**

   The Run dialog box appears.

3. **Type** D:\SETUP.EXE.

   Replace *D* with the proper drive letter if your CD-ROM drive uses a different letter. (If you don't know the letter, see how your CD-ROM drive is listed under My Computer in Windows 95/98/2000).

4. **Click OK.**

   A license agreement window appears.

5. **Read through the license agreement, nod your head, and then click the Accept button if you want to use the CD — after you click Accept, you'll never be bothered by the License Agreement window again.**

   The CD interface Welcome screen appears. The interface is a little program that shows you what's on the CD and coordinates installing the programs and running the demos. The interface basically enables you to click a button or two to make things happen.

6. **Click anywhere on the Welcome screen to enter the interface.**

   Now you're getting to the action. This next screen lists categories for the software on the CD.

7. **To view the items within a category, just click the category's name.**

   A list of programs in the category appears.

8. **For more information about a program, click the program's name.**

   Be sure to read the information that appears. Sometimes a program has its own system requirements or requires you to do a few tricks on your computer before you can install or run the program. This screen tells you what you may need to do, if necessary.

9. **If you don't want to install the program, click the Back button to return to the previous screen.**

   You can always return to the previous screen by clicking the Back button. This feature enables you to browse the different categories and products and decide what you want to install.

10. **To install a program, click the appropriate Install button.**

    The CD interface drops to the background while the CD installs the program you chose.

11. **To install other items, repeat Steps 7 through 10.**

12. **After you've finished installing programs, click the Quit button to close the interface.**

    You can eject the CD now. Carefully place it back in the plastic jacket of the book for safekeeping.

In order to run some of the programs on the *Microsoft Project 2000 For Dummies* CD-ROM, you may need to keep the CD inside your CD-ROM drive. This is a Good Thing. Otherwise, the installed program would have required you to install a very large chunk of the program to your hard drive, which may have kept you from installing other software.

What You'll Find

Here's a summary of the software on this CD arranged by category. If you use Windows, the CD interface helps you install software easily. (If you have no idea what I'm talking about when I say "CD interface," flip back a page or two to find the section, "Using the CD with Microsoft Windows.")

Shareware programs are fully-functional, free trial versions of copyrighted programs. If you like particular programs, register with their authors for a nominal fee and receive licenses, enhanced versions, and technical support. Freeware programs are free, copyrighted games, applications, and utilities. You can copy them to as many PCs as you like — free — but they have no technical support. GNU software is governed by its own license, which is included inside the folder of the GNU software. There are no restrictions on distribution on this software. See the GNU license for more details. Trial, demo, or evaluation versions are usually limited either by time or functionality (such as not being able to save projects).

Internet

The Internet's the thing, so try these cool Internet programs!

MindSpring Internet Service Provider

Commercial Product: In case you don't have an Internet connection, the CD includes sign-on software for MindSpring, an Internet Service Provider.

For more information and for updates of MindSpring, visit the MindSpring Web site at www.mindspring.com.

You need a credit card to sign up with MindSpring Internet Access.

If you already have an Internet Service Provider, please note that the MindSpring Internet software makes changes to your computer's current Internet configuration and may replace your current settings. These changes may stop you from being able to access the Internet through your current provider.

Microsoft Internet Explorer 5.0

Commercial Product: Microsoft Internet Explorer is one of two major players in the Web browser market. However, just in case you don't have the latest version (at the time of publication), we include a copy of Microsoft Internet Explorer 5.0 on this CD. You can always find the latest information about Internet Explorer at the Microsoft support site: www.microsoft.com/ie.

If you are running Windows 98 or 2000, you don't need to install this program because it comes with your copy of Windows.

Project management

Project management is a fast-growing professional discipline. A large and quickly-growing array of project management-related software programs is available to assist novices and professionals in their management tasks. We've included evaluation and demo copies of some excellent project management programs.

Visual Staff Scheduler Pro

Trial Version: If you're responsible for employee scheduling, VSS PRO is for you. It's quick, flexible, and saves you time. Print custom schedules and reports for almost any situation, track time-off, and ensure shift coverage.

For additional information about Visual Staff Scheduler Pro, go to www.abs-usa.com.

Project KickStart

Trial Version: Project KickStart's eight-step planning process focuses your attention on the structure of the project, the goals, resources, risks, and strategic issues critical to your project's success. Your plan is ready in 30 minutes! Schedule your project using the pop-up calendar and Gantt chart. Print out a to-do list or one of the seven presentation-ready reports. Or, for added versatility, "hot link" your plan into Microsoft Project, SureTrak, P3, FastTrack Schedule, Super Project, Project Scheduler 7, Time Line, Milestones Etc., WBS Chart, Word, WordPerfect, and Excel.

For additional information about Project KickStart, go to
www.projectkickstart.com.

Paint Shop Pro 6.0

Evaluation Version: Jasc Paint Shop Pro takes image editing to a new level
of functionality and ease of use. Designed for users who want control, power,
and flexibility, Paint Shop Pro delivers the tools you need to easily capture,
create, enhance, and optimize your graphics projects.

For additional information about Paint Shop Pro, go to www.jasc.com.

Sample files from the book

These files contain all the Microsoft Project practice files used in the book.
You can browse these files directly from the CD by clicking the Browse
button, or you can install them to your hard drive by clicking the Install
button in the CD interface. If you copy them to your hard drive, you can find
them in the Practice folder on your hard drive.

- Smith House3.mpp
- Smith House4.mpp
- Smith House5.mpp
- Chapter 6.mpp
- Award Program 7.mpp
- Award.bmp
- Network Diagram Chapter 8.MPP
- Calendar 9.mpp
- Chapter 10.mpp
- Chapter 11.mpp
- Chapter 12.mpp
- Chapter 13.mpp
- Sample1 Chapter 14.mpp
- Sample2 Chapter 14.mpp
- Sample3 Chapter 14.mpp

- ✔ Sample4 Chapter 14.mpp
- ✔ Chapter 15.mpp
- ✔ Sample1 Chapter 15.mpw
- ✔ Sample2 Chapter 15.mpp
- ✔ Chapter 16.mpp
- ✔ Chapter 17.mpp
- ✔ Chapter 18.mpp
- ✔ Chapter 19.mpp

Sample forms in the book

Chapter 2 contains a form designed to help you plan your project:

- ✔ **Defining.doc:** A Microsoft Word version of a document to help you plan out the tasks and resources in your project.
- ✔ **Defining.wpd:** A WordPerfect version of a document to help you plan out the tasks and resources in your project.

You can browse these forms on the CD by clicking the Browse button or you can install them to your hard drive by clicking the Install button in the CD interface. If you copy them to your hard drive, you can find them in the Practice/Forms folder on your hard drive.

If You've Got Problems (Of the CD Kind)

We tried our best to compile programs that work on most computers with the minimum system requirements. Alas, your computer may differ, and some programs may not work properly for some reason.

The two likeliest problems are that you don't have enough memory (RAM) for the programs you want to use, or you have other programs running that are affecting installation or running of a program. If you get error messages like Not enough memory or Setup cannot continue, try one or more of these methods and then try using the software again:

- ✔ **Turn off any anti-virus software that you have on your computer.** Installers sometimes mimic virus activity and may make your computer incorrectly believe that it's being infected by a virus.

✔ **Close all running programs.** The more programs you're running, the less memory is available to other programs. Installers also typically update files and programs; if you keep other programs running, installation may not work properly.

✔ **In Windows, close the CD interface and run demos or installations directly from Windows Explorer.** The interface itself can tie up system memory, or even conflict with certain kinds of interactive demos. Use Windows Explorer to browse the files on the CD and launch installers or demos.

✔ **Have your local computer store add more RAM to your computer.** This is, admittedly, a drastic and somewhat expensive step. However, if you have a Windows 95 PC or a Mac OS computer with a PowerPC chip, adding more memory can really help the speed of your computer and enable more programs to run at the same time.

If you still have trouble installing the items from the CD, please call the IDG Books Worldwide Customer Service phone number: 800-762-2974 (outside the U.S.: 317-572-3000 ext. 3393).

Index

Notes

Notes

IDG Books Worldwide, Inc., End-User License Agreement

READ THIS. You should carefully read these terms and conditions before opening the software packet(s) included with this book ("Book"). This is a license agreement ("Agreement") between you and IDG Books Worldwide, Inc. ("IDGB"). By opening the accompanying software packet(s), you acknowledge that you have read and accept the following terms and conditions. If you do not agree and do not want to be bound by such terms and conditions, promptly return the Book and the unopened software packet(s) to the place you obtained them for a full refund.

1. **License Grant.** IDGB grants to you (either an individual or entity) a nonexclusive license to use one copy of the enclosed software program(s) (collectively, the "Software") solely for your own personal or business purposes on a single computer (whether a standard computer or a workstation component of a multiuser network). The Software is in use on a computer when it is loaded into temporary memory (RAM) or installed into permanent memory (hard disk, CD-ROM, or other storage device). IDGB reserves all rights not expressly granted herein.

2. **Ownership.** IDGB is the owner of all right, title, and interest, including copyright, in and to the compilation of the Software recorded on the disk(s) or CD-ROM ("Software Media"). Copyright to the individual programs recorded on the Software Media is owned by the author or other authorized copyright owner of each program. Ownership of the Software and all proprietary rights relating thereto remain with IDGB and its licensers.

3. **Restrictions on Use and Transfer.**

   (a) You may only (i) make one copy of the Software for backup or archival purposes, or (ii) transfer the Software to a single hard disk, provided that you keep the original for backup or archival purposes. You may not (i) rent or lease the Software, (ii) copy or reproduce the Software through a LAN or other network system or through any computer subscriber system or bulletin-board system, or (iii) modify, adapt, or create derivative works based on the Software.

   (b) You may not reverse engineer, decompile, or disassemble the Software. You may transfer the Software and user documentation on a permanent basis, provided that the transferee agrees to accept the terms and conditions of this Agreement and you retain no copies. If the Software is an update or has been updated, any transfer must include the most recent update and all prior versions.

4. **Restrictions on Use of Individual Programs.** You must follow the individual requirements and restrictions detailed for each individual program in the "About the CD" section of this Book. These limitations are also contained in the individual license agreements recorded on the Software Media. These limitations may include a requirement that after using the program for a specified period of time, the user must pay a registration fee or discontinue use. By opening the Software packet(s), you will be agreeing to abide by the licenses and restrictions for these individual programs that are detailed in the "About the CD" section and on the Software Media. None of the material on this Software Media or listed in this Book may ever be redistributed, in original or modified form, for commercial purposes.

5. **Limited Warranty.**

   (a) IDGB warrants that the Software and Software Media are free from defects in materials and workmanship under normal use for a period of sixty (60) days from the date of purchase of this Book. If IDGB receives notification within the warranty period of defects in materials or workmanship, IDGB will replace the defective Software Media.

   (b) **IDGB AND THE AUTHOR OF THE BOOK DISCLAIM ALL OTHER WARRANTIES, EXPRESS OR IMPLIED, INCLUDING WITHOUT LIMITATION IMPLIED WARRANTIES OF MERCHANTABILITY AND FITNESS FOR A PARTICULAR PURPOSE, WITH RESPECT TO THE SOFTWARE, THE PROGRAMS, THE SOURCE CODE CONTAINED THEREIN, AND/OR THE TECHNIQUES DESCRIBED IN THIS BOOK. IDGB DOES NOT WARRANT THAT THE FUNCTIONS CONTAINED IN THE SOFTWARE WILL MEET YOUR REQUIREMENTS OR THAT THE OPERATION OF THE SOFTWARE WILL BE ERROR FREE.**

   (c) This limited warranty gives you specific legal rights, and you may have other rights that vary from jurisdiction to jurisdiction.

6. **Remedies.**

   (a) IDGB's entire liability and your exclusive remedy for defects in materials and workmanship shall be limited to replacement of the Software Media, which may be returned to IDGB with a copy of your receipt at the following address: Software Media Fulfillment Department, Attn.: *Microsoft Project 2000 For Dummies,* IDG Books Worldwide, Inc., 10475 Crosspoint Blvd., Indianapolis, IN 46256, or call 800-762-2974. Please allow three to four weeks for delivery. This Limited Warranty is void if failure of the Software Media has resulted from accident, abuse, or misapplication. Any replacement Software Media will be warranted for the remainder of the original warranty period or thirty (30) days, whichever is longer.

   (b) In no event shall IDGB or the author be liable for any damages whatsoever (including without limitation damages for loss of business profits, business interruption, loss of business information, or any other pecuniary loss) arising from the use of or inability to use the Book or the Software, even if IDGB has been advised of the possibility of such damages.

   (c) Because some jurisdictions do not allow the exclusion or limitation of liability for consequential or incidental damages, the above limitation or exclusion may not apply to you.

7. **U.S. Government Restricted Rights.** Use, duplication, or disclosure of the Software by the U.S. Government is subject to restrictions stated in paragraph (c)(1)(ii) of the Rights in Technical Data and Computer Software clause of DFARS 252.227-7013, and in subparagraphs (a) through (d) of the Commercial Computer–Restricted Rights clause at FAR 52.227-19, and in similar clauses in the NASA FAR supplement, when applicable.

8. **General.** This Agreement constitutes the entire understanding of the parties and revokes and supersedes all prior agreements, oral or written, between them and may not be modified or amended except in a writing signed by both parties hereto that specifically refers to this Agreement. This Agreement shall take precedence over any other documents that may be in conflict herewith. If any one or more provisions contained in this Agreement are held by any court or tribunal to be invalid, illegal, or otherwise unenforceable, each and every other provision shall remain in full force and effect.

Installation Instructions

The *Microsoft Project 2000 For Dummies* CD offers valuable information that you won't want to miss. To install the items from the CD to your hard drive, follow these steps.

1. **Insert the CD into your computer's CD-ROM drive.**

2. **Choose Start⇨Run.**

   The Run dialog box appears.

3. **Type** D:\SETUP.EXE.

   Replace *D* with the proper drive letter if your CD-ROM drive uses a different letter. (If you don't know the letter, see how your CD-ROM drive is listed under My Computer in Windows 95/98.)

4. **Click OK.**

   A license agreement window appears.

5. **Read through the license agreement, nod your head, and then click the Accept button.**

6. **Click anywhere on the Welcome screen to enter the interface.**

7. **To view the items within a category, just click the category's name.**

   A list of programs in the category appears.

8. **For more information about a program, click the program's name.**

9. **To install a program, click the appropriate Install button.**

For more information, see Appendix C.

IDG BOOKS WORLDWIDE
BOOK REGISTRATION

We want to hear from you!

Register This Book and Win!

Visit **http://my2cents.dummies.com** to register this book and tell us how you liked it!

- ✔ Get entered in our monthly prize giveaway.

- ✔ Give us feedback about this book — tell us what you like best, what you like least, or maybe what you'd like to ask the author and us to change!

- ✔ Let us know any other *...For Dummies®* topics that interest you.

Your feedback helps us determine what books to publish, tells us what coverage to add as we revise our books, and lets us know whether we're meeting your needs as a *...For Dummies* reader. You're our most valuable resource, and what you have to say is important to us!

Not on the Web yet? It's easy to get started with *Dummies 101®: The Internet For Windows® 98* or *The Internet For Dummies*, 6th Edition, at local retailers everywhere.

Or let us know what you think by sending us a letter at the following address:

...For Dummies Book Registration
Dummies Press
10475 Crosspoint Blvd.
Indianapolis, IN 46256

FOR DUMMIES™

BESTSELLING
BOOK SERIES